Eastern Africa Series

PEACE NOT WAR

Peace Not War

Traditions of Restorative Justice in Imperial Ethiopia, 1769–1960

CHARLES SCHAEFER

JAMES CURREY

James Currey
is an imprint of
Boydell & Brewer Ltd
PO Box 9, Woodbridge
Suffolk IP12 3DF (GB)
www.jamescurrey.com

and of
Boydell & Brewer Inc.
668 Mt Hope Avenue
Rochester, NY 14620-2731 (US)
www.boydellandbrewer.com

Our Authorised Representative for product safety in the EU
is Easy Access System Europe - Mustamäe tee 50, 10621 Tallinn,
Estonia, gpsr.requests@easproject.com

First published 2025

British Library Cataloguing in Publication Data

A catalogue record for this book is available from The British Library

ISBN 978-1-84701-404-7 (James Currey hardback)

Contents

Illustrations

The author and publisher are grateful to all the institutions and individuals listed for permission to reproduce the materials in which they hold copyright. Every effort has been made to trace the copyright holders; apologies are offered for any omission, and the publisher will be pleased to add any necessary acknowledgement in subsequent editions.

While every effort has been made to ensure high-quality image reproduction, some images in this book reflect the condition of the original photographs, which may show variations in clarity, resolution, and detail.

Acknowledgements

First, I must acknowledge my late adviser, Donald Levine, who in discussing matters pertaining to Ethiopia sometime in the late 1990s, listened to my rantings about the possibility of restorative justice modalities being employed in Imperial Ethiopia as part of the peace-building process and convinced me it was worth pursuing. With his validation I began to read the restorative justice literature and probe Ethiopian history. Combining the two took four articles and many years to write this book. Any inaccuracies are my own.

I am deeply indebted to my colleagues in the Department of History at Addis Ababa University for their encouragement, even extending invitations to be the External Examiner for Ph.D. dissertation defenses. Coming unexpectedly, the dissertations stretched my understanding of Ethiopian history and have exposed me to historical material that I would never have encountered. Case in point was the dissertation by Esubalew Belay Fanta on the history of the Ethiopian Imperial High Court that I have used liberally. Gratitude goes to the Director and staff of the Institute for Ethiopian Studies (IES) at Addis Ababa University. Much of the primary material used here was procured from the archives of IES. But more specifically I am beholden to Shiferaw Bekele for his support, encouragement, advice, critiques, and his understanding of nineteenth-century Ethiopia that has shaped my own and that I have appropriated. Without Shiferaw setting the political parameters of the Yejju rulers during the *Zemene Mesafint*, it would have been impossible for me to discern how restorative justice metastasized from a problematic practice that involved one-and-done amnesty to conditional forgiveness that obliged the penitents to atone for their misdeeds according to stipulations set down by those in power. The manner in which restorative justice was adapted to ensure durable peace and reconciliation is the primary thesis of this book. Helping me to sort this out, either directly and/or through their scholarship, are Bahru Zewde, Maimire Mennasemay, Yirga Gelaw Woldeyes, Reidulf Molvaer, Izabela Orlowska, Heran Sereke-Brhan, Aberra Jembere, Richard Pankhurst, Jon Abbink, and many more.

For help with translations, I would like to thank Randa Duvick (French) and Tim Malchow (German), colleagues at Valparaiso University, and Gebru Wolde (Amharic), my neighbor and friend. For advice on transliterating Amharic to English, I owe much to Loren Bliese, Shiferaw Bekele, Alula Pankhurst, and Gebru Wolde who sat with me painstakingly debating the appropriate spelling of Amharic words. For finding obscure sources and then sending them on to me with exceptional efficiency I want to thank Sara Shoppa and Stephanie Frederick, Interlibrary Loan managers at Valparaiso University. Praise for the cover painting of this book goes to Kayden Cotton, a Fine Arts major at Valparaiso University, who applied her artistic sensibilities to magnify justice at the Imperial Court as represented in the photo on page 50. For financial support, I am indebted to Valparaiso University's College of Arts and Sciences for funding summer research trips to Ethiopia, sabbatical support, and travel to countless conferences that allowed me to circulate early iterations of my thesis and receive constructive feedback. I would be remiss if I did not mention the support I received from the Horn of Africa Programme of the Norwegian Institute of Human Rights at the University of Oslo as a Visiting Fellow and subsequently for Research Grants all made possible through the aegis of Kjetil Tronvoll. I owe you.

The manuscript has benefited from suggestions and corrections from many colleagues and friends. Colleen Seguin, my cherished friend and colleague in the Department of History at Valparaiso University, read every chapter, corrected both text and footnotes, and supplied me with an outsider's (non-Ethiopianist) perspective on the clarity of the argument and whether my asides were of the remotest interest to anyone except me. Thank you, Colleen. Other colleagues and friends who have read chapters in early iterations are: Shiferaw Bekele, Alula Pankhurst, Sahlu Mikael Imru my schoolmate from Geneva, Izabela Orlowska, Gebru Wolde, Gretchen Buggeln, Lucas Kelley, Tim Malchow, Tal Howard, and Glenn Petersen.

Lastly, I owe a great deal to my family. As a missionary in Ethiopia, my father, Herbert Schaefer was a history buff and loved to point out the Segale battlefield as we drove to Dessie; on other trips we children were shown the Portuguese castles of Gondar or saw the Ethiopian crown jewels up close which were kept in Axum and brought out and displayed for a few *birr* with only a barbed wire fence between the incalculably precious historical artifacts and our family. My love for Ethiopian history is an extension of his own. My mother, Trudy, always prodded me on any writing project that had something to do with Ethiopia. Her constant questions were annoying at times but came from genuine interest and curiosity. To my daughters, Krista and Sonja, who tolerated my absences and cognitive disengagement as I was thinking about some historical footnote, I want to say thanks. To Kathy, my wife, I am eternally grateful for your support, patience, counsel, and proofreading at our dining room table.

Prologue

A twofold agenda guides *Peace Not War: Traditions of Restorative Justice in Imperial Ethiopia, 1769–1960*. The first agenda item, and by far the principal focus, is a study of the architecture of the state as it changed over time, particularly referencing how justice was served after threats to the existence of the state. In current vernacular, it would be referred to as transitional justice. Specifically, the book historicizes state-level restorative justice initiatives in one country over two centuries. It provides a historical window relevant to all countries about the politics of restorative justice. The form of justice varied from restorative justice to retributive justice as Ethiopia moved into the twentieth century, but the movement was not linear. Restorative justice practiced in the eighteenth and nineteenth centuries was not a giftwrapped package, complete and immutable. The Ethiopian state experimented, discarding notions of justice that unsettled the population and prolonged war. Learning from their mistakes, Ethiopians adopted other judicial modalities that facilitated reconciliation and durable peace. This study assesses state-building over time and, paradoxically, how justice in its various guises contributed to the building of the state. As the book demonstrates, there were many dead-ends and unsatisfactory forays (Chapter 2). Yet, exhibiting flexibility and adaptability, Ethiopians were inventive in designing legal remedies that restored the throne (Chapters 3 and 4) or awarded legitimacy to usurpers (Chapter 5) while also bringing closure to the people.

Today, Ethiopia needs to implement a transitional justice mechanism that works, is respected, and brings about the peace and reconciliation expected of such efforts. The appeals from Ethiopians are widespread. The reason for the clarion call is endless conflict. The more consequential conflicts include: the civil war in Tigray; armed insurrection in Amhara Region and the attempts by *Fano* to transform from a paramilitary into a political party; upheaval in the Oromo Region and the ascendency of the Oromo Liberation Army (OLF-Shane) considering secession; irredentist conflict in the Ogaden as well as periodic skirmishes across the Somali-Afar regional borders; and the killing of civilians in Benishangul as the Gumuz lash out against the incursion of other ethnic groups in the wake of the construction of the Grand

Ethiopian Renaissance Dam on the Blue Nile. Meanwhile, the Renaissance Dam has sparked international tensions between Ethiopia on one side and Sudan and Egypt, who demand unrestricted water supply, on the other. Still assessing international issues, at the end of 2024, countries in the Horn of Africa and Arabian Peninsula are taking sides and building up their militaries in preparation for war over the signing of a Memorandum of Understanding between Ethiopia and Somaliland (an unrecognized inchoate state) giving Ethiopia a naval port in the Gulf of Aden. The prospects of Africa's second most populous country gaining access to the sea upsets the geopolitics of the region. To document abuses in Ethiopia, human rights groups maintain the "Ethiopia Peace Observatory" (launched by ACLED – Armed Conflict Location and Event Data) and EEPA/Africa (Europe External Programme with Africa, Horn of Africa) that concurrently publish weekly reports on the number of firefights, civilian casualties, and public protests. Continued conflict characterizes Ethiopia at the time of this writing.

The second agenda item is more of a plea. A plea for Ethiopian stakeholders to look deep into their history, the record that this account begins to unravel, to reassess their own time-tested strategies to bring about reconciliation. The author acknowledges that circumstances have change radically in Ethiopia from the imperial era to the modern, from a hierarchical feudal society accentuating vertical lines of power, with the emperor at the top, to a parliamentary system legitimated by elections that governs an ethnically divided nation where horizontal ties determine identity and allegiance. Nevertheless, the reasoning, the social understanding, the meting out of justice by Ethiopian monarchs and their attending nobles impart lessons that may ease conflict.

The call for some form of transitional justice to bring about peace basically rests on importing methods developed elsewhere, as in South Africa or Rwanda, and then reworking the modalities as some of the pitfalls of the Truth and Reconciliation Commission or *gacaca* come to light. Currently, the African Union's 2019 handbook *Transitional Justice Policy* is the preferred toolkit for implementing restorative justice because it has more bite, by threatening victim compensation or perpetrator punishment when forgiveness proves insufficient.[1] Ethiopia established a Reconciliation Commission committed to seeking "truth and justice" in 2019[2] yet dissolved it three years later after accomplishing little.[3] Even before its elimination, authorities established the

1 African Union, *Transitional Justice Policy: An Integrated, Prosperous and Peaceful Africa* (Addis Ababa: African Union, 2019).

2 "A Proclamation to Establish Reconciliation Commission," *Federal Negarit Gazette*, Proclamation No. 1102/2018 (February 5, 2019).

3 "Ethiopian Reconciliation Commission Dissolves," *Addis Standard* (March 1, 2022).

Ethiopian National Dialogue Commission in December 2021, during the height of the Tigray civil war, to end conflict and forge a national consensus. Parenthetically, this is a page out of Ethiopian history, for Ethiopians experimented all the time. Using the African Union's toolkit, the commission invited citizens from occupational groups, women, youth, self-help organizations, and the business community to participate. It even reached out to the diasporic community in the United States "to enrich and bolster the ongoing national dialogue process."[4] Inclusion is the benchmark the National Dialogue Commission aspires to, except the commission has not invited Tigrean, Oromo, and Amhara "rebel" leaders to send representatives – all the key players in the ethnic struggles convulsing Ethiopia. Tegbaru Yared views the National Dialogue Commission as an "ahistorical and overambitious conceptualization" that could unintentionally exacerbate ethnic conflict while increasing "the citizenry's political apathy and dwindling trust in the commission."[5]

And still both the government and non-government actors call for some cure-all, some way to dissolve ethnic animus and keep the territorial integrity of Ethiopia intact. *Peace Not War* is by no means a guidebook, but it does give historical context showing how Ethiopians brought about peace and reconciliation in the past. As the Epilogue details, it prods readers to look at indigenous methods of restorative justice implemented in Ethiopia and respected by Ethiopians. *Peace Not War* provides political, social, and cultural insights that should be considered in preference to imported foreign legal remedies.

4 Ethiopian National Dialogue Commission homepage (February 3, 2024) https://ethiondc.org.et/en/home/.

5 Tegbaru Yared, "Ethiopia's National Dialogue needs greater credibility and inclusivity," Institute for Security Studies, *ISS Today* (September 20, 2023), https://issafrica.org/iss-today/ethiopias-national-dialogue-needs-greater-credibility-and-inclusivity.

Introduction

Peace Not War: Traditions of Restorative Justice in Imperial Ethiopia, 1769–1960 provides the field of restorative justice with historically validated cases where restorative justice practices were used to resolve conflict and bring peace to Ethiopia. A general problem with restorative justice is that there are few historically documented examples from Africa, Latin America, North America, or for that matter the Hawaiian Islands. The roots of restorative justice are often attributed to a mythical past, religious beliefs, or cultural traditions – all equally undocumented. But Ethiopia is different. With a writing system, emperors as well as pretenders to the throne chronicled their exploits, both wars and peace-building feats. This book provides the literature on restorative justice with historical examples from as early as 1769 during the *Zemene Mesafint* (Era of the Princes).

Historiographic Critique

As the title *Peace Not War* suggests, this volume is about efforts to build peace. War has held a dominant position in Ethiopian historiography as tussles between feudal adversaries and a persistent struggle to assume the imperial throne have marked its history. Fighting and bloodshed were described in detail in imperial chronicles and the hagiographic literature with great attention given to who allied with whom. European traveler accounts reiterated the war-theme by either recounting battles or the desecration they observed afterwards; moreover, they also parroted secondhand accounts they were told or, for those who mastered an Ethiopian language, had read about. There was a racist objective to depicting Ethiopians as warlike for it validated Europe's civilizing mission. The secondary literature has also dwelt on Ethiopian warmongering. Richard Reid, in *Warfare in African History*, draws extensively from Ethiopia's written record to historicize methods of mobilization, military foundations, violence, and destruction.[1] To

1 Richard Reid, *Warfare in African History* (Cambridge: Cambridge University Press, 2012), ch. 3. Essentially many of the dynastic histories of various

argue that Ethiopia placed high order on peace and reconciliation goes against prevailing historiography. And yet this book contends that restoring the feudal structure of the polity was as important as military victory, and peacebuilding took many forms, but through experimentation – many trials and errors and recalibrations – Ethiopia constructed its own enforceable traditions of restorative justice.

Peace Not War is not a celebration of a unique, surefire Ethiopian strategy to restore political and social ties; rather, it traces Ethiopia's evolving understanding of restorative justice from "forgive and forget," which characterized the *Zemene Mesafint* where perpetrators were exonerated, allowing them to recoup and build their armies to fight another day, to conditional forgiveness. Those conditions were recorded by the court, and offenders were expected to atone for their rebellious ways. If they were not repentant, the terms were readjudicated. Ethiopia's long history of experimentation with different forms of restorative justice demonstrates ingenuity, flexibility, and adaptability.[2]

Using instances when the state faced regime-ending threats, the book analyzes the critical factors facing the victorious and defeated combatants and how reconciliation was nurtured. To this end, the Imperial Court or *chilot* administered justice somewhere on the continuum between lenient and vengeful as circumstances dictated. But as the twentieth century progressed and Ethiopia was drawn into the international community and the incentive to modernize was both for self-preservation as well as infatuation with Western ideas and products, the desire to adopt Western legal codes took hold. Progressing through the chapters, the analysis of justice changes, showing how workable, indigenous forms of restorative justice were sometimes sidelined by Western codified law that emphasized punishment for crimes committed. The memory of the traditions of restorative justice was always there, but its implementation was soon overridden by imported retributive justice procedures.

Historical and Religious Roots of Restorative Justice

The primary contribution of *Peace Not War* to the literature on restorative justice is that it provides historical documentation dating back

emperors elevate warring; for a synthesis of these efforts see, Tsegaye Tegenu, *The Evolution of Ethiopian Absolutism: The Genesis and the Making of the Fiscal Military State, 1696–1913* (Uppsala: Uppsala University, 1996) ; and Tsehai Berhane-Selsssie, *Ethiopan Warriorhood: Defence, Land and Society 1800–1941* (Woodbridge: James Currey, 2018).

2 Charles Schaefer, "Restorative Justice Modalities: What Can Be Learned about Peace and Reconciliation from Imperial Ethiopia?" in *Ethiopia in the Wake of Political Reforms*, ed. Melaku Geboye Desta, Dereje Feyissa Dori, and Mamo Esmelealem Mihretu (Los Angeles: Tsehai, 2020), 231–42.

to the eighteenth century on how emperors and their Imperial Courts built peace. In much of the rest of Africa, restorative justice is ascribed to some murky past or undocumented cultural tradition where precolonial justice functioned as a metaphor and a myth – *ubuntu* – and, in their elevation into functional juridical form,[3] they have been romanticized, covering up "the real story."[4] In Ethiopia there is documentary evidence, for Ethiopia had its own writing system. Ethiopia provides historical context for state-level restorative justice initiatives administered over time in one country.

Unlike South Africa, Rwanda, and most other African countries, state law in Ethiopia was not a transplant of Western legal codes or common law practices that had been forced upon them by a European colonial power. The Imperial Ethiopian state had roots that extended into antiquity with a political hierarchy ruling over the corpus of the land; moreover, it developed ingenious methods of survival based on tribute and usufruct rights to land that resembled feudalism yet were uniquely Ethiopian. Included in Ethiopia's political toolkit was a judicial system that had input from abroad but was far removed from the Western legal framework that most other African states inherited from their colonial metropole. Whereas other African states possessed Customary Dispute Resolution (CDR) institutions (as did Ethiopia) that predated colonialism, these were principally localized justice systems that never resolved disputes beyond the grassroots or inter-ethnic levels, let alone at the state level. In cases like Buganda and a few other precolonial African states where there were well-developed national institutions, they did not have a written language and hence no written archive of judicial procedures or verdicts. Moreover, Buganda's law practices were usurped by European colonials who erected their own legal system above the indigene structures and, over time, systematically undercut the legitimacy of those legal frameworks.[5] By contrast, Ethiopia was never colonized (occupied for six years after the Italian invasion of 1935 but not colonized, see Chapter 6), and therefore its judicial traditions lived on, only incorporating elements of Western legal theory as the twentieth century progressed. Included in Ethiopia's judicial tradition were methods to resolve political disputes that threatened the very existence of the Ethiopian state. These

---

3 Mogobe Ramose, *African Philosophy through Ubuntu*, revised edition (Harare: Mond Books, 2022).

4 Kathleen Daly deconstructs issues involved with "constructing origin myths about restorative justice" in her article "Restorative Justice: The Real Story," *Punishment and Society*, 4:1 (2002): 62.

5 Neil Kodesh connects land tenure to banana cultivation in precolonial Buganda, emphasizing efforts to promote "public healing" as a forum for practical ends, *Beyond the Royal Gaze: Clanship and Public Healing in Buganda* (Charlottesville: University of Virginia Press, 2010), 95; and Benjamin Ray, *Myth, Ritual, and Kingship in Buganda* (Oxford: Oxford University Press, 1991).

were state-level decrees used to bring peace and reconciliation after war, insurrection, or foreign incursion that aligned well with restorative justice practices. Through experimentation and refinement, those restorative justice modalities were recognized by the Ethiopian people to be in their best interest.

A connection between South Africa, Ethiopia, and Rwanda is that all three were state-led processes. In all of them, government devised legal remedies that implicated both victor and vanquished or victim and perpetrator to legitimate the state's version of insurrection, foreign invasion, or genocide that the state believed required adjudicating.

One of the critical oversights in the conversation on restorative justice is this historical dimension. Erik Doxtader's work on South Africa's Truth and Reconciliation Commission (TRC) illustrates the difficulty researchers have had probing ethnographic depths for antecedents. To comprehend *ubuntu* and the synthesis of Christian and South African cultural traditions of restorative justice, Doxtader goes back to 1985, a mere decade before the beginning of the TRC, to reconstruct conversations and formulations by key African National Congress (ANC) and religious figures in South Africa. He claims that "the history of reconciliation in South Africa is a rhetorical history," commencing in the corridors of Robben Island prison or in ANC camps in frontier states in the early 1980s over what the word "reconciliation" means in the context of apartheid.[6] As the end of statutory apartheid drew near, the conversation shifted to very pragmatic issues over how to remain faithful to the agreements – read compromises – between Mandela and de Klerk, while administering some form of justice to mark the end of state-sponsored racism and the beginning of a rainbow nation. To a degree the conversation was historically shallow, though brimming with a consciousness that the TRC possessed the "potential for history-making."[7] Ruti Teitel analyzes the production of history through trials in terms of the state creating an "official" truth about the tragic past to justify current power holders. The narrative is not arrived at democratically and seldom portrays the misdeeds of those in power; rather, through the knowledge that the successor regime has been given the right to shape history, it does so with inclusive discourse that it hopes reconciles the population.[8]

6 Erik Doxtader, *With Faith in the Works of Words: The Beginnings of Reconciliation in South Africa, 1985–1995* (East Lansing: Michigan State University Press, 2009), 4, 35–84.

7 Doxtader, *With Faith in the Works of Words*, 19.

8 Ruti Teitel, *Transitional Justice* (Oxford: Oxford University Press, 2000), 97. For a more developed analysis that has benefited looking in the rearview mirror and uplifting successes of the TRC as well as its failures, see Rita Kesselring, *Bodies of Truth: Law, Memory, and the Emancipation in Post-Apartheid South Africa* (Stanford: Stanford University Press, 2017).

A brief assessment of *gacaca* in Rwanda also illustrates the differences between written history and cultural formulations. Within months following the genocide of 1994, the *Interahamwe* (the most important Hutu extremist leaders) were rounded up and sent to the International Criminal Tribunal for Rwanda (ICTR) in Arusha, Tanzania, where it took fourteen years to convict thirty-five Hutu. However, over 120,000 *genocidaires*, mostly Hutu, were apprehended in Rwanda itself, incarcerated, charged, and finally some tried in Rwandan courts. The court procedures were known more for their shortcomings including reliance upon antiquated Belgian legal codes, prosecution without representation, lack of independence from the executive branch of the government, and excessive use of capital punishment.[9] The Rwandan government tried to fix those problems by issuing the Organic Law of 1996, which spelled out the judicial process to address war crimes and genocide.[10] But those reforms also championed Western jurisprudence that was sluggish, susceptible to corruption, and well-removed from the Rwandan population's conception of justice. Finally the *Gacaca* Law of 2001 was passed to prosecute the vast majority of the 120,000 accused. But it is here where the histories of Ethiopia and Rwanda diverge. Traditionally *gacaca* – literally "justice on the grass" in Kinyarwanda – was one form of grassroots CDR existing in Rwanda, prior to and through the colonial interlude, to mediate disputes by convening elders of a community to hear the disgruntled and seek compromise or restitution.[11] Historically, it had no permanent mandate or judicial underpinning, did not deal with state-level issues, and its form strongly depended on the community in which it operated.[12] Yet because it was widely known and for lack of an alternative, the Rwandan government seized upon it and modified, modernized, and gave it a mandate.[13] Functioning after the genocide, *gacaca* courts were a neocolonial hybrid that brought together community-based CDR institutions with the crime of genocide that in the end legitimated the state's understanding of how the atrocities happened. The similarity with Ethiopia is that they

9 Pietro Sullo, *Beyond Genocide: Transitional Justice and Gacaca Courts in Rwanda* (The Hague: Asser Press, 2018), 159–85.

10 Télesphore Ngarambe, *Practical Challenges in Customary Law Translation: The Case of Rwanda's Gacaca Law* (Addis Ababa: OSSREA, 2015), 17–37.

11 Lars Waldorf, "Rwanda's Failing Experiment in Restorative Justice" in *Handbook of Restorative Justice*, eds. Dennis Sullivan and Larry Tifft (London: Routledge, 2008), 423–6.

12 Nicola Palmer, *Courts in Conflict: Interpreting the Layers of Justice in Post-Genocide Rwanda* (Oxford: Oxford University Press, 2015).

13 Phil Clark, *The Gacaca Courts, Post-Genocide Justice and Reconciliation in Rwanda: Justice without Lawyers* (Cambridge: Cambridge University Press, 2010); Ariel Meyerstein, "Between Law and Culture: Rwanda's *Gacaca* and Postcolonial Legality," *Law and Social Inquiry*, 32:2 (2007): 467–508.

were both expressions of state-level peacemaking.[14] Unlike in Ethiopia, in Rwanda a CDR institution had to be customized to fill the autochthonous void for a mechanism to administer justice and bring about national reconciliation. Ethiopia has written time-tested instruments at the national level to reconcile enemies through processes that line up closely with restorative justice.

This volume sets out to explore traditional ways in which political disputes and wars were resolved at the state level in Ethiopia. Starting in 1769 (the beginning of the *Zemene Mesafint,* meaning the "time of the nobility" or Era of the Princes, 1769–1855) and ending with the abortive coup d'état of 1960, examples will be drawn that illustrate how restorative justice was administered in Ethiopia.

An inference soon arrived at is that concepts of Customary Dispute Resolution – *ubuntu* or *gacaca* –were dexterously selected from a variety of alternatives and changed to fit the social and political needs. To an extent this typifies restorative processes in Sierra Leone, Nigeria, and Ghana;[15] moreover, it appears to be a global phenomenon, for the digital archives of the Artemis Project for Truth Commission Testimonies located at Yale University are equally ahistorical, meaning that the records are about the commissions themselves and the hope is that they will form the historical precedent for future generations. They hold scant historical material prior to the truth commissions for each of the amassed collections of the thirty-two countries transitioning from periods of violence or conflict to stability and peace.[16]

As will become abundantly clear, Ethiopia's traditions of restorative justice were conceived, swaddled, nurtured, and admonished when gone astray by the Ethiopian Orthodox Tewahido Church as described in Chapter 1. Likewise, *Ubuntu* was also born in a manger. Bishop Desmond Tutu's forceful voice in favor of restorative justice placed vague cultural remembrances on a Christian altar.[17] The principal concept borrowed from Christianity was the biblical understandings of forgiveness and less so on atonement.[18] Each and every step in the forgiveness process

---

14 Bert Ingelaere, *Inside Rwanda's Gacaca Courts: Seeking Justice after Genocide* ((Madison: University of Wisconsin Press, 2016); Anuradha Chakravarty, *Investing in Authoritarian Rule: Punishment and Patronage in Rwanda's Gacaca Courts for Genocide Crimes* (Cambridge: Cambridge University Press, 2016).

15 Chandra Lekha Sriram and Suren Pillay, eds., *Peace versus Justice? The Dilemma of Transitional Justice in Africa* (Rochester: James Currey, 2009).

16 Artemis Project, https://ylsmediaserv.law.yale.edu/webwork/trc2005/artemis.htm. For a brief survey see John Perry and T. Debey Sayndee, *African Truth Commissions and Transitional Justice* (New York: Lexington Books, 2019).

17 Desmond Tutu, *No Future Without Forgiveness* (New York: Doubleday, 1999).

18 Megan Shore, *Religion and Conflict Resolution: Christianity and South Africa's Truth and Reconciliation Commission* (London: Routledge, 2009), 69–74; and Richard Wilson, *Politics of Truth and Reconciliation in South Africa: Legitimising*

was analyzed by academics as well as individuals working for the TRC. Almost every critique centered on the concept of truthful apology in exchange for amnesty and forgiveness.[19] Many decried the overly Christian conceptualization of forgiveness which, unavoidably, caused difficulties for South Africans professing African Traditional Religion, Islam, Hinduism, or Judaism. Attached to the critiques was the fact that Christianity was viewed as a colonizing religion. Ethiopia reveals that the Christian elements of restorative justice possessed a foundation in African indigeneity. Ethiopia, it must be remembered, adopted Christianity in the fourth century.

Ethiopia's Contributions to Restorative Justice

Besides historicizing restorative justice in precolonial Africa and arguing that its Christian overtones are equally indigenous to the continent, Ethiopia offers the literature on restorative justice some other insights and corrections. First, it shows that Ethiopians struggled mightily with forgiveness and atonement in much that same way restorative justice advocates are doing today. Second, through trial and error, Ethiopia realized a workable form of restorative justice that brought buy-in by the people of different ethnic and religious backgrounds, and facilitated peace and reconciliation. Third, restorative justice in Ethiopia was indigenously inspired; it was never colonized by Western scholars nor is there an imperative to decolonize it. Fourth, Ethiopia's restorative justice modalities show that history is never static, that ideas, institutions, and jurisprudence change over time, accommodating themselves to pressures both intellectual and material as reflected in legal practices.

The main critique of the TRC was the maxim: amnesty for truth. What bothers victims of apartheid is that its accomplices – those who enforced state-decreed racism and were its willing accomplices – had only to pretend remorsefulness and fabricate "a truth" for which they were given a one-and-done amnesty. With this, white South Africans (primarily) could retain their wealth, property, and privilege, and victims were left with the elusive satisfaction of watching abusers squirm before the panel for a few minutes before returning to their substandard

the Post-Apartheid State (Cambridge: Cambridge University Press, 2001), 120. For a more generalized treatment see Ched Myers and Elaine Enns, *Ambassadors of Reconciliation, Volume I: New Testament Reflections on Restorative Justice and Peacemaking* (New York: Orbis, 2009).

19 Trudy Govier and Wilhelm Verwoerd, "The Promise and Pitfalls of Apology," *Journal of Social Philosophy*, 33:1 (Spring 2002): 67–82; Antjie Krag, *Country of My Skull: Guilt, Sorrow, and the Limits of Forgiveness in the New South Africa* (New York: Three Rivers Press, 2000).

homes, capricious work conditions, systemic poverty, and racial segregation. "Forgive and forget," black South Africans found unjust.[20]

The emphasis on forgive and forget has its rationale. Early twentieth-century theologian H. R. Mackintosh wrote:

> Those people who say that they can forgive but not forget betray the fact, unconsciously for the most part, that their forgiveness has been accompanied by reservations and qualifications which, morally, are fatal ... [I]f pardon is real, the injured man has wholly ceased to regard that past event as determinative of this personal relationships to the offender ... In this sense all true forgiveness forgets the guilt which it pardons.[21]

Nelson Mandela and Desmond Tutu believed this.[22]

In the conversation about forgiving and forgetting, Trudy Govier suggests that forgetting does not ensure a return to a good relationship, rather forgiving has constituent parts. First, forgiving is a process that forever requires work and constant revision; second, forgiving necessitates facing bitterness and anger, and replacing those sentiments with positive ones; and third, foundational to forgiveness is trust, trust in the integrity of the other individual and trust that the process of forgiving, noted above, will be perpetually reenacted.[23] Central to all three parts is the role of memory.

Ethiopia came to those same conclusions. As Chapter 2 demonstrates, "forgive and forget" only perpetuated war in Ethiopia, for the malcontent was left with the freedom and resources to plot insurrection another day. Chapter 3 shows that, through many trials, Ethiopians learned that forgiveness requires atonement, that the malcontent must demonstrate remorse and live according to the conditions of his amnesty, often demonstrated through some form of repair or restitution. This involved the constant evaluation by the memory-keepers tasked with assessing the perpetrators' contriteness, their willingness to live within the requirements set by the state to prove that the trust placed in them was worthy of forgiveness. The term used is "conditional forgiveness."

The second contribution is that conditional forgiveness was predicated on "forgive but never forget." Part of never forgetting involved creating a public spectacle, or as public as premodern Ethiopia would

---

20 Charles Villa-Vicenio and Wilhelm Verwoerd, eds., *Looking Back, Reaching Forward: Reflections on the Truth and Reconciliation Commission of South Africa* (Cape Town: University of Cape Town Press, 2000).

21 H. R. Mackentosh, *The Christian Experience of Forgiveness* (New York: Harper, 1927), 30.

22 Desmond Tutu, *No Future Without Forgiveness* (New York: Doubleday, 1999), 34–5.

23 Trudy Govier, *Forgiveness and Revenge* (London: Routledge, 2002), 43–5.

allow, to ceremonialize honor and shaming. Present at the ceremony or *wurdet* (shaming) were the victorious army, notable aristocracy, and church officials assembled to witness the submission and remember the conditions under which clemency was given. Forgiveness and reconciliation in the Ethiopian context appeared less weighted with notions of personal wrongdoing and instead was grounded in a moral ecology to which all subscribed because of a shared religious and educational background and social worldview that shaped an understanding of fairness and justice.

The emphasis in imperial Ethiopia was on public displays of remorse, in the short term, and on accountability to the conditions of the original forgiveness over longer stretches of time. Life conditionally lived often resulted in full restitution and reintegration. What is a forgivable offence and what is unforgivable may be culturally determined.[24] In Ethiopia the case of *Lij* Iyasu, the emperor who was overthrown in 1916 by a coalition of aristocrats, including *Ras* Tafari (later to take the coronation name Emperor Haile Selassie), and church officials, shows how the unforgivable is determined not by original transgression(s) but by recidivism, the way in which the conditions for forgiveness were abused and thus societal reconciliation jeopardized. In short, punishment represents the loss of trust. The ability to modify a verdict of clemency for apartheid's henchmen based on subsequent actions could quell black discontent in South Africa and other countries that continue to grant one-and-done amnesty through truth commissions gone wrong.

The third contribution to the literature on restorative justice is that restorative justice was endogenously conceived and nurtured in Ethiopia hundreds of years ago. A problem with restorative justice is that it is seen as having been co-opted or colonized by Western academics.[25] The TRC, which focused on rehabilitating a nation by a successor regime after suffering mass violence and gross human rights abuses, was African. The emphasis, during this early phase, was on bringing about peace and reconciliation to South Africa, yet Western academics pounced on it as a solution for the rest of the world. A second problem is that, over the years, restorative justice has broadened its prerogative away from affairs of states to victim/offender mediation and criminal justice reform.[26] These newer studies tend to focus almost exclusively

---

24 Danya Ruttenberg, *On Repentance and Repair: Making Amends in an Unapologetic World* (Boston: Beacon Press, 2022): and Alice MacLachlan, "The Nature and Limits of Forgiveness" (Ph.D. dissertation, Boston University, 2008). For a broad sweep of the strengths and weaknesses of restorative justice see Dennis Sullivan and Larry Tifft. eds., *Handbook of Restorative Justice: A Global Perspective* (London: Routledge, 2008).

25 Mechthild Nagel, *Ludic Ubuntu Ethics: Decolonizing Justice* (New York: Routledge, 2023).

26 The evolution of restorative justice away from national affairs to social and

on the West. An effort is underway to decolonize restorative justice, to bring it back to Africa, to revive *ubuntu*, to make its African origins normative.[27] To an extent, this volume accomplishes that. It scours primary and secondary sources of Ethiopian history to assert the African origins of restorative justice.

The final contribution to restorative justice is more an admonishment. The extensive literature on restorative justice tends to be synchronic; it looks at policy, jurisprudence, and societal reconciliation in the omnipresent. Chapters 2 through 7 show how attention to change over time, the diachronic element, unveils marvelous human understanding and ingenuity coupled with complications, setbacks, and often muddled legal practices, nevertheless – ones that more accurately represent the essence and experience of restorative justice.

Outline of book.

Chapter 1, "Restorative Justice Abstracted," is the most consequential chapter, as it attempts to determine the Judeo-Christian roots of restorative justice encapsulated in the *Fitha Negest* ("Justice of the Kings"). The chapter argues that the Bible was the generative text justifying the terms of forgiveness to be placed anywhere along the continuum between restorative and retributive justice as an individual case warranted.

The chapter probes the biblical origins of justice and how society's moral code became normative. The Ethiopian Orthodox Tewahido Church's gigantic biblical canon has eighty-one books – the most in Christendom. Its unique books concern ecclesiastical order, disciplinary rules, and administration of justice – not salvation. The scriptures modeled justice, yet the imperative to restore the polity rested on land tenure and the insecure political-religious hierarchy (read "feudalism") created to tax the peasantry. It is argued that restorative justice existed to stabilize an unstable social order. The performative aspect of restorative justice centered on honor and shaming. The honor and shaming ceremony or *wurdet*, which emphasized the shaming part, was a highly scripted ritual that functioned as a national signpost unequivocally stating who were the victors and the vanquished. As modalities developed, restorative justice stipulated the terms of conditional forgive-

---

criminal issues is best expressed through the Justice and Peacebuilding's *The Little Book* series, such as Howard Zehr, *The Little Book of Restorative Justice* (New York: Good Books, 2015); Lorraine Stutzman Amstutz, *The Little Book of Victim Offender Conferencing* (New York: Good Books, 2009); David Anderson Hooker, *The Little Book of Transformative Community Conferencing* (New York: Good Books, 2016); and Thomas Norman DeWolf, *The Little Book of Racial Healing* (New York: Good Books, 2019).

27 Nagel, *Ludic Ubuntu Ethics*, 5–12.

ness. Finally, since it was a public ceremony, the aristocracy, clergy, and soldiers were assembled, and functioned as the memory-keepers so that penitents would be forced to atone for their actions against the feudal state.

Chapter 2, "The *Zemene Mesafint*: Restorative Justice Misapplied," is primarily about peacemaking failures, what was learned – after repeated missteps, and how corrections were made to Ethiopia's restorative justice regime. The *Zemene Mesafint* was a time of constant warfare where provincial aristocrats challenged the weak, imperial center. The chapter looks at the way wars were concluded, how rivals were given amnesty, and how there was little consequence for defeat. In fact, it argues that the "forgive and forget" routine was so ingrained that a contender, twice or thrice defeated, was able to resume his position, reassert his patrimony over land and peasants, mobilize his subjects, and wage another war in short order. In other words, blanket amnesties led to more wars. The weakness of the center, and the fact that there was no single, recognized memory-keeper, jeopardized the effectiveness of Ethiopia's mechanisms to bring about social and political reconciliation through restorative justice.

Chapter 3, "Conditional Forgiveness: Restorative Justice Done Right," demonstrates how "conditional forgiveness" operated effectively to bring about peace and reconciliation. This short chapter is the historical highpoint of Ethiopia's restorative justice experiment.

First, however, it assesses how the imperial center was restored under Emperor Tewodros, but how, after his coronation, he became ever more ruthless, killing rivals. Vengeance and retribution dominated. The powers and people, however, remembered why magnanimity was a useful political tool and refashioned restorative justice modalities to include conditions for receiving forgiveness after Tewodros's sudden death.

Reform started with gauging the sincerity of an offender's penitence, in other words, his willingness to live under specified terms of forgiveness. If those conditions were not met, then the Imperial Court reserved the right to add more punitive terms. Ethiopia returned to a biblical understanding of forgiveness and atonement having to do with the relationship between the forgiver and the person seeking forgiveness. This was the idealized "conditional forgiveness" described in Chapter 1, and it worked well into the early twentieth century with many examples that showed the creative and adaptable manner in which restorative justice was applied. Two examples are given to illustrate this workable construct; they have to do with the honor and shaming of *Ras* Menilek and *Ras* Alula

Chapter 4, "The Battle of Adwa: Justice Misinterpreted," describes how Ethiopia's defeat of Italy's army at Adwa was Ethiopia's signature event, guaranteeing the country's independence and establishing it as a beacon for the world's oppressed and colonized populations. "Justice Misinterpreted" applies to the aftermath of the Battle of Adwa in two ways. First, Emperor Menilek was victorious and was duly celebrated for his magnanimity towards Italian officers and soldiers. Yet he encountered significant criticism from the Western press when he did not immediately release all of them. The chapter analyzes how he used Italian prisoners as pawns to ensure that Italy signed a peace treaty. Principally, what is introduced here is the battle between contending judicial systems, Ethiopian versus European, and how Menilek had to acknowledge alien jurisprudence within his sovereign state.

The second issue that it addresses is the amputation of the right hands and left feet of 800 *askaris* (Eritrean soldiers in Italian pay). Again, the West tried to paint Ethiopians as barbarous, but on the continuum between clemency and death that lie within restorative justice modalities, mutilation fits into the spectrum, for the *askaris* were warned on numerous occasions and chose to support the Italians over their own country-kin. As recalcitrant reoffenders, they had to be punished.

Chapter 5, "The Battle of Segale: Justice and Legitimacy," recounts the last time the Ethiopian government resorted to using traditional forms of restorative justice exclusively to settle a national dispute that easily could have torn the country apart. The issue was the short rule of Emperor Menilek's grandson, *Lij* Iyasu. At issue was a widely held belief amongst the aristocracy that *Lij* Iyasu's sexual indiscretions, administrative incompetence, judicial misrule, and conversion to Islam (apostasy) justified regime change. The historiography is contentious; however, this chapter bypasses it by focusing strictly on the efforts the coup-plotters employed to conform to conventional practices of restorative justice. The pageantry of the honor and shaming ceremony was over the top, partly to communicate the legitimacy of Empress Zawditu and *Ras* Tafari as heirs to the throne.

The second half deals with *Lij* Iyasu's noncompliance with the terms of his conditional forgiveness. From luxurious home arrest in Fiche to imprisonment in a musty prison wearing rusty shackles near Harar, this section assesses why more punitive conditions were decreed.

Chapter 6, "Italians, Collaborators, and the Indifferent: Muddled Justice," focuses on post-liberation Ethiopia. After liberation the task of administering justice split the Ethiopian population down the middle: patriots versus collaborators, and the indifferent were obliged to assert that they had always been on the winning side. Naturally collaborators denied their support for the Italians, and over time only a small number were deemed traitors worthy to stand trial. But here is where legal procedures became muddled. In 1941–42 Ethiopia's traditions of restorative justice lived on in the national memory. Yet in the early 1930s, Emperor Haile Selassie had initiated both civil and penal reforms based on codified European laws. Italy, of course, had planted their own courts, thus isolating the Ethiopian public from traditional forms of restorative justice even further. Finally, the British military asserted British military law as yet a third layer of European jurisprudence to confuse legal proceedings. This chapter attempts to explain why restorative justice was overlooked and only resorted to in a few collaborators' cases in which European legal solutions failed.

Chapter 7, "The 1960 Coup d'État: Restorative Justice Ignored," saw the Neway brothers mobilize the Imperial Bodyguard and other allies to overthrow Emperor Haile Selassie. That it failed had much to do with the plotters' negligence to include or neutralize the army and air force in their preparations. The coup attempt was a bloody affair culminating in the brothers gunning down fifteen top officials, including *Ras* Abebe Aregay, hero of the Patriot resistance against the Italians, in the Green Salon of the Imperial Palace.

Germame Neway was killed; his brother Mengistu was captured, tried in court, and sentenced to hanging. The form of justice used was European-inspired retributive justice, but even as the court case was litigated, it appeared societal reconciliation was impossible. Haile Selassie offered restorative justice; Mengistu, knowing full well that capital punishment would ensure his martyrdom, refused it. Much of the chapter analyzes the intellectual currents awash among young, foreign-educated elites. It looks at the progressive ideas discussed among members of the Qachane Club, modeled after the "Free Officers" movement in Egypt and of which Germame was a leader. Members of this group would shape Ethiopian politics for years to come. Their ideologies spanned the spectrum but were decidedly Western in orientation. Finally, this chapter assesses why Ethiopian traditions of restorative justice were ignored or relegated for less important putschists in the all-consuming effort to modernize.

The Epilogue concludes the volume with the more recent Red Terror trials that adjudicated the guilt or innocence of leaders in Mengistu Haile Mariam's military dictatorship. Because of the appeal of modernity and the influence of Marxism, Ethiopia walked away from its own traditions of restorative justice and adopted European penal codes emphasizing punishment. The successor regime, the Ethiopian People's Revolutionary Democratic Front (EPRDF), understood the imperative to deliver justice to the human rights abusers and their victims in order to bring a sense of societal reconciliation for Ethiopian citizens. To this end the EPRDF leadership selected a trial format using Ethiopia's European-based law as well as Ethiopian judges, prosecutors, and defense lawyers. After a fourteen-year trial, the verdict, so to speak, is that the trial brought little peace and no reconciliation. The EPRDF leadership claims they did not even know of Ethiopia's honored tradition of restorative justice.

In terms of form, Chapters 2 through 7 follow a similar pattern. They begin tracing historical developments in Ethiopia, sometimes with an intellectual or legal digression to illustrate how law, in theory and practice, was changing. This is followed by an account of the political and/or military disruption that destabilized the Ethiopian state. This all sets the context for an in-depth analysis on how restorative justice was used to reconstruct society and bring reconciliation to contending parties. Additionally, this is where the modes of meting out justice are studied. They range from forgive-and-forget to conditional forgiveness as restorative justice evolved and added more accountability. As the twentieth century progressed, the book describes instances where restorative justice was sidelined for Western codified law that falls into the category of retributive justice.

While as a historian I am comfortable describing events, the Epilogue bends towards prescriptive recommendations if only to encourage Ethiopians to look at their rich history, extract some of their restorative justice practices that accentuated ingenuity, flexibility, and adaptability and modify and use them to bring lasting peace and reconciliation to a fractured country. It is also hoped that Ethiopia inserts itself into the global discourse on restorative justice by demonstrating its historical roots on the African continent.

1

Restorative Justice Abstracted

This chapter attempts to provide an abstract – albeit a rather thick abstract – on the theory and practice of restorative justice in Ethiopia. The historicity is intentionally left imprecise in order to uplift the ideological roots of justice, their reflection of society's moral code and the normative manner in which understandings of justice were coded into restorative justice modalities. Broken down further the central questions are: Where do Ethiopia's concepts of justice come from? Who adjudicated cases? How were good governance and restorative justice schooled? What was the imperative to restore social order and how tightly was it connected to land tenure and the insecure political-religious hierarchy created to tax the peasantry – a hierarchy characterized by a wobbly social ladder that promoted and demoted aristocrats in near equal numbers? Why was the performative aspect of restorative justice centered on honor and shaming so important? Finally, why be magnanimous?

The chapter intends to leave the reader with four observations or signposts about restorative justice: 1. The Ethiopian Christian Orthodox overtones to restorative justice in both substance and application; 2. The extreme lengths society went to to identify and educate individuals – *debteras* (unordained church clerics) versed in the liturgical poetry known as *qiné* – who possessed superior intellect to decipher the possibility for reconciliation between good and evil in order to produce lasting peace; 3. The role of restorative justice in maintaining a stable mode of production; and 4. The importance of a public honor and shaming ceremony to ensure appropriate penitence associated with conditional forgiveness.

Restorative Justice in Ethiopia

The generative text for Ethiopia's understanding of justice, including restorative justice, was the Bible. The Old and New Testaments offered countless examples from capital punishment to blanket amnesty and included the context under which each choice was made. Forgiveness, atonement, and redemption figure prominently; likewise, vengeance, killing, and war were justified in the Scriptures. Hebraic ideas about justice fall along the whole continuum from vengeance to forgiveness and Ethiopia's understanding reflects the same spectrum.[1]

Little is known about the justice system prior to the coming of Christianity to Ethiopia in the fourth century. The Christianization of Ethiopia, however, is well documented. Two young, well-educated brothers from Tyre, Frumentius and Aedesius were on a boat returning from India when their boat was forced to drop anchor for repairs at the Aksumite port of Adulis on the Red Sea. Tragically, all passengers and shipmates were killed except for the two brothers. Because of their education they were soon brought to the imperial court. The underage king's mother implored the two Syrian Christians to remain in Ethiopia and tradition states that Aedesius became King Ezana's cupbearer and Frumentius, the brighter of the two, became 'guardian of the Law', more accurately steward or scribe to the palace. The story goes on to state that Aedesius eventually returned to Tyre and became a priest, while Frumentius traveled to Alexandria and appealed to the Coptic Patriarch, Athanasius I, to send a bishop to Aksum to convert and baptize those sympathetic to the Christian message and ensure that Ethiopia adhered to the Monophysite creed the Patriarchate championed. Perhaps to Frumentius' surprise, Athanasius consecrated him Bishop and dispatched him back to Ethiopia.[2]

While it is recognized that Ethiopia's conversion was paper thin, confined essentially to Ezana's royal court, two issues stand out. First, Christianity's initial converts were members of the king's court, thus, cementing the connection between priests and politicians. Second, even before Frumentius was made bishop, as 'guardian of the Law' he was in a position to interpret political, military, and legal matters through Christian optics; this continued into the twentieth century as often clerics performed duties as scribes and councilors deciphering secular issues through a Biblical lens. Creed and court henceforth were irrevocably fused.[3]

---

1 Charles Schaefer, "Reexamining the Ethiopian Historical Record on the Continuum between Vengeance and Forgiveness" in *Proceedings of the 15th International Conference on Ethiopian Studies*, ed. Siegbert Uhlig (Wiesbaden: Harrassowitz, 2006), 348–55; and Schaefer, "Forgiveness with Consequences: Scriptures, *Qenē,* and Traditions of Restorative Justice in Nineteenth-Century Ethiopia" in *Displacing the State: Religion and Conflict in Neoliberal Africa*, ed. James Howard Smith and Rosalind Hackett (Notre Dame: University of Notre Dame Press, 2012).

2 Two authors examine the origins of Christianity in detail. Of longstanding repute see Edward Ullendorf, *Ethiopia and the Bible* (London: Oxford University Press, 1968); for contemporary interpretation see Ephraim Isaac, *The Ethiopian Orthodox Täwahïdo Church* (Trenton: Red Sea Press, 2012).

3 Perhaps the most insightful, yet brief, analysis of this fusion of politics and

In the early 1600s, Jerome Lobo observed, "It would not be easy to determine whether the Abyssins are more Jews or Christians."[4] Traveling through Ethiopia in 1809, Henry Salt similarly noted, "The reader conversant in Scripture, cannot fail ... to remark ... the general resemblance existing throughout between the manners of [Ethiopians] and those of Jews previously to the reign of Solomon."[5] Edward Ullendorf, one of the early deans of Ethiopian studies, observed that the form of Christianity in Ethiopia syncretized elements of pre-Talmudic Judaism with spirit worship or *zar* to form an "Abyssinian Christianity" that emphasized the Old Testament as much as the New Testament.[6] Emphasizing both testaments widened the range for what were considered appropriate legal solutions on the continuum from vengeance to forgiveness.

This fusion of religious and political ideology, found in the *Kibre Negest*,[7] defined the institution of the emperor and prescribed how to govern.[8] Its mythology, invented in the twelfth century and passed down to us in its final redaction in the early fourteenth century, is centered on legitimating Ethiopian emperors by claiming their descent from Menilek I, the offspring of King Solomon's consummated lust for the Queen of Sheba.[9] The national epic has Menilek coming of age and

religion – the "King-Priest" – is provided by Taddesse Tamrat, "Feudalism in Heaven and on Earth: Ideology and the Political Structure of Medieval Ethiopia" in *Proceedings of the Seventh International Conference of Ethiopian Studies*, ed. Sven Rubenson (Addis Ababa: Addis Ababa University Press, 1984), 195–200.

4 Jerome Lobo, *A Voyage to Abyssinia*, trans. Samuel Johnson (London: 1735), 310.

5 Henry Salt, *A Voyage to Abyssinia and Travels into the Interior of that Country*, reprint (London: Frank Case, 1967), 306. For an alternate view on the connection between scripture and power see Manuel Joao Ramos, "Machiavellian Empowerment and Disempowerment: The Violent Political Changes in Early Seventeenth-Century Ethiopia" in *The Anthropology of Power: Empowerment and Disempowerment in Changing Structures*, ed. Angela Cheater (London: Routledge, 1999), 191–205.

6 Edward Ullendorf, *The Ethiopian: An Introduction to Country and People* (London: Oxford University Press, 1965), 97–9; also Ullendorf, *Ethiopia and the Bible*, 73–130.

7 *Kebra Negast (The Glory of the Kings)*, ed. and trans. Miguel Brooks (Kingston, Jamaica: LMH Publishing Limited, 2001).

8 Yirga Gelaw Woldeyes, *Native Colonialism: Education and the Economy of Violence Against Traditions in Ethiopia* (Trenton: Red Sea Press, 2017), 23–56. Despite what the title implies, Donald Crummey's article principally discusses the political rationale for buying into the ideology of the *Kibre Negest*, see "Imperial Legitimacy and the Creation of Neo-Solomonic Ideology in 19th-Century Ethiopia," *Cahiers d'Etudes Africaines*, 109:28 (1988): 13–43.

9 The disconnect between being authored in the twelfth century CE while the events took place in the tenth century BCE are difficult to reconcile, but mythology tends to slight history. The purpose Jacques Rancière observes

leaving his mother in Ethiopia to travel to Israel to visit his father and acquire statecraft, knowledge and wisdom. Much of what defined good governance, therefore, was lifted straight from the Old Testament specifically the books of Judges and Kings. Yirga Gelaw Woldeyes argues, "What is considered important is the significance of the book [*Kibre Negest*] in framing social consciousness and organizing political life in Ethiopia."[10] The ultimate legitimation was the abduction of the Ark of the Covenant from Jerusalem to Axum and God's proclamation that Ethiopia was the new Zion. That the historicity of the *Kibre Negest* is problematic for many reasons, including linearly drawing succession between Old and New Testaments without emphasizing Christ's new covenant to all gentiles, seems not to trouble Orthodox Ethiopians. It is the social modeling contained within to which believers adhere. Again, Yirga Gelaw Woldeyes notes that the Ark of the Covenant is a physical entity as well as the word of God or *Egzia'biher*. *Egzia'biher* "means Lord of country or place. The Ark of the Covenant is believed to be that place where God chose to emplace himself in order to give law and mercy to the world."[11]

This fusion between divine and profane is seen in many of the unique books included in the Ethiopian Orthodox Tewahido Church's gigantic biblical canon. The Protestant biblical canon contains 66 books in both testaments, the Catholic 73, the Eastern Orthodox 78, and the Ethiopian Orthodox 81, in which the Wisdom literature, decreed by both the Orthodox and the Roman Catholic churches to be canonical, is prized.[12] What is revealing about those additional canonical books unique to the Ethiopian Orthodox Tewahido Church is how they model ecclesiastical order – when to be firm, when to give. The Ethiopic book of Meqabyan I (it should be noted that the three books of Meqabyan are not identical to Maccabees though there is some similarity) recounts how King Tserutsaydan persecuted three sons of Benjamin, a Jew, how this led to

---

is that national epics, or democratic politics, are not about establishing the correct origin story; the origin is a retroactive discovery, constructed to legitimate contemporary conditions, *Hatred of Democracy* (London: Verso, 2007), 51. Harald Aspen grounds the *Kibre Negest* in the space between history and myth, "Sacred History: The Solomonic Myth" in *Amhara Traditions of Knowledge: Spirit Mediums and their Clients* (Wiesbaden: Harrassowitz Verlag, 2001), 49–54. Also see I. Shâhid, "The *Kebra Nagast* in the Light of Recent Research," *Le Muséon*. 89 (1976): 133–78.

10 Yirga Gelaw Woldeyes, *Native Colonialism*, 26.

11 Yirga Gelaw Woldeyes, *Native Colonialism*, 29.

12 Canonization of books in the Ethiopian Orthodox Tewahido Church is less stringent than most other churches. Many Christian texts and synodical reports from Alexandria and other Monophysite synods filtered down to the Aksumite kingdom and once there were revered. It was only in the twelfth century that Zera Yaqob attempted to limit the canon to 81 by assessing their broader spiritual basis and ecclesiastical import, see Peter Brandt, "Bible Canon" in *Encyclopaedia Aethiopica*.

Tseerutsaydan's fall and finally his shaming, atonement, and redemption.[13] To follow JAH (Yahweh) and keep his laws had societal implications: "Love Me, and I shall love your welfare."[14] Like the other two, Meqabyan III depicts the struggle between good and evil saying that "when [the sinner] has knowledge, he might return and enter repentance, and that JAH might forgive him his sin."[15] Fascination with law, order, and reconciliation is seen in the Ethiopian Orthodox Tewahido Church's broader New Testament canon. The struggle between good and evil dominates The Ethiopic Book of Enoch with prescribed paths for the faithful to "practice uprightness and peace" (Enoch 92.1).[16] The transmission and reception of Enoch was conveyed through the sale of amulets and icons to show alternate understandings of good and evil (including justice and injustice) "which introduces successive interpretations."[17] Chapters 96 through 100 admonish believers with countless expressions of "Woe to you" about ambition, avarice, and malice that (a) pervert their relationship with God, and (b) destroy community.[18]

Senodos (translated as 'assembly, meeting, council', alternately Sinodos) is arguably considered the most important of canonical collections of the church because it deals with church appointments, functions of the ecclesiastical hierarchy, disciplinary rules and moral practices often attributed to the Apostles. "Sinodos is the Corpus juris Ecclesiastic" with two books devoted to the "Hortatory discourse to believers who desire to walk in the paths of wisdom and knowledge."[19] All of these practical stories about methods to govern and lessons on how to administer justice were applied to the secular sphere.

While Scriptures were read by a few literate priests and educated aristocrats, Zera Yaqob, a model fifteenth-century emperor, stipulated the whole Bible was to be read in its entirety during church services in the course of the year and that special emphasis be placed on the Law and the Prophets. Scriptures shaped language, idiomatic expression, metaphor, and, in fact, the ideation of the world and society. This is seen repeatedly in the hagiographic literature where emperors are referred to in biblical terms. In reading the royal chronicles of Zera Yaqob, Amde Seyon, Tekle Giorgis, Galawdewos, Yohannes, and even

---

13 Feqade Selassie, trans. *Ethiopian Books of Meqabyan 1–3, in Standard English* (New York: Netsanet Publishing, 2008).

14 Feqade Selassie, *Meqabyan I*, ch. 29.

15 Feqade Selassie, *Meqabyan III*, ch. 10.

16 M. A. Knibb, *The Ethiopic Book of Enoch* (Oxford: Clarendon Press, 1978), 222.

17 Bruk Ayele Asale, *I Enoch as Christian Scripture* (Eugene: Pickwick Publications, 2020), 88.

18 Knibb, *Enoch*, 228–35.

19 "Canon Law" *The Ethiopian Orthodox Tewahedo Church Faith and Order* https://www.ethiopianorthodox.org/english/canonical/books.html; Alessandro Bausi, "Senodos" in *Encyclopaedia Aethiopica.*

Menilek II, a case can be made that Ethiopian imperial history is simply the history of Israel with Ethiopian names superimposed, for the personalities, wisdom imparted, victories and defeats and their resolution are all comparable to the Old Testament prophets and kings like Elijah, Elisha, Saul, David, and Solomon.[20]

Under Zera Yaqob, legal procedure became more formalized. While the *Kibre Negest* legitimated the restoration of the Solomonic dynasty over the Zagwe dynasty, Emperor Zera Yaqob felt compelled to go beyond and codify law. First he directed the compilation of religious legal precedents into the *Fawse Manfasawi* (literally 'spiritual remedies' or 'canonical penances'). When the limitations of Ethiopian customary law became apparent, Zera Yaqob ordered the translation of the *Fitha Negest* ('Justice of the Kings') from Arabic into Ge'ez, the court and liturgical language of Ethiopia at that time.[21] The *Fitha Negest* is a compilation of Roman-Byzantine law collected by the Coptic Church of Alexandria following the Council of Nicaea. Again these laws fused Old and New Testaments, endorsed Orthodox synodical agreements, and included other ecclesiastical and secular remedies the Coptic Church judged suitable for Ethiopia's legal code.[22] The first twenty-two chapters are about ecclesiastical order, with the remainder given to social directives cementing the fusion between church and society.[23] The initial impact of the *Fitha Negest* may have been negligible due to the variety of court practices operating in Ethiopia from adjudicating divorce to state-level decisions; however, by the sixteenth-century Portuguese Catholics working in Ethiopia began to refer to it, possibly because of its reference to Roman-Byzantine law with which they were moderately familiar.[24] While it is difficult to determine when the *Fitha Negest* was cited in court cases, it was only formally incorporated into the Ethiopi-

---

20 For two English translations that communicate this point see, G. W. B. Huntingford, *The Glorious Victories of 'Amda Seyon King of Ethiopia* (Oxford: Clarendon Press, 1965); and H. Weld Blundell, *The Royal Chronicle of Abyssinia 1769-1840*, reprinted (Osnabrück: Otto Zeller Verlag, 1989).

21 Paulos Tzadua, trans., *The Fetha Nagast: The Law of the Kings*, reprint (Durham, NC: Carolina Academic Press, 2009).

22 Aberra Jembere, *An Introduction to the Legal History of Ethiopia, 1434–1974* (Munster: Lit Verlag, 2000), 3, 187–92.

23 Negussie Andres Dominic, *The Fetha Nagast and its Ecclesiology* (New York: Peter Lang, 2010) develops the nature and structure of church order applied to Ethiopia.

24 F. Alvares who resided in Ethiopia between 1506 and 1520, described the Imperial Court and lesser court proceedings and made reference to *Fitha Negest* in *The Prester John of the Indies*, trans. C. F. Beckingham and G. W. B. Huntingford (Cambridge: 1962), 439–40. To comprehend how extensive Ethiopia's contacts were with Europe through the seventeenth century, see Verena Krebs, *Medieval Ethiopian Kingship, Craft, and Diplomacy with Latin Europe* (Cham: Palgrave Macmillan, 2021).

an legal system in 1908 when Emperor Menilek II formalized government structure and specified the duties of each ministry. According to Mahteme Sellassie Welde Mesqel, prominent official and intellectual titan, the Minister of Justice "shall control whether any decision has been given in accordance with rules incorporated in the *Fetha Negast*."[25]

Who Adjudicated Justice?

Aberra Jembere describes Ethiopian laws as "legal pluralism,"[26] he goes on to analyze influences on the law-making process that have to do with natural law, religious principles, and customary law all determined by whether a community practiced African Traditional Religion, Islam, or Christianity, whether a group was pastoralist or agrarian, or whether they were located in the highlands of central Ethiopia or the lowlands of the Awash. The variety of legal procedures is impressive. Perhaps the earliest comparative study of Ethiopian jurisprudence was written in 1888 by Antoine d'Abbadie describing court practices in the highlands and among the Gurage and Oromo.[27] Over a century later Alula Pankhurst and Getachew Assefa in their edited volume, *Grass-roots Justice in Ethiopia: The Contribution of Customary Dispute Resolution*, study ethnic interpretations of dispute resolution from the Afar to the Sidama and beyond. Yet within each ethnic group, the volume shows, there is considerable variation and levels of adjudication that are unique to their language and kinship structure.[28] Marco Bassi's in-depth study *Decisions in the Shade: Political and Juridical Processes among the Oromo-Borana* addresses how the *Gada* system brokered justice in southern Ethiopia.[29] In the Ethiopian highlands, people resolved disputes through the "road-side court," an informal people's court that often availed itself by waylaying a local governor or some

---

25 Mahteme Sellassie Welde Mesqel quoted in Aberra Jembere, *Legal History of Ethiopia*, 195.

26 Aberra Jembere, *Legal History of Ethiopia*, 2. For a more robust analysis of legal pluralism applied to the Horn of Africa, see Lyda Favali and Roy Pateman, *Blood, Land, and Sex: Legal and Political Pluralism in Eritrea* (Bloomington: Indiana University Press, 2003).

27 Antoine d'Abbadie, "La Procédure en Éthiopie," *Nouvelle revue historique de droit français et étranger*, vol. 12 (1888): 462–71.

28 Alula Pankhurst and Getachew Assefa, eds., *Grass-roots Justice in Ethiopia: The Contribution of Customary Dispute Resolution* (Addis Ababa: Centre Français d'Études Éthiopiennes, 2008).

29 Marco Bassi, *Decisions in the Shade: Political and Juridical Processes among the Oromo-Borana* (Trenton: Red Sea Press, 2005). The *Gada* system, practiced by the Oromo, is a traditional method of governance and jurisprudence that tends to be more democratic.

other ranking aristocrat to listen and offer a verdict.[30] Donald Crummey further extends the terrain of who was able to litigate showing that, as far back as the 1750s, Amhara women frequently pleaded before courts to claim their usufruct rights to land.[31] Geography, gender, class, religion, and culture were all factors that contributed to Ethiopia's legal pluralism. However, the focus of this study is on the highest court of the land, the *zufan chilot,* translated as the Imperial Court or Crown Court, where matters of state were decided.

While the *Fitha Negest* influenced state decisions, the subtleties, the political calculations, and the implications a decision could have on a group or region was left for the *zufan chilot,* the Imperial Court – made up of the emperor, the *techiwoch* and the *afa negus* – to resolve. The *techiwoch,* those who listen to a case and render a verdict, comprised trusted members of the *mekwanint* or the high ruling class consisting of nobles, provincial governors and high-ranking military and ecclesiastical officials;[32] the *afa negus* literally means 'the Mouth of the emperor' and was equivalent to a Chief Justice. The manner in which the *zufan chilot* resolved treasonous acts, gross human rights abuses, or political crimes was decided using Ethiopia's traditions of restorative justice.

Administration of justice was a collective affair. Supporting this notion, the *afa negus* ideally employed up to twenty-four *wember*s (high religious judicial figures) with differing expertise to advise him on particular cases, for there was a proverb, "One stick does not light, one man may not give a judgement."[33] Likewise the emperor relied upon the *mekwanint.*

Members of the *mekwanint* were homogeneous and heterogeneous at the same time. They were a homogeneous social class in that many elite families had remained in the aristocratic ranks for generations and cemented their position by arranging single or double intermarriages to other leading families. Marriage took many forms and at the highest levels was strictly political.[34] Family genealogies were complicated by

30 The "road-side court" is similar to the Old Testament practice of *mishpat* (meaning justice or judgement in Hebrew) or justice at the gate where the 'courthouse' was in a public forum at the entry-gate to the town (Amos 5:15).
31 Donald Crummey, "Women and Landed Property in Gondarine Ethiopia," *International Journal of African Historical Studies,* 14:3 (1981): 444–65; also see Allan Hoben, *Land Tenure among the Amhara of Ethiopia* (Chicago: University of Chicago Press, 1973), 61.
32 *Mekwanint* literally is translated as 'nobles' as the word itself is plural. The *mekwanint* includes the *masafent* at the very top of royal bloodlines and descends to the *balabbat* or local elites. For this study *mekwanint* is used for a central feature of the Ethiopian aristocracy – its impermanence, its fluidity, which will be explained below.
33 Craven H. Walker, *The Abyssinian At Home* (New York: AMS Press, 1933), 151.
34 Bairu Tafla, "Marriage as a Political Device: An Appraisal of a Social-

the fact that a father could marry off his daughter to an ally and then, when political fortunes changed, annul the marriage and give her to a rival to ensure protection and reduce the likelihood of future conflict. Multiplied over generations, kinship tied almost every prominent family together. There was a negative side to this, as Heran Sereke-Brhan writes: "The rate at which marriages were arranged and dissolved and the number of men elite women were married to over their lifetimes seems to place them as vulnerable victims of their political machinery."[35] Yet Heran Sereke-Brhan acknowledges that the political nature of marriage "continued to weave a matrix of an increasingly shared identity in proximity to power."[36] When Taytu Betul (better known as Empress Taytu) finally married Menilek, he was her fifth husband; similarly Menilek left Bafena for the stronger alliances Taytu brought through her family connections to Semen, Yejju, and Begemdir.[37] Heran Sereke-Brhan's brilliant dissertation diagrams the prevalence of intermarriages among the power elites, even showing how three of Emperor Haile Selassie's grandchildren were married to members of Wallega aristocratic families, thus, tying his Amhara line with Oromo lineages.[38] Marriages also cut across the Christian/Muslim divide when politically advantageous, especially during the *Zemene Mesafint* where Christians and Muslims frequently intermarried.[39] Creed was less important among these hybridized families than sharing "certain aspirations, common value systems, self-interests and perceptions."[40]

Simultaneously the *mekwanint* were remarkably heterogeneous. Not only was there ethnic intermarriage between northerners and southerners or between Christians and Muslims, but there was a constant infusion of new bloodlines from those lower in the social hierarchy. Social mobility was exceptionally fluid in Ethiopia with individuals and families moving up and down the social ladder in near equal numbers.

political Aspect of the Menilek Period 1889–1916," *Journal of Ethiopian Studies,* 10:1 (1972): 24–48.

35 Heran Sereke-Brhan, "Building Bridges, Drying Bad Blood: Elite Marriages, Politics and Ethnicity in 19th and 20th Century Imperial Ethiopia," Ph.D. dissertation, Michigan State University (2002), 132.

36 Heran Sereke-Brhan, "Building Bridges, Drying Bad Blood," 101.

37 Chris Prouty, *Empress Taytu and Menilek II: Ethiopia, 1883–1910* (Trenton: Red Sea Press, 1986), 24–5.

38 Heran Sereke-Brhan, "Building Bridges, Drying Bad Blood," 197.

39 Two authorities have assessed this connection in detail, see R. A. Caulk, "Religion and State in Nineteenth Century Ethiopia," *Journal of Ethiopian Studies,* 10:1 (1972): 23–41; and Donald Crummey, *Priests and Politicians: Protestant and Catholic Missions in Orthodox Ethiopia, 1830–1868* (Oxford: Clarendon Press, 1972).

40 Heran Sereke-Brhan, "Building Bridges, Drying Bad Blood," 87.

A warrior distinguished on the battlefield was often rewarded with *gult* rights, which, in overly simplistic terms, meant the right to demand tribute from peasants working the land who, themselves, had recognized usufruct rights to land. Those usufruct rights, known as *rist* rights, enabled farmers and their children the right to cultivate their *rist* lands in perpetuity. A shrewd *gult*-holder could parlay his position through additional meritorious service to his Lord, through upwardly mobile marriages or through exploitative acts to ever higher positions on the social ladder. Likewise, a *debtera*, an educated, unordained church cleric, who was often revered for his knowledge while feared for his magical powers, could use his expertise in customary law and his oratorical skills to successfully argue that he had *rist* rights to more and more land, ultimately positioning himself to become the local *chiqa shum* (village chief and/or tax collector for the *gult* holder). Once there, the ambitious *debtera* was positioned to ascend into the lower ranks of the aristocracy and acquire *gult* rights to become a *balabbat* (local chief). It could take one or more generations but, nevertheless, upward social mobility was possible. Taddesse Tamrat wrote, "Under favourable circumstances such a resourceful local prince could easily grow into a serious rival of the monarch himself."[41] Brave, competent, articulate progeny could move up; less gifted sons and daughters could just as easily move down.

There was another avenue for downward mobility based on the vertical clientage ties between the *gult* holders and *rist* holders – lords and peasants – for the former's position and prosperity depended on the latter's support and willingness to be taxed at appropriate levels as well as fight the aristocrats' political battles. But those ties were easily broken when the peasant was pressed into military service and the constellation of elites, which formed the vertical ties he fought for on the battlefield, were defeated. At such a time a peasant often joined the victorious lord's army and assumed a new patron-client relationship. It was all about earning merit and honor, superior and inferior, victor or vanquished.[42]

It takes little imagination to see why scholars have equated Ethiopia's land tenure system with European feudalism for conceptually there were many similarities especially when focusing on reciprocal feudal obligations versus tribute.[43] Conversely, European feudalism was static

41 Taddesse Tamrat, *Church and State in Ethiopia, 1270–1527* (Oxford: 1972), 96.

42 John Iliffe, *Honour in African History* (Cambridge: Cambridge University Press, 2005), 63.

43 Defining whether the Ethiopian polity was feudal or not took on urgency prior to the Ethiopian Revolution of 1974 and continued to be hotly debated for another decade as the feudal mode of production was so convenient a term in asserting Ethiopia's trajectory to communism, see Addis Hiwet, *Ethiopia: from Autocracy to Revolution* (London: 1975) and Negatu Alemu (writing in a quarterly published by the EPRP), "On the Modes of Production in Ethiopia," *Ethiopian Marxist Review*, 1 (August 1980): 7–42. But there were those who

Figure 1 Provincial court of justice. Attribution: Photographic Collection of the Institute for Ethiopian Studies, Addis Ababa University.

with social classes defined by birth; whereas Ethiopia championed meritocracy, enabling assertive social climbers ways to ascend on approved paths or aggressive malcontents to use the institution of the *shiftnet* (an acknowledged form of banditry) to challenge authority and if successful in battle to become aristocrats.[44] The point, even for the *shiftnet*, was not social disruption but rather an alternate path for inclusion.

---

adamantly argued that Ethiopia's relationship between elites and peasants was unique, see Gene Ellis, "The Feudal Paradigm as a Hindrance to Understanding Ethiopia," *Journal of Modern African Studies*, 14 (1976): 275–95. And then there were those who, perhaps objectively, tried to appease both sides by coining the term "Abyssinian feudalism" a phrase that accounts for the idiosyncrasies of Ethiopia along with its similarities to Europe, see Donald Crummey, "Abyssinian Feudalism," *Past and Present*, 89 (1980): 115–38. For a last word, based on thorough archival research complemented by years of fieldwork see Svein Ege, *Class, State, and Power in Africa: A Case Study of the Kingdom of Shäwa (Ethiopia) about 1840* (Wiesbaden: 1996). While many scholars have weighed in on whether Ethiopia was feudal, two old ethnohistorical studies stand out in terms of their deep ethnographic analysis, see Hoben, *Land Tenure*; and Joanna Mantel-Niećko, *The Role of Land Tenure in the System of Ethiopian Imperial Government in Modern Times*, trans. K. A. Bobiński (Warsaw: Wydawnictwa Uniwersytetu Warszawskiego,1980).

44 Timothy Fernyhough, "Social Mobility and Dissident Elites in Northern Ethiopia: The Role of Banditry, 1900–1969" in *Banditry, Rebellion and Social Protest in Africa*, ed. Donald Crummey (London: James Currey, 1986), 151–72; Donald Crummey, "Banditry and Resistance: Noble and Peasant in Nineteenth Century Ethiopia" in *Proceedings of the Seventh International Conference of*

The *mekwanint* was made up of a diverse group of men yet they all were similarly educated, shared a deep-seated allegiance to the Ethiopian monarchy and were experienced judges. Indeed, *mekwanint* is the plural of *mekonnen*, which means governor or judge, for the two are consider synonymous. As Samuel Gobat observed, during the *Zemene Mesafint*, political, judicial and military offices were one: "for all the governors are civil judges, and all the civil judges are military men."[45] Guébrè Sellassié in his *Chronique du règne de Ménélik II* devotes a chapter each to three judgements Menilek issued, shortly after having been sprung from captivity at Maqdala in 1865 as he reentered his patrimonial lands and consolidated power.[46] Why did Guébrè Sellassié choose to elaborate on those three thorny rulings? To confirm that Menilek had the ability to lead Shewa and ultimately the whole of Ethiopia as emperor, military prowess was not enough.

In the 'feudal' structure of Ethiopia there were governors and subgovernors throughout the kingdom each authorized to collect taxes, provide services (few that there were), command the provincial army or local militia, ensure ecclesiastical order, and maintain peace which, obviously, involved adjudicating disputes.[47] Listening to and resolving disputes comprised a sizeable block of time every day at the governor's provincial court, known as the *shaleqa fird bet*.[48] Land disputes, financial maleficence, and divorce were routinely settled; more complex cases involved political spats caused by an ever-changing social hierarchy where an ambitious social climber challenged a complacent placeholder. A governor had to consider what was best for his realm. Were the patron-client relations of the placeholder sufficiently strong that to replace him would disrupt tax revenue and jeopardize the governor's ability to mobilize a specified number of peasant/soldiers? Or was it time to cast about and consider whether the more competent social climber

Ethiopian Studies, ed. Sven Rubenson (Addis Ababa: Addis Ababa University Press, 1984): 263–77; and Richard Caulk, "Bad Men of the Borders: *Shum* and *Shifta* in Northern Ethiopia in the Nineteenth Century," *Proceedings of the Second Annual Seminar of the Department of History of AAU*, Vol. I (Addis Ababa: 1984), 39–104.

45 Samuel Gobat, *Journal of a Three Year's Residence in Abyssinia* (London: 1834), 335.

46 Guébrè Sellassié, *Chronique du règne de Ménélik II, Roi des Rois d'Éthiopie*, vol. 1 (Paris: Librairie Orientale et Américaine, 1930), chaps. XX–XXII.

47 Shiferaw Bekele, "Kassa and Kassa: The State of Their Historiography," *Kasa and Kasa: Papers on the Lives, Times and Images of Tewodros II and Yohannes IV (1855-1889)* (Addis Ababa: Institute for Ethiopian Studies, 1990), 294–5.

48 Aberra Jembere, *Legal History of Ethiopia*, 222–4.

would be a superior ally? In short, each governor or sub-governor was well versed in considering issues of state in his own province.[49]

Antoine d'Abbadie, a French explorer/entrepreneur with a legal background, provides insight into the manner in which broader considerations were taken into account when rendering judgements in the nineteenth century. He claims, *Ras* Mikael overruled talion law – eye for eye, tooth for tooth (Leviticus 24:19–21) – that victims demanded in a certain case, profiting from his powers to see both sides and long-term consequences as the judge to commute the sentence, like King Solomon.[50]

However, the *mekwanint* were required to split their time between their governorate and the royal court. Heeding imperial summons, they came and stayed at the court to function as royal counselors to the emperor for a significant portion of the year. The emperor's motives were thinly disguised; he sought their advice on issues of state but, more importantly, he wanted them physically close to ensure loyalty. Likewise, self-interest of a particular governor often countermanded that of the imperial court, but collectively the *mekwanint* were a remarkably cohesive group guided by "'the invisible hand' that makes them tick as a group."[51]

The *zufan chilot* was an institution devised to promote consensus. There were a few permanent members, including the *afa negus* ('Mouth of the emperor') and an elite clique of churchmen that at times included the full participation of the *abuna* (Archbishop or head of the Ethiopian Orthodox Tewahido Church), the *echege* (Chief Prior of the monastery of Debre Libanos in Shewa, who functioned as the ecclesiastical head of the Church and chief of all monasteries), the *qes atse* (the Imperial Chaplain), the *aqabe sa'at* (guardian of the canon), the *liqa memmheran* (chief of the learned scholars associated with the *Meshaf Bet*), and the *liqa debtera* (chief of the scribes and cantors associated with a *Qiné Bet* – School of Poetry).[52] When there was a legitimate emperor who ruled over all of Ethiopia, these permanent members functioned as a team of memory-keepers for the court.

In contrast, the revolving door of the *mekwanint* to the *zufan chilot* was constantly turning, for all had obligations in their home provinces, which drew them away from the imperial court, yet their role in court proceedings was critical.[53] Hearing cases at the *zufan chilot*, these

49 For a description of the duties and obligations of governors see R. H. Kofi Darkwah, *Shewa, Menilek and the Ethiopian Empire 1813–1899* (London: Heinemann, 1975), 124–33.

50 Antoine d'Abbadie, "La Procédure en Éthiopie," 470–1.

51 Shiferaw Bekele, "Kassa and Kassa," 298.

52 Ephraim Isaac, *Täwahïdo Church*, 91–2.

53 Stanley Z. Fisher, "Traditional Criminal Procedure in Ethiopia," *American Journal of Comparative Law*, 19:4 (1971): 712–16.

aristocrats were known as *ras wember* or superior judges. Shiferaw Bekele wonderfully describes how the *zufan chilot* functioned. The court was called into session when important issues of state needed to be addressed or important civil or criminal cases heard. Once seated, the lower ranks in the *techiwoch* voiced their opinions with more senior members following in order of rank. The emperor was the last to speak and his word, ideally, reflected the consensus of the court and rendered equitable and impartial justice. Often the *afa negus,* the 'mouth of the king' or chief justice pronounced the judgement in civil or criminal cases, less often on issues of state where the emperor typically announced his decision. For those whose opinions were rejected, the fact that they were able to articulate their views acted as a pressure valve – something analogous to parliament for modern states – and made them an integral part of the Imperial Court.[54] The *zufan chilot* provided a forum for the emperor "to rally opinion and to mobilize support against rebels, conspirators and others who defied his authority."[55] Yet court procedure gave plaintiffs time to plead their case, seek justice, and request reinstatement scripted by the restorative justice protocols around forgiveness and atonement. The emperor was not removed from society, just the opposite as the ultimate arbiter he was involved daily in civil and criminal cases. In Shiferaw Bekele's words,

> the monarchy was believed to have absolute authority. But the royal council [*zufan chilot*] was not only a very important check, at least on this absolutism, but also a mechanism that enabled the *mekwanint* to partake in some of the powers. Hence, it was a truly central, coordinating and key institution.[56]

Schooling Shared Values

The 'the invisible hand' that made the *mekwanint* into a likeminded group was education.[57] As stated above, Scriptures were the generative text for concepts of justice and governance that became normative. Clemency as well as conflict was all around, iterated in Mass, fasting

54 Shiferaw Bekele, "Kassa and Kassa," 294–6. For the origins and early history see Taddesse Tamrat, *Church and State,* 103–6; and Aberra Jembere, "Chilot" in *Encyclopaedia Aethiopica.*

55 Shiferaw Bekele, "Kassa and Kassa," 296.

56 Shiferaw Bekele, "Kassa and Kassa," 295.

57 Teshome Wagaw's, *Education in Ethiopia: Prospect and Retrospect* (Ann Arbor: University of Michigan, 1970) provides an excellent analysis of traditional church education. More analytically, Reidulf Molvaer provides perhaps the most detailed study of traditional methods of education in Ethiopia on the behavior and motivations of Ethiopians, see *Socialization and Social Control in Ethiopia* (Wiesbaden: Harrassovitz Verlag, 1995).

days,[58] the veneration of the saints and the *Kibre Negest*.[59] All this was shaped by religious education.[60]

From the arrival of Christianity to highland Ethiopia every village had its church and nearly every church its school.[61] For illiterate Ethiopians lessons were taught through religious art and iconography. Orthodox hagiographic literature is overrun with examples of the miracles of Jesus, various angels, saints and especially the Virgin Mary. The veneration of saints was a prominent feature of Ethiopian orthodoxy. Around their veneration developed an iconic tradition whereby a person prayed to a saint while holding the icon of that saint for it was believed to be a talisman possessing some of the saint's power.[62] Saints represent many human characteristics from powerful warriors, like St. George and St. Mikael, to St. Tekla Haymanot and St. Mary, "Mother of Peace," who were viewed as intercessors bringing peace and understanding. Much of this was depicted in church paintings and thus made comprehensible to the illiterate.[63] Even the *tabot*, the representative wooden ark found in the inner sanctuary of each church, was personified by the saint to whom the church was dedicated; thus, "arks of Mikael are vengeful while arks of Mary are compassionate."[64]

---

58 Donald Levine, *Wax & Gold: Tradition and Innovation in Ethiopian Culture* (Chicago: University of Chicago Press, 1965), 60. Although the number of days varies by region, if strictly counted Levine maintains there are over 260 religious days to be observed in Debre Damot in the early 1960s.

59 Marilyn E. Heldman and Stuart Monro-Hays, *African Zion: The Sacred Art of Ethiopia* (New Haven: Yale University Press, 1993); and Raymond Silverman and Neal Sobania, *Ethiopian Church Art: Painters, Patrons, Purveyors* (Los Angeles: Tsehai, 2022).

60 Yirga Gelaw Woldeyes' chapter, "Traditional Schooling and Indigenous Knowledge Production," provides a comprehensive overview of traditional education, *Native Colonialism*, 57–93.

61 Ephraim Isaac, "Social Structure of the Ethiopian Church," *Ethiopian Observer*, 14:4 (1971): 240–88.

62 Stanislaw Chojnacki, *Ethiopian Icons: Catalogue of the Collection of the Institute of Ethiopian Studies, Addis Ababa University* (Milan: Skira Editore, 2000) provides reproductions and explanations of hundreds of icons. Exploring the relationship between icons and the image of Christ and the saints in the broader ecclesiology of Eastern Orthodoxy see Constantine Kalokyris, *The Essence of Orthodox Iconography*, trans. Peter Chamberas (Brookline, MA: Holy Cross Orthodox Press, 1985), 85–87. Describing how Ethiopian crosses shape religious beliefs and socio-political values see Maria Evangelatu, *A Contextual Reading of Ethiopian Crosses through Form and Ritual: Kaleidoscopes of Meaning* (Chicago: Gorgias Press, 2018).

63 Jacques Mercer, *Vierges d'Ethiopie* (Montpellier: L'Archange Minotaure, 2004); Raymond Silverman and Neal Sobania, *Ethiopian Church Art: Painters, Patrons, Purveyors* (Los Angeles: Tsehai, 2022).

64 Hoben, *Land Tenure*, 68.

Lessons on appropriate social conduct were conveyed through religious art. On church walls or parchments images of the saints communicated their place on the spectrum between wrathful and forgiving. If a saint was depicted with a dove near or even entering his/her head that meant the saint brought love and peace to the world. If a lion was on the left side of the saint that signified order and tranquility; if a monkey, leopard or hyena was either on the lower left or upper right, that connoted evil, anarchy, or disharmony, as did a dragon, signifying pestilence, like the one beneath the horse of Saint George who is spearing it.[65] Priests' sermons were illuminated by murals on church walls, and Bibles were illustrated with pictographs for all congregants to see and learn.

Formal religious education was the primary motivation to teach literacy before the twentieth century.[66] Much was simply memorization, but memorization quickly led to literacy. In the fifteenth century, religious instruction became part of religious service which included educating Ethiopia's elites. The parish church was the center of all social activity. The liturgical calendar offered some observance for nearly every day of the year.[67] Of course, Sunday *kidassie* (mass and communion) was a fixture, while religious festivals were organized around the church calendar involving fasting which affected everyone. Other activities centered around the church, for example, *mahbers* – religious mutual self-help associations – were outgrowths of parish funeral societies, the church porch was a convenient meeting place for old men to gather and talk, a shady tree in the church courtyard often served as the courtroom to resolve local disputes, and school took place on the same porch or under the same tree.[68] At the lowest level the village priest started out teaching the Ethiopic syllabary, simple arithmetic, and memorization of verses from the Gospels ultimately leading to study of the Psalter. Some exegetical motifs centered around the four elements (wealth, earth; mercy, water; power, fire; judging, wind) all of which were taken into consideration in applying restorative justice.[69] The moral component was there from the beginning. "The student was

65 Mercer, *Vierges d'Ethiopie*, 41, 52; Chojnacki, *Ethiopian Icons*, 38; and Heldman, *African Zion*, 97–8.

66 Alaka Imbakom Kalewold, *Traditional Ethiopian Church Education*, trans. Mengistu Lemma (New York: Teachers College Press, 1970).

67 Emmanuel Fritsch, "The Liturgical Year of the Ethiopian Church: The Temporal: Seasons and Sundays," *Ethiopian Review of Cultures*, Special Issue, Vols. IX–X (2001).

68 Girma Amare, "Aims and Purposes of Church Education in Ethiopia," *Ethiopian Journal of Education*, 1:1 (June 1967): 2.

69 Roger W. Cowley, *Ethiopian Biblical Interpretation: A Study in Exegetical Tradition and Hermeneutics* (Cambridge: Cambridge University Press, 1988), 235.

being constantly assessed by his teacher for other qualities such as honesty and personal integrity."[70] Beyond basic instruction in reading and writing, education followed two tracks. The first track taught priests Scriptures, liturgy, doctrine and the *Fitha Negest,* with the goal of ordination into the priesthood. The vast majority of Orthodox priests were limited to this basic religious instruction. The central tenet was memorization. Among the elite, aristocratic families, a priest or deacon was hired to provide this elementary education to their sons.

Beyond primary education, there was a second track that emphasized praise and composition. This more creative realm of religious study can be divided into three stages. The first stage was the *Zema Bet* or School of Church Music where either priests or *debteras* (highly educated but non-ordained clerics) learned rhythm and singing to be used in church services. This often took three years of study. Most of those who passed through the *Zema Bet* became priests ministering in remote parishes. The *debteras*, however, tended to gravitate to larger churches, where they were intimately involved in church administration and participated in worship life as cantors. They were not required to live the pious lives of monks or priests. "The monk's life is normally given to sensual renunciation; the *debtera* is normally an acknowledged sensualist."[71]

The second stage was the *Qiné Bet* or the School of Poetry where *debteras* enrolled to learn rhyme and to develop their vocabulary, especially their lexicon of multiple meanings of Ge'ez words often appositionally juxtaposed to illuminate a wider context.[72] *Debteras* were respected for their learning and their ability to use biblical teachings as commentary on everyday occurrences in the form of a liturgical poetry known as *qiné. Qiné,* it will be shown, epitomizes Ethiopians' ability to perceive the multiple threads of justice; it encouraged decision-makers, whether clerics, leading political figures or local *chiqa shums*, to consider alternate ramifications for each action. The third stage, attained by a very select group of the educated elite, graduated Christian theologians from the *Meshaf Bet,* literally 'the House of Books and Interpretation' (perhaps equivalent to schools of theology).[73] Yet it should be noted that this third track was uncommon.[74] As Asma Giyorgis laments,

70 Girma Amare, "Aims and Purposes of Church Education," 8.

71 Girma Amare, "Aims and Purposes of Church Education," 1–4; Levine, *Wax & Gold*, 172.

72 Hiwot Teffera has written a novel about *qiné* schools and all the struggles and sacrifices involved in being a *qiné* student, *Mine to Win* (Addis Ababa: Eclipse Printing, 2016).

73 Sylvia Pankhurst, *Ethiopia: A Cultural History* (Essex: Lalibela House, 1955), 233–83.

74 Yirga Gelaw Woldeyes notes that select, bright students spent five years learning Ge'ez in a *Qiné Bet* and another seven years to learn interpretation in the special school of *Tirguamme Bet* (The House of Interpretation), "Colonial

"[The clergy] have no education … The sum total of their education is the *Zema* of Yared. One could hardly find thirty people versed in *qiné* among a hundred singers of the *zema*; nor are there five of the thirty versed in *qiné* who can interpret the Old and New Testaments or who know the Ge'ez language thoroughly."[75]

The importance of *qiné* cannot be overemphasized for it provides insight into the indirect and secretive communication patterns of educated Amharas and Tigreans where parable and symbolism were prized, and ambiguity was treasured.[76] Girma Amare states, "The study of Kene [*qiné*] derives its significance from the fact that this is the most highly refined expression of Ethiopian culture, which … is characterized by ambiguity, vagueness and secretiveness."[77] How does it work? Ge'ez, Amharic, Tigray and other Semitic languages of Ethiopia tend to have imprecise stress indicators on words; thus, depending on where the stress is placed the word *belew* can mean "tell him" or "strike him"[78] – radically contradictory meanings. But *qiné* was not always about comprehending an adversary's darker intentions, it fostered self-actualization and most importantly the discipline to seek truth. Again, as Girma Amare states, "Kene may be defined as the art of detecting others' ambiguities which increases the subtleties of one's own."[79]

Abstractly stated, what does the discipline of composing and comprehending *qiné* provide? Before detailing *qiné*, the defining study by Maimire Mennasemay, *Qiné Hermeneutics and Ethiopian Critical Theory*, summarizes its intellectual and therefore religious, social and judicial offerings. Maimire Mennasemay states that "[*qiné*] expresses a passion for critically reflecting on and interpreting earthly issues: social practices, ideas, ideals, norms, hope, joy, love, work, injustice, power, poverty, friendship, oppression, sorrow, death, and other aspects of human life."[80] At root, "Questioning is the active spirit that animates the *qiné* practice of composition and interpretation. The *qiné* tradition

---

Rewriting of African History: Misinterpretations and Distortions in Belcher and Kleiner's *Life and Struggles of Walatta Petros*," *Journal of Afroasiatic Languages and Culture*, 9:2 (2020): 151.

75 Bairu Tafla, editor and translator, *Asma Giyorgis and His Work: History of the Gälla and the Kingdom of Sawä* (Stuttgart: Franz Steiner Verlag Weisbaden, 1987), 343.

76 Donald Levine, *The Flight from Ambiguity: Essays in Social and Cultural Theory* (Chicago: University of Chicago Press, 1985), 25.

77 Girma Amare, "Aims and Purposes of Church Education," 3.

78 G.E. Gorfu, "A Brief Introduction to Qene" unpublished paper (December 26, 2003).

79 Girma Amare, "Aims and Purposes of Church Education," 3.

80 Maimire Mennasemay, *Qiné Hermeneutics and Ethiopian Critical Theory* (Los Angeles: Tsehai, 2021) 50. While portions of his study were published earlier, Maimire Mennasemay successfully connects multiple features of *qiné* in this book.

of questioning involves transgressing the given, the accepted, and the boundaries of meanings that the hegemonic order establishes."[81]

Qiné is an exceptionally sophisticated liturgical doubletalk that in poetic form carries a superficial "wax" level of meaning, perhaps an exegesis of a biblical text, but its ambiguous "gold" level may be arguing against the common biblical interpretation, urging the listener to consider an alternate understanding of the text that recommends compassion. *Sem inna werq* or "wax and gold" is foundational to a uniquely Ethiopian hermeneutic that extends well beyond theology.[82] Maimire Mennasemay maintains that "the *sem* plays a key role as the raw material in the production of *sem inna werq*." And that "the *werq*, once produced, retroactively throws light on the *sem*, brings out its limitations or distortions, reorders the relation of the *sem* (the particular) to the *werq* (the universal), and serves as a regulative principle for reinterpreting the subject matter of the *qiné* in a way that brings out its universal aspect(s)."[83] He goes on to say that the "practitioner opens parallax views, critical alternatives, unforeseen options, novel meanings, and possibilities of a new or more comprehensive understanding."[84]

Some scholars like Donald Levine, my graduate adviser, emphasized negative consequences of the "wax and gold" ideology which included (a) providing "an inexhaustible supply of humor," (b) uplifting the individual over the community, (c) demeaning others and insulting them in cryptic code, and (d) serving as a medium to criticize authority.[85] In short, Levine accentuates the profane aspects of *sem inna werq* that ensured Ethiopia's underdevelopment and lack of democratic values. By contrast, Messay Kebede may overemphasize its religious connotations that probed interpretations of biblical texts to understand the mysteries of God or differentiate between secular paths and divine truth.[86] This historical analysis leans upon Maimire Mennasemay's middle ground, which scrutinizes the hermeneutics of reason, critical thinking and truth, both religious and secular, to better comprehend how the ideology of "wax and gold" influenced adjudicating restorative justice.[87]

---

81 Maimire Mennasemay, *Qiné Hermeneutics*, 52.

82 Mohammod Girma, "Whose Meaning? The Wax and Gold Tradition as a Philosophical Foundation for an Ethiopian Hermeneutic" *SOPHIA* 50 (2011): 175–87.

83 Maimire Mennasemay, *Qiné Hermeneutics*, 53.

84 Maimire Mennasemay, *Qiné Hermeneutics*, 67.

85 Levine, *Wax & Gold*, 9.

86 Messay Kebede, *Survival and Modernization, Ethiopia's Enigmatic Present: A Philosophical Discourse* (Trenton: Red Sea Press, 1998), 180–2.

87 Maimire Mennasemay, *Qiné Hermeneutics*, 53–5 and ch. 5, 83–133. This position is also reflected in Mohammod Girma, "Whose Meaning?" 185–6.

To become an accomplished *qiné* composer takes years of study. Each verse of *qiné* is supposed to be unique with strict rules of meter and rhyme.[88] Lines must end with the same consonant and vowel, if not the poet is ridiculed. Moreover, there are complicated formulas for stanza length and meter within *qiné*, yet all poems must be original.[89] Once composed it enters the public domain to be committed to memory by listeners (meaning the Orthodox Christian population); thus, there is an improvisational aspect to *qiné*. It should be obvious that not everyone can compose *qiné* for it takes superior intelligence and wisdom on a level seldom encountered in political or legal circles anywhere, and yet in Ethiopia is was twined into the social fabric of the nation.

Once in the public domain, though, lines and whole poems can be repeated hundreds of times in houses and public spaces and ruminated upon as part of a robust oral tradition. "It must never fail in suitability for singing. Moreover, it must be rich in content, revealing a deep knowledge of the Bible, of Ethiopian history and the stories and legends which have gathered during the centuries around the great personalities and events of religious and national tradition."[90]

While *qiné*'s rules of prosody were very complex, most educated Amhara and Tigreans loved to try their hand either repeating poems or extemporizing verse at feasts, weddings, or *tegg bet*s (bars). Maimire Mennasemay calls this a "simplified form" of *qiné* emphasizing *sem inna werq* that championed the double-entrendre to express peoples' repressed sentiments from joy and love to anguish and oppression.[91] Extemporizing became professionalized among the *azmari*, usually a poetess who sings verses composed about the individuals attending a bar or about contemporary events. The best *azmaris*' use of double meanings or obscure allusions are often found in Amharic proverbs and poetry.[92] Indeed, much practice was given to refining *sem inna werq* meanings in order to bury "the covert insult beneath the commonplace."[93] Political humor has had a long history in Ethiopia.[94] Burying

88 It should be noted that there are numerous forms and styles of *qiné*, many of which do not follow the wax and gold dictum, yet, as a probable overstatement, the vast majority attempt to unveil "truth." Alaka Imbakom Kalewold states that there are seventeen major *Qiné Bet*, see *Traditional Ethiopian Church Education*, 26–7.

89 Alaka Imbakom Kalewold, *Traditional Ethiopian Church Education*, ch. 5; Sylvia Pankhurst, *Ethiopia*, 244; and Levine, *Wax & Gold*, 269–71.

90 Sylvia Pankhurst, *Ethiopia*, 245.

91 Maimire Mennasemay, *Qiné Hermeneutics*, 54.

92 Fisseha Demoze and William Armstrong, *Ethiopian Amharic Proverbs* (Washington D.C.: 2019); Getie Gelaye, *Amharic Oral Poems of the Peasantry in East Gojjam* (Hamburg: Lit Verlag, 2001); and Tuquabo Aresse, "A Note on Tigrinya Proverbs," *Ethiopian Journal of African Studies*, 3/2–4/1 (1984): 73–9.

93 Iliffe, *Honour in African History*, 61.

94 Hewan Semon Marye, "The Rhetorics and Polemics of Humor in Addis

covert insults morphed into veiled, yet not-so-veiled, political critiques during the oppression of the Derg dictatorship years in the twentieth century,[95] and recently political satire aimed at Prime Minister Abiy Ahmed.[96] Conversely, proverbs could also equated common understandings with deep issues of law and justice.[97] As Jon Abbink translates: "no grain without harvest, no judgment without judge/court" implying that court decisions must be respected to bring justice just as grain must be harvest to nourish the body.[98] The point of the excursive on "simplified forms" of *sem inna werq* is to underscore that literary knowledge about complexities, relationships, conflicts, injustices, and things that could not necessarily be resolved or reconciled permeated the social and political environment of Imperial Ethiopia.[99] There was no getting around it.

Debteras most adept at capturing deep meanings and/or subtle criticism of prevailing socio-political conditions in the country became celebrities. *Qiné* could be pro-vengeance or pro-forgiveness on the surface and just the opposite at the deeper level. To an extent *qiné* epitomized the Ethiopian personality that Levine borrowed for the title to his seminal and much disputed book *Wax and Gold*. He notes, "The ambiguity symbolized by the formula 'wax and gold' colors the entire fabric of Amhara life. It patterns the speech and outlook of every Amhara."[100] Many *qiné* verses became proverbs almost indistinguishable from either psalms or parables and were memorized and widely dispersed in civil society. *Sem inna werq*, that embodies the polysemic nature of Ethiopia's Semitic-based languages, ensured that Ethiopians are comfortable with ambiguity. Ethiopians think in oppositional terms with both positive and negative consequences.[101] Central is the ability to see both sides of an argument.

Abäba, 2005-2019" Ph.D. dissertation, University of Hamburg (2021).

95 Fekade Azeze, *Unheard Voices: Drought, Famine and God in Ethiopian Oral Poetry* (Addis Ababa: Addis Ababa University Press, 1998).

96 Anonymous, "Wax and Gold: Satire is Flourishing in Ethiopia," *The Economist* (March 23, 2019): 75–6.

97 One of the earliest and more complete collections of saying and proverbs was compiled by Walker, *The Abyssinian At Home*, which, in his words, "are the statements of natives taken down in their actual speech." Many of them are about justice, social norms and importance of reconciliation. All compiled in the early 1930s.

98 Jon Abbink, "Traditional Ethiopian Legal Culture: Amharic Proverbs and Maxims on Law and Justice" *Studies in Ethiopian Languages, Literature, and History: Festschrift for Getatchew Haile*, ed. Adam Carter McCollum (Harrassowitz Verlag, 2017), 10.

99 Maimire Mennasemay, *Qiné Hermeneutics*, 147–58.

100 Levine, *Flight from Ambiguity*, 27.

101 Molvaer, *Socialization*, 84–128.

For example, warfare may lead a *ras* to victory, but *qiné* may show the long-term or unintended consequences of conquest like the destruction of established patron-client relations that were the basis of a well-functioning tributary system. Likewise, retribution may be the preferred way to deal with an enemy, but *qiné* may contend that forgiveness would be more salutary ten or twenty years down the line. Conversely, clemency may have been granted to a defeated army, but the poet might argue for stiffer punishment based on the insincerity of the vanquished lord. Impulsiveness is not considered a virtue in Ethiopia. This is one reason that Emperors Tewodros and *Lij* Iyasu were considered outliers in Ethiopian history; they appeared disinclined to consider the long-term or unintentional ramifications of their actions.

While extraordinarily difficult to translate the ambiguity in *qiné* with all its subtle messaging, Levine provides a translation of one *qiné* poem that probes the "wax and gold" meanings of this tercet.

> *Ya-bähetäwi lij sifalleg le'llennä*
> *Ya-kritosen mesht telänt washama-nnä*
> *Qetal betähono qarrama-nnä*
>
> The son of a hermit, high rank to display,
> Made love with Christ's wife yesterday;
> When she fed him leaves he wasted away.[102]

The wax meaning refers to an ambitious man who makes love with Christ's wife, metaphorically the world's highest-ranking woman, in order to raise his social status. However, she fed him medicinal leaves and he wasted away. On the surface this is an unassuming parable about living simply, which is enforced with the reference to a hermit and his rejection of worldly goods. In the gold meaning "son of a hermit" refers to hunger, "Christ's wife" symbolizes fasting. Therefore, a hermit's hunger is heightened by fasting and diminishes when he eats leaves, the ultimate diet of a hermit.[103] But "high rank to display" poses the question "Why?" and never offers an easy answer yet perhaps has cautionary soteriological implications against earning one's way to heaven.

The ability to perceive contradictions and ambiguity also had metaphysical roots in Orthodox theology. The Ethiopian Orthodox Tewahido Church did not appropriate Western ethical dualism – good and evil as distinct and separate – rather "the Ethiopian conception of dualism assumes a non-essentialized and flexible other, and a compassionate self or soul. These two concepts are embodied in the idea of *irq*, which presupposes the possibility of negotiation and reconciliation between good and evil."[104] Theologically, of course, *irq* iterated

---

102 This translation is found in Levine, *Flight from Ambiguity*, 27.

103 Levine, *Flight from Ambiguity*, 27.

104 Yirga Gelaw Woldeyes, *Native Colonialism*, 48. Maimire Mennasemay calls

through *qiné* influenced how Ethiopians thought about the Judgement Day and salvation. The lessons of *qiné* touched the highest aristocrat and the poorest peasant and could function as a political soapbox from which to articulate social justice ideas. As one proverb states: "A king desiring reconciliation will be reconciled by a peasant; but a peasant not wanting reconciliation will not be reconciled by a king."[105] Many of them were remembered as proverbs and dictums on law and justice as part of a dynamic tradition "with a shared language and hegemonic 'code'"[106] used by the *mekwanint* and others in authority.

Qiné could also argue for more profane things related to government policy. In one example, recorded by Asma Giyorgis, *qiné* argued for an ecclesiastical realignment. He claims the *debtera* implored Emperor Menilek to favor the authority of the important monastery of Debre Libanos on theological and ecclesiastical grounds over that of the Enderta monastery that Emperor Yohannes had promoted. While the theological differences were real, the true reason to seek this shift had everything to do with power and the perception of power, and the author, using allegory, appealed to the vanity of Emperor Menilek to make this change and assure Menilek's place in history.[107]

Ethiopian elites, including the *mekwanint*, were taught by tutors, some of whom instructed them in the martial arts including equestrian skills and use of shield and spear;[108] other tutors provided literacy and religious instruction. According to Cornwallis Harris, a nineteenth-century traveler to the Shewan court, both of Sahle Sellasie's sons, Haile Malakot (father of Menilek II) and Sayfu Sellasie, were sent to different monasteries for theological and legal studies plus horsemanship and warfare. Tight discipline was adhered to and the scions were required to attend church services and observe fasting days.[109]

Yet the *mekwanint*'s formal education concentrated less on Christian dogma and more on issues of justice. Priests drilled aristocratic students in the *Fitha Negest* and how to adjudicate cases based on customary law, which included such issues as land rights, marriage and divorce, inheritance, and administration. Students were also coached on how to effectively argue court cases by appealing to biblical passages as

---

this "duality without dualism," *Qiné Hermeneutics*, 53–4, 158.

105 Abbink, "Traditional Ethiopian Legal Culture," 12.

106 Abbink, "Traditional Ethiopian Legal Culture," 17.

107 Bairu Tafla, *Asma Giyorgis and His Work*, 693.

108 Mehteme-Sillase Welde-Mesqel, *Zekra Nagar* [Recollection of Things Past] (Addis Ababa: 1962 Ethiopian calendar); a portion is translated as "*Portrait Retrospectif d'un Gentilhomme Ethiopien*" in *Proceedings of the Third International Conference of Ethiopian Studies* (Addis Ababa: Haile Selassie I University Press, 1966), 60–2.

109 W. Cornwallis Harris, *The Highlands of Ethiopia* (London, 1844 reprinted Farnborough: Gregg International Publishers, 1968), vol. 3, 15–16.

well as social customs, first by emulation then through invention.[110] But most important for the *mekwanint* was cultivating the ability to perceive ambiguity; here noted *debteras* were sought to help the elites' sons comprehend the complexities of human nature – *irq*. From infancy, the scions of the *mekwanint* were recounted proverbs. Later they memorized Bible passages. Still later they listened to *qiné* and heard its various interpretations all for the purpose of perceiving the multiple arms of justice in order to develop their own sense of right and wrong. The goal was to find "compromise" – *irq*. As the nineteenth-century French traveler and ethnographer Antoine d'Abbadie observed, the Ethiopian judicial system emphasized compromise and compromise more often brought about real justice as opposed to the application of tort law.[111] Aberra Jemberre notes that the traditional mode of litigation or *tatayyaq muget*, which was not confined to the *mekwanint* but nevertheless commonly practiced by them, involved sophisticated interrogation and cross-examination techniques that used oral and documentary evidence, privileged the art of advocacy and rebuttal (*wurd menzat* or *bela labelah*) and rendered judgements.[112] Bridging the gap between "wax and gold" ideation and court argumentation was "a special form of litigation poetry called *iset-ageba* developed" in Wollo that played upon the ambiguity of justice and restitution.[113]

Mehteme-Sillase Welde-Mesqel lists four characteristics of elite education: the primacy of religious instruction, a love for the country, a commitment to the social hierarchy, and a sense of justice. Of the four, Mehteme-Sillase Welde-Mesqel opines that justice is the most important. But to his mind justice is not codified, rather it is circumstantial, it tries to be impartial but more important it attempts to promote social harmony.[114] In matters of state, lessons in conflict resolution or societal reconciliation proved invaluable to the emperor and the *techiwoch*.

The Imperative to Restore Social Order

The *zufan chilot* was called into session to rally the emperor's allies when the state was threatened or, after victory, to determine an appropriate resolution to deal with the defeated rebels. Often, many members of the *mekwanint* resided in the capital at any given time and were

110 Girma Amare, "Aims and Purposes of Church Education," 8.

111 Antoine d'Abbadie, "La Procédure en Éthiopie," 468.

112 Aberra Jemberre, "'Tatayyaq Muget' the traditional Ethiopian mode of litigation" in *Proceedings of the Eighth International Conference of Ethiopian Studies*, ed. Tadesse Beyene (Addis Ababa: Institute of Ethiopian Studies, 1988), I: 245–52.

113 Pankhurst and Getachew Assefa, *Grass-roots Justice*, 13.

114 Mehteme-Sillase Welde-Mesqel, *Zekra Nagar*, 63–4.

readily available to assist the emperor on such matters. Recall that the emperor insisted that each governor and sub-governor spend considerable time at his court to assist him in governing or adjudicating cases, but ancillary to that was to keep an eye on them and preempt insurrections and disloyalty. What complicated the matter was that prior to the late nineteenth century the emperor's court was often a tent city that roved the countryside moving from one population center to another. The itinerant capital made communications and logistics difficult and disorganized. There was ample opportunity for a wayward governor to ignore a summons using the excuse that he had not received the message. The roving capital also had another serious downside; by moving around the country, supply chains never had a chance to develop sufficiently to bring food and resources to the capital in a sustainable manner. During Louis XIV's reign in France it was said, "all roads lead to Paris." French supply chains were formalized, and food, commodities, weapons, and luxury items passed smoothly from countryside or seaport to Paris and Versailles.

Ethiopia was radically different. Trade routes crisscrossed Ethiopia but were chiefly extractive; like colonial railroads, trade routes were built to ferry commodities, such as slaves, ivory, hides and skins, from the interior to the coast.[115] Theoretically, it was more profitable to avoid population centers where rulers could levy taxes, but the parasitic nature of government did not allow this to happen and trading posts developed along those routes precisely for the revenue they generated and over time led to shifts in population centers. The point of this aside is to clarify that farmers markets dominated the Ethiopian economy. With the exceptions of salt and some spices, foodstuffs did not come from long distances; rather, local farmers and herders took their produce to village markets and mostly bartered them for items they needed.[116] Soon the local production of teff, vegetables, and livestock was exhausted, and the tent capital picked up and moved to another locale where foodstuffs were available. Surplus extraction needed to grow large towns and cities was negligible. The vast majority of the Ethiopian population was tied to land. Society revolved around sun, soil, and season, so much so that wars were initiated and concluded between sowing and harvesting or in the offseason. Elites – emperor, *mekwanint*, *gult* holders

115 There is a voluminous literature on trade, trade routes and taxation, for Ethiopia, perhaps most notable are the works of Richard Pankhurst, *An Introduction to the Economic History of Ethiopia* (London: Lalibela House, 1961), and Mordechai Abir, *Ethiopia and the Red Sea* (London: Frank Case, 1980).

116 For the nature of commodity exchange through barter and coinage barter – the complex use of commodity currencies primarily the Maria Theresa thaler, see Charles Schaefer, "Enclavistic Capitalism in Ethiopia, 1906–1936: A Study of Currency, Banking, and Informal Credit Networks" Ph.D. dissertation, University of Chicago (1990), ch. 4.

and clergy – constituted a small percentage of the populace. Peasants, despite their lowly position and endless exploitation, were crucial to maintaining the state. The whole system of restorative justice was fabricated around ensuring an ample supply of peasants to till the soil. Without them famine and calamity were guaranteed.[117]

In answering the question, "What was the imperative to restore social order?" the focus must turn to land tenure and the insecure political-religious hierarchy created to ensure its continuation. As stated above, lord and serf existed as *gult* and *rist* holders. In terms of security, *rist* holders had durable claims to work the land that could not easily be revoked. A peasant's risk was primarily confined to his or her siblings' claim to that same plot of land upon the death of their parents or kinsmen through an ambilineal descent system that allowed the one possessing the most persuasive verbal skills to argue that they deserved the majority of their parents' land. Of course, this usually involved litigation in a court comprised of community elders under the shady parish tree. The judgement as to whose usufruct rights to their parents' land was stronger was based on which sibling had superior communication skills. Once divided, the land stayed with that son or daughter until infirmity or death prevented them from exploiting the land, at which point the litigation process reignited with the next generation. There were other ways to increase access to land, most notably through marriage, divorce, and remarriage.[118] The bedrock of Ethiopian society, to state yet again, was the peasant cultivator. Restorative justice functioned as a means to minimize disruption of the agrarian mode of production.

Knowing that feudal societies are dependent on their cultivators, Tsegaye Tegenu describes how Ethiopian aristocrats mobilized peasant/soldiers according to cultivation's seasonal demands and made efforts to start or stop campaigns accordingly.[119] Also knowing that revenge against rank-and-file peasant/soldiers would only hurt the economy and citizenry of the conquered areas, Ethiopian rulers seldom, if ever, sought retribution against agriculturalists. Peasants were accorded respect in the Royal Chronicles, in *qiné*, and implied in the guarantee of peasants' *rist* rights to land.

Understanding that the whole political-religious hierarchy rested on peasant labor, the elites sought to ensure that producers were left in place and that the mechanisms of taxation remained strong. Often this

117 Richard Pankhurst, "The Great Ethiopian Famine of 1888–1892: A New Assessment," *Journal of the History of Medicine and Allied Sciences,* 21 (1966): 95–124.

118 Hoben, *Land Tenure*, 144–59.

119 Tsegaye Tegenu, *The Evolution of Ethiopian Absolutism.*

meant putting aside the desire for revenge and punishment against a rebel *ras* knowing that to replace him would disrupt the taxes and tribute wrested from peasant-producers, for the patron-client "trust" – often a mixture of fear and self-interest – that existed between the wayward *ras* and his allies to exploit the peasants could take years to reconstruct. Better to invent a way to forgive and move on.

The situation for the lords, more accurately a layered stratum of *gult* holders from as low as a soldier-settler rewarded for his valor on the battlefield to the highest noble, was far more tenuous. As stated above, Ethiopia possessed a wobbly social ladder with many missing rungs that promoted and demoted *gult* holders in near equal numbers. The elites were an ever-changing social hierarchy where an ambitious social climber could challenge a complacent placeholder. Theoretically this meritorious system rid the aristocracy of its incompetent and weak members, ensuring that the ruling class remained strong and engaged. Or so the theory goes. But those on the upper rungs of the social ladder seldom wanted to see their less gifted progeny descend a rung or two for that was a reflection on them. Devices were developed to assure some security for those who had achieved a higher position on the social ladder to pass on their station to their children. This included arranged marriages, forced divorces and prearranged remarriages, for each of those new kinship bonds enhanced the position of the less-gifted progeny by obscuring their incompetence in the larger, more powerful kinship circle into which they had wed. But there were more subtle devices. Sociologists studying Ethiopia have long written about distrust and heightened suspicion of others as national characteristics and impediments to social change.[120] Change, to an extent, was what social climbers sought; the status quo was what placeholders dearly wanted to preserve. And at any given time, there were far more placeholders than social climbers, and the former cultivated suspicion and elevated doubt about those who represented change, for they perceived themselves as vulnerable – vulnerable to loss of status and power. While confining his analysis to the Amhara, Reidulf Molvaer states:

> A perhaps peculiar aspect of Amhara society is the almost self-destructive envy or jealousy (*miqqenninnet*, which can mean spite) people feel towards each other, predisposing them to try to destroy opportunities for others, even if they themselves in the "process" should suffer or lose more than the one they try to harm – even if they are aware of this loss to themselves. At the base of this attitude there may be a strong belief in "zero growth" – that if another person gains something, he gets an advantage over others at their expense, and will use it to suppress others when he comes into a position of power.[121]

[120] Molvaer, *Socialization*, 123–8; Levine, *Wax and Gold*, 86–94.
[121] Molvaer, *Socialization*, 125.

The *mekwanint* and lesser aristocrats were the social class with the most to lose and best placed to erect safeguards to insure their privilege. From the emperor demanding that his governors stay a good portion of the year at his tent-capital, to a sub-governor obstructing a rival's promotion, the devices invented to thwart perceived rivals were limitless.

For the elite class, restorative justice functioned both in positive and negative ways to restore social order. On the positive side, there was a recognition that the land tenure system had to be preserved with minimal disruption. Wars between contending *ras*es were a given. In a hierarchical political structure with the emperor on top, there were always going to be plots and counterplots to topple the politician above and take territory, but more importantly vanquishing a rival could mean controlling more of the peasants working the land in the disputed territory. Mechanisms to bring reconciliation were devised to minimize the disruption that mobilized armies marching through the countryside living off peasant producers could cause, or post-battle retribution that could maim or kill countless peasant/soldiers. These mechanisms, often embodied in the protocols of restorative justice, did just that.

Restorative justice allowed Ethiopian society to return to equilibrium as if nothing had happened. It allowed defeated *ras*es to return to their provinces and resume their activities. To an extent, restorative justice played into the hands of the complacent placeholder or the *ras* fearful that his sons would be pushed out of the aristocracy if his patron-client relationships were severed. It played a role analogous to the Old Testament's Jubilee Year (once every fifty years) where debtors' debts were forgiven and other luckless individuals' lands were restored, on the premise that they deserved the opportunity to have a second chance to pursue a gainful livelihood. On the negative side, restorative justice was less about taking the state in a new direction and punishing rebels. Rather, it was about returning to the status quo where the political order was reaffirmed – yet again – and the entrenched elites, both victors and vanquished, were allowed to retain the power and patron-client networks they held prior to the insurrection. Social change was antithetical to restorative justice.

Honor and Shaming; Forgiveness and Atonement

The aftermath of most battles was especially noteworthy. Some nineteenth-century European travelers, such as W. Cornwallis Harris, recount "revolting barbarities" where Abyssinians "butcher children and old men without distinction, mutilate all who fall into their hands, and enslave females upon every opportunity."[122] But to an extent this

122 W. Cornwallis Harris, *Adventures in Africa* (Philadelphia: T. B. Peterson,

was in Europeans' racialized self-interest to characterize horrendous brutality to justify colonialism's "civilizing" mission. Castration was one barbarity that particularly caught Europeans' attention. Young Frenchmen Edmond Combes and Maurice Tamisier exploring Ethiopia in the 1830s noted scrotums decorating lances, shields and the bridles of horses as sign of strength and prowess.[123] But this was not unique to Ethiopia. Castration was widely practiced throughout the Ottoman Empire and was common in the Middle East and Indian Ocean littoral.[124] Physical emasculation had deep socio-religious roots both in Orthodox Ethiopia as well as in the Islamic countries surrounding it. If men survived the ordeal they could be sold as eunuchs commanding very high prices; in more punitive terms a neutered male was denied inclusion into kinship structures like age-groups thus denying him marriage rights.[125] Castration effectively separated men from society. Yet the vast majority of talismanic scrotums were sliced from dead enemy soldiers, not dissimilar to the taking of an ear, a hand or a scalp in other societies.[126] The following analysis in no way negates accounts of blood and brutality during and after battle; rather, the intent is to demonstrate an equally valid antithesis, one of concern and generosity shown to defeated comrades-in-arms.

Other Europeans residing in Ethiopia for longer periods with better access to the court and in-depth knowledge of cultural traditions, wrote about who paid tribute to whom, what political marriages allied one ruler to another and, of course, dynastic wars. Their firsthand observations about the aftermath of battles were remarkably different. Henry

---

1843), 183; and James Bruce, *Travels to Discover the Source of the Nile*, reprint (New York: Horizon Press, 1964), 181.

123 Edmond Combes and Maurice Tamisier, *Voyage en Ethiopie, dans le pays des Galla, de Choa et d'Ifat: précédé d'une excursion dans L'Arabie-heureuse, et accompagné d'une carte de ces diverses contrées* (Paris: L. Desessert, 1838), 1: 221–2.

124 For a comprehensive analysis of the practice of castration of African slaves by Ottomans see George Junne, *The Black Eunuchs of the Ottoman Empire: Networks of Power in the Court of the Sultan* (London: I. B. Tauris, 2016).

125 Florence Bernault, "Body, Power and Sacrifice in Equatorial Africa," *Journal of African History*, 47 (2006): 207–39.

126 Zachary Brown assesses the prevalence of scalping before and during the American Revolutionary War where Indian, Patriots, and British soldiers were all involved, "The Rhetoric and Practice of Scalping," *Journal of the American Revolution* (September 1, 2016). https://allthingsliberty.com/2016/09/rhetoric-practice-scalping. Margaret Sewall Ball pushes the timeline back by documenting the imposition of bounties for Indian scalps collected by white settlers in Massachusetts Colony, "Grim Commerce: Scalps, Bounties, and the Transformation of Trophy-Taking in the Early American Northeast, 1450–1770" Ph.D. dissertation, Department of History, University of Colorado (2013). On castration see Gary Taylor, *Castration: An Abbreviated History of Western Manhood* (New York: Routledge, 2000).

Dufton, who was in a position to witness the transformation of Emperor Tewodros into the cruel despot he later became, noted that in his early reign Tewodros acted with magnanimity: "Whether from policy, or in obedience to the better impulses of his nature, he did not allow his conquests to be marked by even the ordinary cruelties of Abyssinian warfare ... He exercised the utmost clemency towards the vanquished, treating them rather as his friends than his enemies."[127]

Arnauld d'Abbadie, Antoine's brother, who lived in Ethiopia from 1836 to 1848 and took part in a number of battles during the *Zemene Mesafint*, describes how rank-and-file soldiers demonstrated chivalrous behavior after battle. Despite committing "revolting barbarities" on the battlefield, afterwards they appeared remorseful and showed consideration towards defeated soldiers:

> Ethiopian soldiers are so secure in the solemnity of warfare that these beliefs contribute to their ability to show clemency to the vanquished. One observes the victorious and the defeated recognizing each other, embracing, inquiring with concern about the wellbeing of their recent adversaries, or interposing in order to improve the fortunes as if they were friends.[128]

For the peasant/soldier the shame of defeat was not conferred to him. He was simply obeying orders. "There was no punishment for a common soldier who deserted, provided he left his gun behind, nor was it dishonourable to preserve one's life by flight before a stronger enemy."[129] In contrast, the peasant/soldier had everything to gain on the battlefield, even possibly the conferral of *gult* rights over other peasant-producers if recognized by his superiors for his strength, bravery, and ruthlessness during the fight and his honorable conduct afterwards. The unspoken assumption was that all soldiers found themselves in similar situations having been mobilized by their sovereign to fight his battle against his enemies. Often, similar to feudal Europe, the peasant/soldier did not know his master's master, the reason for the skirmish, or whether they were fighting to usurp or defend the imperial or provincial throne.

As argued above, the peasant/soldier was a valued subject for agrarian production and military engagement. Demographic guestimates tend to infer a steady line, births cancelling out deaths, prior to Africa's

---

127 Henry Dufton, *Narrative of a Journey through Abyssinia 1862–3*, reprint (Westport, CT: Negro University Press, 1970), 134.

128 Arnauld d'Abbadie (brother of Antoine quoted above), *Douze ans de séjour dans la Haute-Éthiopie (Abyssinie)*, reprint (Vatican: Biblioteca Apostolica Vaticana, 1980), 455. "Les soldats éthiopiens sont convaincus de la versatilité des positions, et cette croyance contribue à les render cléments envers les vaincųs. On voit de vainqueurs et des vaincus se reconnaîs, embrasser, s'informer avec solicitude de leurs récents adversaries ou s'interposer auprès d'un compagnon afin d'améliorer le sort de quelque ami."

129 Iliffe, *Honour in African History*, 63.

demographic shift in the twentieth century. While no reliable data exists for Ethiopia's population in the eighteenth and nineteenth centuries, the royal chronicles report that famines and plagues were devastating because they depleted the peasant base of society. The *Fitha Negest* confirms this, stating that: "Whosoever is forcibly compelled to kill shall not be held responsible, if he who compelled him is the master of [his] body."[130] Wanton killing contradicted social stability for all and was recognized as aberrant by all.

The *mekwanint* treatment of peasant/soldiers pretty much followed the warrior-to-warrior scenario that Arnauld d'Abbadie describes – forgiving them for supporting their rival knowing that they had little choice in the matter. Changing allegiance was common. The peasant/soldiers were either encouraged to return to their farms to attend the crops or lured into the victorious *ras*'s army – affording them a chance to graft onto new patronage trees. As a seventeenth-century Portuguese traveler observed:

> They [peasant/soldiers] are ordinarily changeable and inconstant, and so today they are with one lord and tomorrow will leave him and take another. They readily swear to any agreement and then break it as if they had not sworn. Hence arise incessant rebellions and most often, if things go badly for the rebel and his followers, they ask the Emperor's pardon and obtain it.[131]

Again, the concept of *irq* – the Ethiopian Orthodox penchant to view the world as open to the idea of negotiation and reconciliation, not the dueling forces of good and evil as in the West – partially exonerates the peasant/soldier for being drafted by his master to fight. Of course, there were exceptions, perhaps the situation that W. Cornwallis Harris described where lowly warriors were executed or, according to other reports, mutilated,[132] but cases of vengeance were comparatively rare. Under certain circumstances, as in the case of the *askaris* (Eritrean soldiers fighting for Italy) after the Battle of Adwa in 1896, there were valid reasons to withhold clemency in that they had been repeatedly warned to stop aiding the foreign enemy from invading Ethiopia – see Chapter 4. The mutilation that some of the *askari* suffered was in keeping with Ethiopia's rules of war.[133] Ransoming peasant/soldiers was another option open to a victorious *ras* for there were levels of *gult*-holders, from where they came, who relied upon their labor and were willing – under duress – to pay for their return.[134]

---

130 Paulos Tzadua, trans., *The Fetha Nagast*, 289.

131 C. F. Bechingham and G. W. B. Huntingford, eds., *Some Records of Ethiopia 1593–1646* (London: Hakluyt Society, 1954), 58.

132 Cornwallis Harris, *Adventures in Africa*, 183; d'Abbadie, *Douze ans*, 454.

133 Iliffe, *Honour in African History*, 60.

134 d'Abbadie, *Douze ans*, 454.

The way *mekwanint* treated each other after battle was more elaborate. Believing in a providential God grounded their attitude; at minimum there was an assumption that God foreordained the outcome, good or bad, and that to gloat about victory or bemoan defeat was an affront to divine order.[135] But the manner in which forgiveness and atonement were ordained was ceremonialized. Acceptance of surrender and treatment of defeated foes was highly scripted and addressed what was at the core of restorative justice – honor and shaming.[136]

Ethiopia adopted many attributes of honor-shame cultures from the Middle East and Arabian Peninsula.[137] Honor and shame had deep roots in both the New and Old Testaments, as scholars are discerning.[138] Conflating the Ethiopian idea of honor were ideals of Greek heroic warriors embellished in *The Iliad* with the Christian duty of protecting the faithful. Yet Christian duty won out: "Our story is (written) not (from) vainglory nor to display (our power) to the sight of men, but that we may tell of the goodness of God."[139] Honor, thus, was a double-edged sword; it glorified strength, courage and cunning while uplifting duty to God, country and countrymen. The latter invoked the ideology of the *Kibre Negest* with all its allusions to grace and understanding bound up in being magnanimous or vengeful as circumstances dictated. In Amharic, cognates of the word honor, *keber*, are defined as a rich person (elite), a respected person (elder), or an impartial person (judge).[140] Another definition of honor was "fearless uprightness, honesty, generosity and eloquence of speech"[141] – the latter harkening back to the polysemic meanings found in *sem inna werq*. Remarkably absent were masculinity, strength, and courage which so define Western notions of honor.[142]

---

135 Paulos Tzadua, trans., *The Fetha Nagast*, 261.

136 For overviews of honor-shame culture, see John K. Campbell, *Honor, Family and Patronage* (Oxford: Oxford University Press, 1964) for honor and John Braithwaite, *Crime, Shame and Reintegration* (Cambridge: Cambridge University Press, 1989) for shame.

137 J. G. Peristiany, ed., *Honour and Shame: the Values of Mediterranean Society* (Chicago: Midway reprint, 1966).

138 Jerome H. Neyrey, *Honor and Shame in the Gospel of Matthew* (Louisville: Westminster John Knox Press, 1998); David A. deSilva, *Honor, Patronage, Kinship & Purity: Unlocking New Testament Culture* (Downers Grove: InterVarsity Press, 2000); and David A. deSilva, *Despising Shame: Honor Discourse and Community Maintenance in the Epistle of the Hebrews* (Atlanta: Scholars Press, 1996).

139 G. W. B. Huntingford, ed., *The Glorious Victories of Amda Seyon* (Oxford: Oxford University Press, 1965), 96.

140 Iliffe, *Honour in African History*, 57.

141 Bereket Habte Selassie uses these words to describe the charisma and character of his widely respected father, *The Crown and the Pen: The Memoirs of a Lawyer Turned Rebel* (Trenton: Red Sea Press, 2007), 11.

142 J. G. Peristiany, ed., *Honour and Shame: The Values of Mediterranean Society*

If honor was defined by society's acceptance and admiration, shame connoted its censure and contempt – but with the hope for reintegration.[143] As one scholar, writing about conceptions of honor, said, "you know you are good or bad by what your community says about you."[144] Disapproval magnified through the "mechanics of gossip" were powerful inducements to conform or be remorseful.[145] In Ethiopia, favorable public opinion was vitally important for maintaining a person's stature and rank in society and in the *chilot.* Moreover, honor-shame was directly tied to patronage in a complex manner that was both inclusive and exclusive, replicating practices throughout the Islamic world as well as Biblical lands.[146]

Rarely were battles fought to eliminate a foe; rather, victory was declared when it was apparent that one side was significantly weakened and disequilibrium self-evident. After battle, assuming the leaders of the defeated army were still alive, submission was rather perfunctory. The battlefield was the place to resolve issues that negotiation and mediation could not. Often wars were fought over contending claims to political power, which could start over contests for the imperial throne or could descend to provincial claims for office. Refusal to pay tribute was reason enough. Wars also could be fought over conflicting lineage claims to land or more accurately *gult* rights to exploit the peasantry on the land.[147] In all cases, combat declared a winner and a loser. Acts of submission, from the loser's perspective, were designed to acknowledge the winner as superior and consent to his claim for

---

(Chicago: University of Chicago Press, 1966); and J. G. Peristiany and Julian Pitt-Rivers, eds., *Honor and Grace in Anthropology* (Cambridge: 1992). That the concept on honor and shame stretches across the Atlantic Ocean see, Bertram Wyatt-Brown, *Southern Honor: Ethics and Behavior in the Old South* (New York: Oxford University Press, 1982); and Robert Elder, *The Sacred South: Evangelicalism, Honor, and Identity in the Deep South, 1790–1860* (Chapel Hill: University of North Carolina Press, 2016).

143 Braithwaite, *Crime, Shame and Reintegration*, 4–97; Herbert Thomas, *The Shame Response to Rejection* (New York: Albenel, 2006).

144 Andy Crouch, "The Return of Shame," *Christianity Today,* 59:2 (March 10, 2015): 32.

145 Nathan Harris and Shadd Maruna, "Shame, Shaming and Restorative Justice: A Critical Appraisal" in *Handbook of Restorative Justice*, ed. Sullivan and Tifft, 454, 457–8; Braithwaite, *Crime, Shame and Reintegration,* 75–7.

146 deSilva, "Patronage & Reciprocity: The Social Context of Grace" in *Honor, Patronage, Kinship & Purity* ch. 3; and Raymond Jamous, "From the Death of Men to the Peace of God: Violence and Peace-making in the Rif" in Peristiany and Pitt-Rivers, *Honor and Grace*, 167–91.

147 Shiferaw Bekele, "The State of the Zamana Masafent (1786–1853): An Essay in Reinterpretation," *Kasa and Kasa: Papers on the Lives, Times and Images of Tewodros II and Yohannes IV (1855–1889)* (Addis Ababa: Institute for Ethiopian Studies, 1990), 32.

office and/or land. Typically, an act of submission involved taking an oath on a cross or on the Gospels administered by the priests who inevitably accompanied both armies. In a real sense military engagement resolved disputes potentially leading to the restoration of peaceful relations between rivals by declaring a winner and loser. But post-battle submission rituals had limitations. Usually, battlegrounds were remote places and soldiers who fought could remain faithful to their defeated lord or be lured to the victor's army and into his stronger patron-client network. Soldiers' loyalty was feckless. But these quick, impromptu submission rituals had some advantages for the loser. A defeated lord could go through the rites of submission, lose a percentage of his warriors, acknowledge the superiority of the victor, yet essentially keep his obeisance private and his honor intact. With his honor intact he could return home, remain angry and dedicate his energies to redressing his humiliation by starting a new war at a later date.

To preempt this possibility a shaming ceremony or *wurdet* (literally translated as shaming, dishonor, humiliation, obeisance) was devised whereby the loser had to come before the winner and all his allies and formally submit, acknowledging the honor and superiority of the victor. Ideally this took place sometime after the conclusion of the battle giving adequate time for a raft of issues to be sorted out ahead of time, not least of which was to give enough time for reason to prevail and all the elites and the local population to travel to the victor's court to witness the shaming ceremony. But more important the delay enabled details to be sorted out: who was to submit, who was to confer forgiveness (*mihret*), what circumstances needed to be considered ahead of time including all of the political and tributary considerations written about above, whether penalties were to be imposed and how punitive they were to be, was recognition and even promotion to be granted, in short, how humiliating was the shaming ceremony to be.[148] Was simply kissing the ground in front of the victor on his throne sufficient or was the vanquished to appear with exposed shoulders carrying a stone as a sign of servanthood and utter humility? Influencing the shaming ceremony was the recognition that almost every ruler had submitted at one time or another. Humiliation had been experienced by one and all; for as recounted in a letter from *Ras* Walda-Sellase to Henry Salt, an early nineteenth-century traveler: "As for submission, everyone has sub-

148 An insightful analysis of the details that went into these negotiations is supplied by Izabela Orlowska who compares three Ethiopian-authored chronicles about the submission of Menilek to Emperor Yohannes in March 1878, "Performance and Ritual in Nineteenth-century Ethiopian Political Culture" in *Proceedings of the 16th International Conference of Ethiopian Studies,* eds. Svein Ege, Harold Aspen, Birhanu Teferra, and Shiferaw Bekele (Trondheim, 2009), 78–81.

mitted."[149] Time allowed the shaming ceremony to be negotiated and moderated. Part of the calculus was what John Braithwaite describes as reintegrative versus disintegrative; in other words, creating a forum whereby the guilty admit remorse and therefore were willing to reconcile, versus publicly stigmatized to the point that "humiliation, disrespect and ridicule" provoked violent rebellion.[150]

The shaming ceremony, when finally set, was a highly visual spectacle full of symbolism.[151] Globally, from Japan to Cuba, from ancient Rome to twenty-first century Norway the modalities of shaming are culturally specific.[152] In Ethiopia the victor and his retinue were often arrayed under an open tent or canopy with the emperor or victorious *ras* in the center and aristocrats arranged in descending rank on either side all attired in splendid robes and lion mane headdresses. Conversely, the defeated leader and his officers had to walk towards the tent hunched over according to rank often with the top lord appearing last. The performance was choreographed to demonstrate superiority and inferiority, and those who submitted were expected to show diffidence and respect by physically humbling themselves. One way this was done was by draping a *shemma* (a heavy hand-woven cotton shawl) tightly around his waist, leaving his shoulders bare as well as his whole face exposed.[153] One definition of the Amharic verb *tattaq* describes "folding a *shemma* around one's waist as a mark of respect."[154] The *shemma* was an item of clothing worn by everyone for warmth during the rainy season. When working it was wound around the waist to free arms for labor – a symbol of subservience associated with peasant labor. In the shaming ceremony, the concept of wrapping a *shemma* around the waist, known as *metat'eq*, was a public manifestation showing acceptance of lower status.[155] Draping the *shemma* over the right shoulder

---

149 Sven Rubenson, ed., *Acta Aethiopica: Correspondence and Treaties, 1800–1854,* vol. 1 (Evanston: Northwestern University Press, 1987), 17.

150 Braithwaite, *Crime, Shame and Reintegration*, 54–5; and James Gilligan, *Violence: Our Deadly Epidemic and its Causes* (New York: Grosset/Putman Books, 1996), 110.

151 Orlowska, "Performance and Ritual," 78–83.

152 Braithwaite, *Crime, Shame and Reintegration*, 58, 72.

153 The use of the *shemma* to connote superiority and inferiority was widely observed, see d'Abbadie, *Douze ans*, 463. The first generation of ethnographers noted how status was conferred by the way a *shemma* was worn among the Amhara and Tigreans, Levine, *Wax & Gold*, 254; Simon Wessing, "The Highland-plateau Amhara of Ethiopia" Ph.D. dissertation, University of Pennsylvania (1957), 329; and Dan Franz Bauer, "Land, Leadership and Legitimacy among the Inderta Tigray of Ethiopia," Ph.D. dissertation, University of Rochester (1972), 54–5 along with Plates 7–10 illustrating how to wear a *shemma,* or what Bauer refers to as a *kuta*, for different occasions.

154 Orlowska, "Performance and Ritual," 81.

155 Orlowska, "Re-imagining Empire: Ethiopian Political Culture under

Figure 2 Empress Zawditu holding court with *Ras* Tafari, the Regent on left. Attribution: Rosita Forbes, *From Red Sea to Blue Nile* (Macaulay, 1925).

leaving only the left side of a chest exposed was a slight variation that a man of higher status could invoke.

For the victor, the *shemma* was worn loosely covering almost his entire torso and part of it was pulled over his head and face only revealing his eyes, or only a small portion was pulled over his lower face ensuring that the crown and other royal headgear were visible. An emperor or powerful rival often wore *lebsa mangest*, literally clothes of the throne (state), to accentuate his or her superiority yet still covered his or her nose and mouth (see above image of Empress Zauditu). The symbolism was justice personified. Lady Justice in western images and statues is depicted with a blindfold to convey the idea that her pronouncements are impartial. In Ethiopia, the offender came before the law, his identity exposed for all to see. The sovereign/victor/judge, however, concealed his identity – at least symbolically by covering his lower face – so that his verdict would be perceived as equitable and unbiased. In Ethiopia justice was wide-eyed but faceless: eyes wide open to see the social implications of all possible judgements, and faceless to demonstrate that justice was administered impartially by an unidentifiable individual without known kinship ties and political base – or at least in theory.

Not only was style of dress important but posture and gestures were part of the pageantry to show shame and humility. In walking up to

Yohannis IV, 1872–89" Ph.D. dissertation, School of Oriental and African Studies, University of London (2006), 230–2.

submit before the imperial tent, the offender had to bow and look contrite and would, if negotiations decreed it necessary, kiss the ground before the sovereign.[156]

To accentuate shaming, an offender carried a heavy stone, often a millstone, on his shoulders. "Generally the most culpable, puts a large stone upon his neck, and, approaching the other, asks for pardon: the other, in saying to him 'May God forgive you!' ... A master ... contents himself, on forgiving his servant [inferior], with taking the stone from his neck and putting it into his hands."[157] Carrying a stone invoked servanthood, a clear sign of respect, repentance, subordination and was a gesture for seeking forgiveness. In many of the nineteenth-century chronicles it was shouldering a stone that was noted as proof of submission. While these shaming ceremonies constituted the pageantry that was an integral part of restorative justice, the political calculus was measured well beforehand in the negotiating stage where motivation and circumstance were calibrated.

Forgiveness is a reciprocal process; the forgiver must determine if the person seeking it warrants forgiveness. It puts power into the hands of the grantee, whether they are victors on Ethiopian battlefields or victims of Apartheid, to decide whether pardon, amnesty, or clemency is granted. Reciprocally, the person seeking forgiveness must demonstrate that they are worthy of forgiveness. This includes all the performative pageantry of the shaming ceremony to prove they are contrite, but more important their commitment to atone for their actions and promise fidelity to their overlord. Related to atonement and demonstrating the depth of their remorse, the honor and shaming ceremony allowed the defeated or perpetrators to apologize in public to representatives of the public. Penitence figures prominently in both the Old and New Testaments and was an essential part of Ethiopia's understanding of restorative justice.

Penitence and punishment were closely related. Depending on how penitent the forgiver believed the person seeking forgiveness was, sentences could range from promotions or amnesty, to demotion or other more serious punishments. An emperor could determine that his challenger had shown sufficient humility and, to redress the public shaming, could decide to give him a promotion in rank along with sovereignty over more lands to placate his vanity and assimilate him into the emperor's political hierarchy. Promotion involved the bestowing of titles, which gave the recipient power over those of lower rank for they were required to recognize him as their souverain.[158] Often this was sealed through an arranged marriage. Conversely, the emperor

156 Bauer, "Land, Leadership and Legitimacy," 55.
157 Gobat, *Journal of a Three Year's Residence*, 359.
158 Shiferaw Bekele, "Zamana Masafent," 34.

might decide to simply allow the challenger to return to his province – an act tantamount to amnesty – because the emperor was aware of the fragility of the tributary system in that area, the unrest a change in land tenure would cause, and how disruptive imposing a new patron would be on the peasant tax base. Finally, the emperor might distrust the offender, because he previously abused the condition under which the terms of restorative justice had been granted and put in place steps to weaken and demote him by sending him to another province far removed from his patronage network. Demotions, known as *gizot*, to peripheral areas were considered severe punishment; severe because it removed a wayward ruler from his patrimony. A *gizotenna* (a person subject to *gizot*) was prevented from actively participating in politics through expulsion from the court. *Gizot* connoted denunciation, demotion, and relocation yet, paradoxically, there was a notion of respect conferred to a *gizotenna* in recognition of their legitimate provincial powerbase.[159] *Gizot*, while relatively rare at the beginning of the nineteenth century, became more common by the end and increasingly frequent in the twentieth century under Emperor Haile Selassie.

Other punishments included house arrest, binding in chains (sometimes gold or silver plated as a symbolic gesture to honor a person of high office), chaining in iron shackles, imprisonment, or some combination thereof. In extreme cases of repeated treasonous acts, especially when they involved siding with a foreign invader, punishment could involve amputation of limbs, usually the right hand and left foot, or even execution.

One more issue needs to be addressed. Shaming was done in public or in as public a forum as pre-modern circumstances allowed.[160] The public aspect was vital for a crowd witnessing a shaming could amplify the megaphone of gossip.[161] Without witnesses either side could misconstrue the terms and conditions of the ritualized forgiveness and atonement ceremony. In short, the shaming ceremony was intended to be memorialized, and those who witnessed it were designated memory-keepers. Their function was twofold, albeit decidedly weighted in favor of the victor. First, memory-keepers were tasked with remembering the terms under which forgiveness was granted by the victor and the explicit conditions under which atonement or penitence was expected

159 Correspondence with Shiferaw Bekele (February 12, 2010).

160 Shaming remains a tool for the enforcement of human rights norms today. It is more successful when other parties ascribe to the protocol and participate in the modalities, like the public forum in pre-modern Ethiopia. Rochelle Terman argues that the politicization of shaming is integral to success, *The Geopolitics of Shaming: When Human Rights Pressure Works – and When It Backfires* (Princeton: Princeton University Press, 2023).

161 Braithwaite, *Crime, Shame and Reintegration*, 75–7.

to be carried out.[162] Second, the *mekwanint* and clergy, who typically formed the core of the memory-keepers, were responsible for holding the victors to their original terms, thus halting capricious and harsher recalibration of those terms and conditions. Within Christian theology, forgiveness is immensely problematic for it recognizes that the act of forgiveness is the easy part; it is how forgiveness is lived out that is more difficult for both giver and receiver. Imperial Ethiopian history attests to this for Ethiopians experimented mightily before getting it right and in those experiments pursued many mistaken paths. One final word, the public forum announced, unequivocally, who the losers were. *Wurdet* or submission on the battlefield could easily be misconstrued or ignored because of its remote location and lack of a public forum. Submission before the *mekwanint*, clergy, and hundreds or thousands of spectators at a central place cemented in the minds of soldiers who were the winners and whom to fight for.

Why be Magnanimous?

Eighteenth and nineteenth-century accounts depict the ideal ruler being magnanimous, exhibiting many of the learned traits priests taught them in their religious education. Charity, mercy, and understanding were all predicated on society's projection that they represent a compassionate and just leader. The Royal Chronicles of the *Zemene Mesafint* states that "the King of Kings Takla Giyorgis [was a] treasure-house of clemency and patience."[163] Samuel Gobat writes in 1834 of "*Ras* Googsa, whose death is still regretted, on account of his justice and peaceful disposition."[164] The *Fitha Negest* praises reconciliation, "A peaceful settlement is commanded by the word of Our Lord in the Gospel" and "The Apostles have also said that the servants of Christ must not be the enemies of each other."[165]

The coronation ceremony iterated the ideals by which each new emperor promised to rule.[166] After placing the crown on the emperor the Bishop says:

[162] David Swinburne, *Responsibility and Atonement* (Oxford: Oxford University Press, 1989).

[163] Blundell, *The Royal Chronicle of Abyssinia*, 256.

[164] Gobat, *Journal of a Three Year's Residence*, 339.

[165] Paulos Tzadua, trans., *The Fetha Nagast*, 261.

[166] As an illustration of the pageantry and the performative acts involved in imperial coronations in Ethiopia see Orlowska, "Feasting and Political Change: Tafari's Ascent to Power in Early 20th century Geber," *Annales d'Ethiopie*, 28 (2013): 45–67; and Orlowska "Re-imagining Empire: The Coronation of Yohannis IV as an expression of Historical Memory" in *Wälättä Yohanna: Ethiopian Studies in Honour of Jaanna Mantel-Niećko*, eds. Witold Witakowski and

> May God grant that his crown be a halo of holiness and glory. May you be pure in heart even as this gold is pure. To this blessing the emperor replies, "Amen." The emperor is given a sword known as the "Sword of Solomon," with the exhortation: "By this sword execute true justice, protect the Church, the widows, and the orphans, restore that which needs to be restored, chastise the wicked, render honour to the righteous; and with it serve our savior Jesus Christ.[167]

Names taken by emperors upon their coronation also reflected the merciful ideals they sought to uphold: Sahle Selassie means "clemency (or mercy) of the Trinity." Haile Selassie means "power of the Trinity." Being judicious was good politics; ruling benevolently was good form.

Laura Lykowska (Warsaw: Warsaw University, 2006), 173–80.
167 Ephraim Isaac, *Täwahïdo Church*, 137.

2

The *Zemene Mesafint*: Restorative Justice Misapplied

The *Zemene Mesafint* (1769–1853), also known as the Era of the Princes, alternately as the Era of the Judges,[1] was a time of incessant war and constant peacebuilding. The anomaly, as will be argued, has everything to do with trying to preserve the state. Those who challenged the emperor sought to revitalize the imperial court that they perceived was weak; those who supported the emperor professed loyalty to the man but more so to the institutions and political alliances he represented. Neither desired wholesale change, for eighteenth- and early nineteenth-century Ethiopia was secluded and content in being so.[2] Scholars have fixated on the struggles of the *Zemene Mesafint*: its military alliances, mobilizations, movement of armies, wanton plundering of the countryside for foodstuffs, and fierce battles with grossly high casualty counts. Their conclusion appears obvious, that war and the *Zemene Mesafint* are synonyms.[3] In the recesses of their works, though, are indications that peacebuilding was also of paramount concern. Careful reading of the battles shows that the same cast of malcontent aristocrats and provincial *ras*es challenged each other and the emperor time and time again. An obvious question is, how could this be?

How could a *ras*, defeated multiple times, be able to resume his position, reassert his patrimony over land and peasants, excise tax and

[1] The Era of the Judges in many ways is a more accurate characterization of not politics but the political ideation of the period, which was steeped in the lessons and wisdom of Elijah, Elisha, and other judges of the Old Testament, see Paul Henze, *Layers of Time: A History of Ethiopia* (New York: St. Martin's Press, 2000), 121.

[2] In Edward Gibbon's words Ethiopia was, "forgetful of the world, by whom they were forgotten." *The Decline and Fall of the Roman Empire* (New York: Heritage Press, 1946), 1601.

[3] Researchers include Mordechai Abir, *Ethiopia the Era of the Princes: The Challenge of Islam and the Re-unification of the Christian Empire, 1769-1855* (London: Longmans, Green & Co., 1968); Crummey, *Priests and Politicians: Protestant and Catholic Missions in Orthodox Ethiopia*; and Sven Rubenson, *The Survival of Ethiopian Independence* (London: Heinemann,1978). More recently, the idea that the Zemene Mesafint represents "vicious total war, ruthlessly rational in economic and political terms" has been championed by Robert Reid, *Frontiers of Violence in North-east Africa: Genealogies of Conflict since C.1800* (Oxford: Oxford University Press, 2011), 41.

tribute, use that income to procure arms, mobilize his subjects, and wage another war within one to five years with the ambition, yet again, to topple the emperor and assume the throne himself? The point of this chapter is that the persistence of war in Ethiopia was a result of the over-effectiveness of its restorative justice modalities. During the *Zemene Mesafint* Shiferaw Bekele argues,

> Ethiopia's rulers spent probably as much time making peace as warfare ... Indeed the history of the country over the last three centuries suggests that peace making was an integral part of the political and institutional architecture of the Ethiopian polity. The chronicles and other sources shed light on numerous peace building efforts.[4]

Forgive and forget was the modus operandi; this is in contrast to the modification to restorative justice practiced later on, which emphasized conditional forgiveness. The *Zemene Mesafint* was a learning experience, a failed lesson that needed to be corrected, a teaching moment extended over eighty years. The weakness of the center and the fact that there was no single, recognized memory-keeper, jeopardized the effectiveness of Ethiopia's mechanisms to bring about social and political reconciliation through restorative justice. Paradoxically, in an era when as much effort was given to reconciling enemies as to war itself, the experience taught Ethiopians about the shortfalls of forgiveness.[5]

Zemene Mesafint: Restorative Justice Too Freely Given

The *Zemene Mesafint* is widely viewed as a period of incessant war when centrifugal forces flung order, stability, in fact the whole Solomonic construct into chaos and disorder. In assessing the period, Margery Perham, in 1948, makes the claim: "The country did, indeed, fall to pieces."[6] The claim that the Ethiopian state tends to entropically spiral outward is a longstanding trope of Ethiopian scholarship.[7] Richard

---

4 Shiferaw Bekele, "The Peace Making Process in the History of Ethiopia," unpublished paper, July 2001. His analysis was further developed in "The Chronicle of Täklä Giyorgis I (first r. 1779–1784): An Introductory Assessment" in *Studia Aethiopica – In Honour of Siegbert Uhlig on the Occasion of his 65th Birthday*, ed. Verena Böll, Denis Nosnitsin, Thomas Rave, Wolbert Smidt, and Evgenia Sokolinskaia (Wiesbaden: Harrasowitz Verlag).

5 Many of these shortfalls inherent in forgiving and granting amnesty to bring about socio-political reconciliation have been documented extensively in critiques of South Africa's Truth and Reconciliation Commission, perhaps most critically articulated by Antjie Krag in *Country of My Skull: Guilt, Sorrow, and the Limits of Forgiveness in the New South Africa* (New York: Three Rivers Press, 2000).

6 Margery Perham, *The Government of Ethiopia*, reprint (Evanston: Northwestern University Press, 1969), 48.

7 Taddesse Tamrat pushes the genius of centrifugal forces to the reign of

Reid recently reiterated, "Ethiopia had been ripped apart by centrifugal forces."[8] Yet the counterfactual question that this chapter poses is how could a state of chaos and disorder endure from 1769 to 1853? Without centralized political institutions, without courts, without enduring religious beliefs, without agrarian production, without adequate surplus extraction, without long-distance trade, how could a state continue to exist, after eighty-six years of disintegration, and come out on the other side a recognizable polity with all institutions of statehood still intact? Shiferaw Bekele's reinterpretation makes a counterclaim that: "The Zemene Mesafint was the era of the Wara Sheh Mesfenate and not, as hitherto believed, an era of disintegration and of the State."[9] Moreover, he goes on to demonstrate that the centrifugal and centripetal forces often offset each other, yet "with ... the centripetal tendency being the predominant trait."[10] Bahru Zewde concurs stating that "The regional conflicts ... showed scarcely any centrifugal tendencies. The moves of the regional lords were to dominate the centre, not go away from it."[11] Allowing for factional politics and acknowledging a weak center, Shiferaw Bekele nevertheless maintains, "there were structural elements which bound governors and regional lords to the centre. These were the central institutions of the State, the system of military organization and the basic tenets of the national ideology";[12] these were, in other words, many of the social, religious, and political issues discussed above in regard to the theory of restorative justice in imperial Ethiopia.

At this point it is time to assess how restorative justice during the *Zemene Mesafint* contributed to maintaining the viability of the emperor and the *zufan chilot*, yet, paradoxically, dismembered the state by giving clemency to contenders determined to overthrow the emperor or, conversely, pursue regional autonomy. This section first describes political order during the *Zemene Mesafint*, making every attempt to perceive what was stable in the midst of political and societal flux. To

---

Amdä Siyon in the fourteenth century arguing that regional autonomy of provincial governors was always being mitigated by the emperor by building up the central institutions, his military forces, and wrapping the imperial throne in religious garb, *Church and State*, 90, 97–8. Donald Crummey observes that, "Abyssinian political history has a major motif of centrifugal tendencies, which are associated a great deal more with the drives of the nobility towards maximum local autonomy than with the ethnic or regional identities ... These centrifugal forces triumphed from the 1770s to the 1850s in the period known as the *Zamana Masafent*, "Abyssinian Feudalism," 124–5.

8 Reid, *Warfare in African History*, 92.

9 Shiferaw Bekele, "Kassa and Kassa," 290.

10 Shiferaw Bekele, "Reflections on the Power Elite of the *Wärä Séh Mäsfenate*," *Annales d'Ethiopie*, 15 (1990):168.

11 Bahru Zewde, *A History of Modern Ethiopia, 1855–1991*, 2nd ed. (Oxford: James Currey, 2001), 14.

12 Shiferaw Bekele, "Kassa and Kassa," 293.

a large extent, the description of Ethiopia's political economy during this period borrows unabashedly from Shiferaw Bekele's two articles: "The State in the Zemene Mesafint (1786–1853): An Essay in Reinterpretation" and "Reflections on the Power Elite of the *Wärä Séh Mäsfenate*." The aim here is to assert the continuity of imperial Ethiopia even after the fall of the Solomonic dynasty and the assumption of the throne by Yejju rulers who created the Wara Sheh Mesfenate. Second, attention will be given to characterizing the nature of jurisprudence during the *Zemene Mesafint* demonstrating where restorative justice fits into the mix. Finally, a hypothesis will be suggested that restorative justice when misapplied – meaning giving general amnesty freely along the lines of forgive and forget – can generate war and exacerbate political instability.

The Wara Sheh Mesfenate

While the *Zemene Mesafint* was characterized by constant warfare, each battle was of comparatively short duration, often a day, meaning considerably more time was devoted to recalibrating political forces – peacemaking – between skirmishes. The year 1755 marked the passing of Iyasu II (the Great) and the end of the Solomonic dynasty for a century until Kassa Haylu crowned himself *neguse negest*, King of Kings or Emperor Tewodros II at Darasgé Maryam church in 1855. Between 1755 and 1769 when Mikael Sehul was appointed *ras bitwedded*, literally meaning "head of the governors or lords," Ethiopia was engulfed in fighting, yet wars were primarily over succession – who was to control power in Gondar – not wars of secession. The *Ras bitwedded* had all the powers of an emperor yet acknowledged the heredity of the office of *neguse negest*, that at times was filled by Solomonic puppet emperors like Iyasu III. Various princes were not content with the title *ras bitwedded* and tried to revive the monarchy. The last to proclaim himself *neguse negest* was Tekle Giorgis in 1779, yet his brief tenure on the throne should be considered more of an interregnum than a reign, for a powerful coalition of lords, including the future Ali I, defied him from the start, finally defeating him in 1784. In the chronicles he was nicknamed *tafsameta mangest* or "end of the monarchy."[13]

Control of the state did not disappear; rather, the Solomonic monarchy took an extended hiatus and government functions were consolidated under the office of the *ras bitwedded*. From approximately 1784 to 1853, struggles for sovereignty alternated between attempts to rid Ethiopia of the ruling *ras bitwedded* and take over the office, or to use religious/ethnic justifications to seize power and reestablish the throne of *neguse negest*, and revive the Solomonic, Christian dynasty in lieu of

13 Shiferaw Bekele, "Reflections," 160.

the office of *ras bitwedded*. The commonality between the two motivations was to commandeer the court, the epicenter of all the centripetal elements that made up the state. Whether the prince was Christian or Muslim, his challenge did not intend to jettison or replace the political order but simply to personally assume the responsibilities of governing, meting out justice and ensuring that the political and religious hierarchy remained intact, while observing court decorum and the whole assemblage of functions, practices, and rituals of government. The reward for the usurper was asserting his authority over all the tributary provinces his former overlord controlled.

After yet another succession struggle Ali Gwangul I assumed the title of *ras bitwedded* in 1786. He reigned for only two years but in that short time managed to consolidate sufficient power to ensure that his Yejju descendants ruled Ethiopia for the next sixty-seven years by creating the Wara Sheh Mesfenate.[14] Wara Sheh was the designation of a family from the Yejju region, currently near the town of Waldiya in Wollo province, who years before were part of the Oromo migration that settled in the area. They originally professed Islam but later converted to Christianity. Shiferaw Bekele, basing his argument on two contemporary chroniclers, Alaqa Taye and Takla Sadiq, contends that the state was referred to as *mesfena* and was ruled by a *mesfen*, and thus can be referred to in modern phrasing as "mesfenate." He argues there is one overriding advantage to depicting the Wara Sheh's rule as a "mesfenate," that being it sharply differentiates the limitations of their government from a typical monarchical dynasty. This included the fact that they were content with the title *ras bitwedded*.[15] The apex of the Wara Sheh Mesfenate was reached under Gugsa (1803–1825) who asserted his authority over all the lords of Gojjam, Begemdir, Wollo, Lasta, and Semen and required them to pay tribute. Upon his death it was said that Gugsa "ruled the whole world except Shewa and Tigre."[16]

While the Wara Sheh Mesfenate was a loose confederation of regional principalities, it still dominated politics. In discussing the heyday of the Solomonic dynasty, Taddesse Tamrat observes that a dominant king was able to ask his vassals to collect and submit "the king's tributes accruing from a region, and ... to contribute an adequate fighting force to the king's army during a national crisis or to send contingents against local rebellions in the name of the king when called upon to do so."[17] The Wara Sheh rulers from Yejju were able to demand all these

14 A detailed history of Yejju and the Wara Sheh is provided by Éloi Ficquet, "Understanding *Lïj* Iyassu through his Forefathers: The Mammedoch *Imam*-s of Wello" in *The Life and Times of Lïj Iyassu of Ethiopia: New Insights*, ed. Éloi Ficquet and Wolbert Smidt (Zurich: Lit Verlag, 2014), 5–29

15 Shiferaw Bekele, "Zamana Masafent," 49.

16 Blundell, *The Royal Chronicle of Abyssinia*, 485.

17 Taddesse Tamrat, *Church and State*, 96.

things from the provinces they dominated, including Tigray at various times. Yet these two issues, tribute and fighting forces, also provoked constant rebellion and were central to the peacemaking efforts embodied in restorative justice that will be addressed below.

The *ras bitwedded* of the Wara Sheh Mesfenate had many other characteristics of a dominant hegemon. They could bestow titles, but they only granted promotion up to *ras* (prince or governor) as they themselves were only one rank above. They had the power of *shum shir*, the ability to assign or reassign governors and other titleholders to offices in districts throughout their state. They assumed an absolute right to confirm and assign *gult*. In addition and in continuity with past imperial dynasties, the Wara Sheh Mesfenate used single and double marriages to cement alliances and assure loyalty; they saw to it that the national elite class remained remarkably stable and homogeneous; they "shared common ways of life, value systems and self-perceptions" nurtured by a traditional Orthodox religious education;[18] they endowed churches and promoted Christianity even though others accused them of being Muslim;[19] and they maintained time-honored military practices while integrating "much-feared infantry and cavalry" formations associated with the militaristic pastoralism that their Oromo ancestry brought with them.[20]

The Wara Sheh rulers understood their own limitations. As previously mentioned, they did not seek the title emperor, *neguse negest*, or attempt to revive the Solomonic dynasty. Nor did they aspire to rule from Gondar, the traditional government citadel, but moved the capital to Debre Tabor, the administrative seat of Yejju. This shifted the seat of power to the southeast requiring travelers and traders to draft a new map of the empire. Lastly, the Wara Sheh rulers suffered from being perceived as non-Christian even though they professed Christ as their Savior. Oromo descendants of the Wara Sheh had migrated north during the Oromo migrations in the seventeenth century. Oromos had settled in many parts of the highlands but particularly along the eastern escarpment, primarily in Yejju and Wollo.[21] Many remained Muslim even though they intermarried with Christian families. Other Oromos converted to Christianity from Islam and observed Christian fasting days, festivals, marriage and burial rights, were given Christian education, and even endowed churches. Yet they lived in close proximity to their Muslim neighbors, respected Muslim beliefs and

18 Shiferaw Bekele, "Reflections," 162, 164–5.

19 Donald Crummey, *Land and Society in the Christian Kingdom of Ethiopia* (Addis Ababa: Addis Ababa University Press, 2000), 158.

20 Reid, *Warfare in African History*, 55, 91.

21 Hussein Ahmed, *Islam in Nineteenth-Century Wollo, Ethiopia: Revival, Reform and Reaction* (Leiden: Brill, 2001), 14–27.

cultural practices, allowed Muslim *gult* holders, and either recruited Muslims into their power structures or allowed them to continue ruling their districts. In some ways it looked like Christianity and Islam had become syncretized. Couple this with the widespread practice of *zar* (spirit worship) by both Christians and Muslims, and there appeared reason to doubt the exclusivity of Christ's message "I am the way, the truth and the life" (John 14:6).

The height of the Wara Sheh Mesfenate was under *Ras Bitwedded* Gugsa Marsu who provided twenty-two years of relative stability and peace by skilfully subduing the most rebellious rivals, often enticing them into his patronage through marriages and promotions as opposed to resorting to armed conflict. One effective deterrent was his ability to mobilize huge armies by calling upon his vassals to contribute their provincial armies to join his own. The number of warriors was simply daunting to his enemies. His nephew, Ali Alula, known as Ali II, also ruled for twenty-two years and arguably had equal authority over his vassals and ensured relative peace throughout most of his reign using the same tactics as Gugsa.

Justice during the Zemene Mesafint

Laws governed land, inheritance, taxes, marriage, divorce, and other issues families or neighbors found impossible to resolve. Ethiopia has been referred to as a nation of litigants, forever taking their grievances to court. Local courts, as stated above, often were conducted on the church porch or somewhere on the premises of the parish simply because it was the acknowledged public square in rural Ethiopia. Judges were usually elders from the community who could render a verdict since they were part of the social fabric and implicitly understood the importance of kinship ties. Aggrieved plaintiffs, however, could always appeal to a higher court. These higher courts mirrored the social hierarchy all the way up to the governor's *shaleqa fird bet* (governors' courts, see Illustration 1 above). These provincial courts were called into session mostly to resolve weighty civil or criminal cases. To lessen the burden on the *shaleqa fird bet*, significant effort was given to adjudicating disputes in lower courts. In addition, the governor's *shaleqa fird bet* replicated the emperor's *zufan chilot* in that the governor could require his own vassals to come to his court to deliberate on issues of state; this, of course, included whether to heed the *ras bitwedded*'s demand to mobilize the provincial army or to impose new taxes on the people and remit the extra to the center. And this is where problems arose.

Debre Tabor was the capital of the Wara Sheh Mesfenate but lacked the grandeur and history of Gondar. Wara Sheh rulers at times had difficulty compelling their regional lords to come to Debre Tabor, remain in residence for months out of every year and deliberate in the Wara Sheh's *chilot* precisely because it was not viewed as the imperial court.[22] Recall that the purpose of the *zufan chilot* was twofold: to adjudicate court cases or bring about consensus over issues of state; and to keep their vassals under close surveillance to ensure loyalty. Even Gugsa and Ali II were less successful than their Solomonic predecessors in doing the latter.

The Wara Sheh *chilot* used restorative justice as a deliberate strategy to reconcile contending forces to the new power dynamics decided on the battlefield. From the battlefield emerged a winner and a loser. This was reflected in the pageantry of the shaming ceremony for victor and vanquished were visually recognized by observers. Included in these post-battle ceremonies were negotiations detailing how fidelity was to be observed and what taxes and other dues were expected. Restorative justice was central to peacebuilding, but the prompt battlefield ceremonies and negotiations were too easy to ignore.

Restorative justice misapplied

The point of this chapter is that restorative justice was misapplied or too freely given to produce meaningful, long-lasting political/social reconciliation. To an extent, the constellation of contenders to the throne regenerated themselves because of the frequency and leniency of restorative justice modalities associated with the honor and shaming ceremony, *wurdet*. Central to this was the lack of specificity about how the defeated lord was to atone for his offenses thereafter. Four issues need to be investigated. First was the effect of a weak center. Second was the lack of national memory-keepers, persons, or institutions whose pronouncements became part of the state record. Third was the allegation or rather the suspicion that Ethiopia was no longer an exclusively Christian country. Fourth was a cultural belief among senior members of the *mekwanint* that the institution of *Kibre Negest* gave them as much right to the *alga* (throne) as anyone else, thus justifying rebellion.

First, Debre Tabor never carried the élan of Gondar; moreover, the Wara Sheh Mesfenate understood their limitations. While they controlled the majority of highland Ethiopia, they were sandwiched between two semi-independent states. To the south was Shewa, at the height of its power during the rule of *Negus* Sahle Selassie, 1795–1847. Sahle Selassie's rule spanned the summit of the Wara Sheh Mesfenate under Gugsa and Ali II, and he provided steady leadership throughout without the succession upheavals that plagued the Yejju rulers. Sharing a long border, the Wara Sheh rulers were only too aware of

22 Shiferaw Bekele, "Reflections," 167.

Sahle Selassie's power. Sahle Selassie controlled vast fertile territories and long trade routes to the south and west. Most of Ethiopia's slaves were captured and ivory collected in the southwestern regions and the most lucrative trade route passed through Ankober and Aleu Amba right in the center of Sahle Selassie's kingdom. In exchange for primary commodities and slaves, Shewans were able to barter for arms coming in through Zeila, Berbera, and other ports along the Red Sea. Shewa received some of the first breech-loading firearms to enter Ethiopia. With arms, money, and food, fortress-Shewa looked unassailable to Yejju. Sahle Selassie's patron client network was solid; his *mekwanint* paid regular tribute and spent significant time at his *chilot* attending to matters of state and administering justice. He demanded loyalty and those who challenged him were brought to account and shamed into submission. Sahle Selassie's title *negus* theoretically outranked *ras bitwedded*; in addition, he could legitimately claim Solomonic lineage. In many respects Sahle Selassie's Shewa was the model of good governance and political stability during the *Zemene Mesafint.*

Tigray possessed many of the same attributes as Shewa. For years it remained separated from the Wara Sheh Mesfenate, yet at other times was either directly ruled or dominated by allies of the Wara Sheh. It never, however, had a leader of Sahle Selassie's stature nor was it perceived as impenetrable – just the opposite. Yejju was frequently at war with Tigray. Economically, Tigray benefited from its location on Ethiopia's foremost trading route to Mitsiwa (historically referred to as Massawa in Western literature). Armaments poured into Ethiopia through Tigray and to an extent Tigreans influenced their distribution. The Amhara population, including the Yejju, was caught between the two main thoroughfares in and out of Ethiopia and consequently Tigray and Shewa benefited most from economic growth in the nineteenth century. Noting Tigrean and Shewan autonomy, other provincial *ras*es rebelled against Yejju domination. As Shiferaw Bekele argues, the aim was a conservative rearward looking rebellion for which wars were fought either for the office of the *ras bitwedded* or in defiance of Ali I and his descendants who were viewed as interlopers.[23]

Second, justice operates best under a unified system where all verdicts are decreed by a recognized authority and pronouncements recorded in a court ledger so to speak. It was vital that one entity be tasked with recording details of a court case or the messier, more ambiguous expectations that were associated with restorative justice. In instances of restorative justice, a national memory-keeper's function was to note the conditions under which forgiveness was granted and monitor compliance with those stipulations to certify whether the offender was truly remorseful. Immediately problems arose when a sole voice

23 Shiferaw Bekele, "Reflections," 160, 168.

of authority did not exist. For starters, Yejju, Shewa, and Tigray plus all the semi-autonomous *ras*es who disputed Yejju power, offered their own restorative justice practices and supplied their own memory-keepers.

Recall that, when there was one recognized monarch, the *zufan chilot* (Imperial Court) had a number of permanent members who functioned as memory-keepers for the state, these men included the *afa negus*, the *abuna*, the *echege*, the *qes atse* (the Imperial Chaplain), and about three or four other prominent church leaders.[24] However, the head of the Church, the *abuna* was an Egyptian Copt and not necessarily aware of political subtleties within Ethiopia. By contrast the *echege* and other church leaders were deeply immersed in state and society and were required to remember the pronouncements of the court especially concerning matters of state and the conditions of restorative justice.[25] However, during the *Zemene Mesafint*, the church hierarchy was as dispersed as politics was decentralized. The *abuna* could be in Debre Tabor, capital of the Wara Sheh Mesfenate, or in another province under the sway of a rival governor, as in 1840–1842 when *Abuna* Salama III was under *Dejazmach* Wube's influence. Traditionally the *echege* stayed in the monastery of Debre Libanos in Shewa, which was controlled by *Negus* Sahle Selassie. Other church dignitaries were likewise scattered.

Sahle Selassie's fortress-Shewa administered its own restorative justice. Tigray did the same thing. In fact, many provincial rulers forgave their adversaries and demanded penitence in very real and tangible ways that often overlapped, duplicated, or negated submission protocols leveraged by other powerbrokers including the Wara Sheh's *chilot*. To repeat, *Ras* Walda Sellase stated: "As for submission, everyone has submitted."[26] In a loose confederation of provincial powers where rivalries were commonplace, shaming and submission was equally common. Each victor decreed different levels of penitence over the vanquished. If punishment was too severe there was little incentive to abide by the decree and a huge incentive to find another powerful patron that could (a) offer protection, (b) deliver financial incentives, and (c) reduce or override punishments. Peacemaking processes became entwined in war posturing and political gamesmanship and had everything to do with consolidating patronage. Over time, terms of submission were diluted to the point where, because of a robust marketplace for better conditions for submission, the terms for receiving forgiveness sunk to the point that the only acceptable term was "forgive and forget."

Penitence, contrition, atonement, in a phrase, the obligations inherent in receiving forgiveness, were cast aside. Each principality had its own memory-keepers whose authority to enforce compliance with the

24 Ephraim Isaac, *Täwahïdo Church*, 91–2.
25 Ephraim Isaac, *Täwahïdo Church*, 133–9.
26 Rubenson, *Acta Aethiopica*, 17.

original terms of forgiveness was either circumnavigated by another lord or modified to keep the offending vassal from quitting the modest terms of his lord's patron-client relationship.

Third, the conviction that Ethiopia was no longer a Christian country played into the loss of respect for restorative justice. As described above, the whole ideation of restorative justice was founded on Christian principles. The suspicion that the Yejju rulers were Muslim or even sympathetic to Muslims, whether true or not, diluted the theological precepts of forgiveness and atonement. Without Christianity, justice could become more retributive – an eye for an eye, a tooth for a tooth – or could sink to a state where it possessed no bite whatsoever. That the diluted, "forgive and forget" form of restorative justice survived, even thrived, had more to do with the common values of honor and shaming that all the Abrahamic religions shared.

Compounding the religious underpinning of the state was an inadequately resolved controversy over the nature of Christ. Prior to the *Zemene Mesafint*, Ethiopian orthodoxy was profoundly shaken by Portuguese Jesuit missionaries espousing Catholic theology stating Christ was fully man while ministering on earth, thus, his suffering on the cross was real. Ultimately the Portuguese were ejected but the church splintered over orthodox responses over the nature of Christ. The dominant theological group was known as the *tewahido* (union) and they espoused a strict Monophysite belief in the *Hulat Ledat* (Two Births) where Christ was both God and man. Other interpretations of orthodox doctrine were known as *Qebat* (Unction) that had a strong following in Gojjam, and *Ya Sagga Lej* (Son through Grace) with similar allegiance in Gondar.[27] While these doctrinal disputes were resolved in favor of the *tewahido*, thus the appellation the Ethiopian Orthodox Tewahido Church agreed upon at the Council of Bora Meda in 1878, theological controversy continued to be exploited by political rivals from Gojjam and Gondar, and still others, like *Dejazmach* Wube, who viewed Yejju support for *tewahido* doctrine as tepid.

Finally, impacting the manner in which the atonement phase of restorative justice was carried out during the *Zemene Mesafint*, was the belief, deeply embedded in the ethos of the *Kibre Negest*, that Ethiopians were God's chosen people and that all were equal in God's sight. Therefore, senior members of the *mekwanint* had as much of a right to the throne (*alga*) as anyone else, which justified rebellion. In the event they were unsuccessful, the issue deliberated within the appropriate *chilot* had less to do with how to punish and seek revenge and more about how to restore the unsuccessful claimants to their rightful – though inferior – position in a newly constituted political hierarchy.

27 Bahru Zewde, *Modern Ethiopia*, 14.

Dejazmach Wube's recidivism

There were many provincial *ras*es who experienced submission multiple times, but none as poignantly as *Dejazmach* Wube Hayle Maryam.[28] He suffered the humiliation of the shaming ceremony multiple times; paradoxically, he lived contritely and ruled for long periods under conditions Wara Sheh rulers had set. He gained power and status throughout his career, and judged cases and advocated for restorative justice both as a member in good standing within the Wara Sheh *chilot* as well as in his own court. *Dejazmach* Wube epitomizes the full range of restorative justice applications and yet his recidivism, his constant thirst for more power, his lifelong aspirations for grandeur guaranteed that he would remain a "thorn in the flesh" to the Wara Sheh Mesfenate. *Dejazmach* Wube provides the ideal case study to question the hypothesis that restorative justice when misapplied can generate war and enhance political instability.

Other provincial *ras*es may have rebelled more frequently and in some cases more successfully, yet, because of *Dejazmach* Wube's proximity to the court and the interest he garnered from foreign travelers and missionaries, his exploits and foibles were extensively recorded in their travelogues. Rivals, in loose chronological order, included *Ras* Walda Sellase followed by *Dejazmach* Sebagadis Weldu, both of Tigray, *Ras* Aligaz and his son *Dejazmach* Faris Aligaz of Lasta, and *Dejazmach* Beru Goshu from Gojam who were in constant rebellion either alone or in alliance with one another.[29] For example, *Dejazmach* Beru at one time allied with Ali II and married his daughter to reinforce their cooperation. Perhaps as an omen *Dejazmach* Beru turned against his own father; therefore, it was not surprising that in 1842 he allied with *Dejazmach* Wube to overthrow his father-in-law, *Ras Bitwedded* Ali II. The plot failed, he submitted perfunctorily and retired to Gojam where he built his power base, exploited his tributary system and continued to defy Ali until the end of the Wara Sheh Mesfenate. Arnaud D'Abbadie claims that throughout the 1840s Ali mounted an annual campaign to subdue *Dejazmach* Beru,[30] yet Beru remained in power. The conditions for submission embedded in restorative justice modalities at that time must have been exceptionally soft. As an epitaph, *Dejazmach* Beru was defeated by Kassa Haylu, later to become Emperor Tewodros II, and was imprisoned at Maqdala only to be released in 1868 after Tewodros's defeat by the British.[31] Tewodros had learned the lesson of peacemaking during the *Zemene Mesafint*: no restorative justice, no leniency.

---

28 Perhaps the most thorough examination of *Dejazmach* Wube is found in Rubenson, *Survival*, 82–140.

29 Shiferaw Bekele, "Reflections," 168.

30 D'Abbadie, *Douze ans*, 127.

31 Sven Rubenson, "Bərru Goššu" in *Encyclopaedia Aethiopica*.

In 1826 *Dejazmach* Wube Hayle Maryam succeeded his father, *Dejazmach* Hayla Maryam of Semen. During the successional struggle after Gugsa's death, *Dejazmach* Hayla Maryam rose up against Gugsa's son, Yimam.[32] Yimam Gugsa handily defeated him and in the first of a number of seemingly illogical political moves (Move #1) appointed Wube, son of a defeated and dishonored father, the governor of Semen and promoted him to the rank of *Dejazmach*. Depending on where his loyalties lay, *Dejazmach* Wube either could have been grateful and loyal to Yimam who had given him power or defy Yimam in order to restore the name of his shamed father and satisfy his own ambitions. He chose the latter, "Takla Iyasus and Asmé [two contemporary chroniclers] have transmitted to us the tradition that ... Wube himself declared his rebellion against Yimam. But Wube was defeated."[33] Before the requisite cooling-off period needed to determine the conditions for restorative justice, whether to be punitive or lenient, Yimam died and was succeeded by his brother Marye Gugsa.

In illogical political Move #2, though defeated it appears *Dejazmach* Wube retained his power and refused to obey Marye's summons to Debre Tabor to pay homage and promise loyalty – the humiliation of *wurdet* (the honor and shaming ceremony) may have been too much for Wube's ego. The message was clear: Wube remained recalcitrant. Marye confronted Wube and defeated him yet immediately reinstated him. Only after this second defeat, D'Abbadie observed in June 1830, did Wube submit and accept his vassalage.[34]

Ras Bitwedded Marye invited *Dejazmach* Wube to follow him up to Tigray to deal with another rebellious lord, *Dejazmach* Sebagadis Weldu. Wube accepted, for in late 1830 Sebagadis ravaged Semen, defeated Wube and forced him out of his capital. Wube's forces were in the advance guard of Marye's army and in one of the bloodiest battles of the *Zemene Mesafint* Sebagadis's army was defeated, but toward the end of the battle Marye was killed. In contrast to the normal rules of war, after the Battle of Debre Abbay, Sebagadis was executed "at the hands of the Oromo soldiers who wanted to revenge the death of their leader Marəyye."[35]

Dori Gugsa, the third brother, took over the Yejju throne and rewarded Wube by appointing him governor of Tigray, a far larger region than his own Semen. This was done with the rationale that inserting Wube into Tigray would thwart the ambitions of three other contentious Tigrean ruling families with pretensions to the throne and would serve Yejju interests. The fact that Wube was an Amhara also ethnically

---

32 Shiferaw Bekele, "Zamana Masafent," 35.
33 Shiferaw Bekele, "Zamana Masafent," 35.
34 D'Abbadie, *Douze ans*, 187-89.
35 Tsegay Berhe, "Säbagadis Wäldu" in *Encyclopaedia Aethiopica*.

and religiously insulated the Yejjus from their Tigrean rivals.[36] Dori, however, only ruled for three months, and was succeeded by his nephew, Ali II, who ruled Ethiopia for twenty-two years from 1831 to 1853.

In the early years of Ali's rule, 1831–1838, *Dejazmach* Wube was a dutiful servant, paying an estimated 8,000 thalers per annum in taxes, attending Ali's *chilot* in Debre Tabor, and marching with Ali against rivals like *Dejazmach* Faris Aligaz. Sometime in his loyal-vassal phase, Wube gave his daughter in marriage to Ali II to solidify the alliance further. In accordance with the conferral of the governorship of Tigray, Wube invested enormous efforts in consolidating his authority over the province by constantly marching his army to crush Tigrean rivals. By 1838 he was the undisputed ruler of Tigray, his patronage system matched Ali's, his tax base was reliable, he controlled the major northern trade route to Mitsiwa and by strengthening contacts with European powers he had procured modern weapons. Abir writes: "By the second half of 1838 it was an open secret that Dajazmatch Wube was actively plotting to overthrow Ras Ali."[37]

Open secret or not, Wube's preparations were painstaking. Understanding that the outcome of battle was short-lived and that peacemaking was equally inconsequential if appropriate measures to legitimize the conditions of restorative justice were not made beforehand, *Dejazmach* Wube put in motion an agenda to coopt the Ethiopian Orthodox clergy by taking it upon himself to bring a new *abuna* (Archbishop) from the Coptic Patriarchate in Alexandria to preside over the Ethiopian Orthodox Tewahido Church. Salama III arrived at the end of 1840 and added to the prestige of Wube.[38] The fact that Ali II abdicated this fundamental responsibility to ask the Coptic Patriarch of Alexandria to send a new *abuna* delegitimized his authority. That he abdicated this responsibility to *Dejazmach* Wube, a Christian ruler from the Amhara region, only strengthened the impression that Ali did not care about the ecclesiastical order of the church. *Dejazmach* Wube laid the foundation to construct a united Ethiopia – minus *Negus* Sahle Selassie's fortress-Shewa – so that his conditions for administering restorative justice, assuming he was victorious, would carry weight. While the *echege* or *qes atse* may have adjudicated in other provincial courts, Wube had secured the Archbishop in his lair, immeasurably enhancing his legitimacy by coopting the most prestigious memory-keeper. Evidently, he was persuasive for in the ever-revolving assortment of

36 Shiferaw Bekele, "Zamana Masafent," 36.

37 Abir, in *Ethiopia, the Era of the Princes*, 108, appears to be relying on D'Abbadie's firsthand account of Wube's political maneuvering and the anxiety it caused in Debre Tabor and Gondar and why Wube opted to postpone challenging Ali II, see *Douze ans*, 188–9.

38 Denis Nosnitsin, "Wəbe Haylä Maryam" in *Encyclopaedia Aethiopica*.

enemies and friends, Wube allied with former enemies Beru Goshu of Gojam and Faris Aligaz of Lasta, making their combined territory and army larger than Ali's.[39]

The Battle of Debre Tabor was perhaps the most momentous of all conflicts during the *Zemene Mesafint* – and its aftermath the most perplexing. The combined armies of Wube Hayle Maryam and Beru Goshu marched on Debre Tabor on February 7, 1842 and engaged Ali and his tributary lords. Towards the end of the bloody battle when it looked like defeat was imminent, *Ras Bitwedded* Ali II, the recognized ruler of Ethiopia, fled and sought safety in Wadla, a remote village. Wube had won. Except that *Dejazmach* Beru Aligaz, one of Ali's relatives and a powerful lord from Yejju, arrived at the battleground with his army to support Ali. Finding the victorious forces celebrating and thus out of formation, Beru Aligaz's surprise attack routed the enemy. Wube and *Abuna* Salama were captured, Beru Goshu ran away. Beru Aligaz, holding all the cards to assume supreme power himself, spent a week looking for Ali and once located, escorted him back, and re-seated Ali on the *alga* in Debre Tabor.[40]

In praise for his loyalty and dedication, Ali quickly rewarded Beru Aligaz with a minor governorate, yet, astonishingly, gave Semen and Tigray – the territorial crown jewels he could have offered – to Wube's brother *Dejazmach* Marso Hayla Maryam.

In illogical political Move #3, no sooner had *Dejazmach* Marso arrived in Semen and declared himself the new governor, than Ali demoted him and reappointed his brother *Dejazmach* Wube, the same person who had unabashedly challenged the political and religious authority of the Wara Sheh Mesfenate for years prior to the Battle of Debre Tabor. This was the same person who had defeated Ali and technically, during the brief post-victory celebrations, was the absolute ruler over Ethiopia. This traitor, this malcontent, this disloyal rival who never showed remorse was forgiven, and all his territories restored. The story goes that within the Wara Sheh *chilot*, Wube's allies plus *Abuna* Salama convinced Ali to return to the status quo and argued that restoring Wube was preferable to dealing with unknown leaders. As a postscript, *Dejazmach* Wube remained loyal to Ali II from 1842 to the end of the Wara Sheh Mesfenate in 1855; maybe forgiveness, thrice given, did ensure loyalty.

Evidently an Ethiopian chronicler was perplexed by Ali's remarkably swift change of heart. Emphasizing the polysemic nature of Amharic, in his line extolling the wisdom of Ali, the chronicler offered a "gold" critique where he credits what may be incomprehensible on earth to the omniscience of God's design: "And all the world was astonished at the

---

39 Shiferaw Bekele, "Zamana Masafent," 38.

40 Rubenson, *Survival*, 93.

generosity of Ras Ali. What happened at Debre Tabor was marvelous and amazing; however, the Lord rules all nations."[41]

Three times *Dejazmach* Wube had challenged the ruler of Ethiopia and three times he had been forgiven, his treachery forgotten, and his power enhanced as reward. All appear illogical and bear repeating. First, Wube was selected to succeed his defeated father as governor of Semen and promoted to *Dejazmach*, and yet immediately repudiated the duties and responsibilities of vassalage to the king who appointed him. Second, Wube's rebelliousness was communicated in his refusal to come to Debre Tabor and endure the humiliation of the submission ceremony as a sign of his obeisance. This provoked *Ras Bitwedded* Marye, the first brother to succeed Yimam, to send an army to defeat him. Only then did he submit. Almost immediately afterwards, the reward for submission was stupendously generous. In return for *Dejazmach* Wube joining Marye to defeat Sebagadis Weldu's Tigrean usurpers, Wube was appointed governor of Tigray making him sovereign over lands equal in size and population to his Yejju masters. Third, after consolidating power in Tigray and meticulously developing his tributary patronage system and coopting the Orthodox religious establishment, Wube marched on Debre Tabor and defeated *Ras Bitwedded* Ali II. Yet in quirky circumstances the loyal comrade-in-arms, *Dejazmach* Beru Aligaz, who defeated Wube and saved the Wara Sheh Mesfenate was rewarded with minor territorial concessions while traitor Wube was restored to all his previous lands. What does this say about restorative justice?

It says that during the *Zemene Mesafint* efforts to reconcile were paramount, arguably more important than war or justice. With political instability inherent in the whole matrix of power and tribute, the calculus was on how to retain the status quo; how to preserve that which was known; how to ensure that the placeholders held on to their land; and how the hierarchy, who were tied to the peasants working the land, remained in place, for to tamper with anyone could destabilize the whole feudal order. Peace was not really part of the equation, for peace often required recasting the political order, a step avoided at all costs. In the Era of the Princes, the jostling to assume the imperial throne was primarily motivated by two considerations: personal ambition and, second, to restore the Solomonic dynasty and resurrect Ethiopian Orthodoxy's lineage back to Menilek I. Wara Sheh rulers understood their own limitations and consented to operate within those limits. Marshaling the evidence, Shiferaw Bekele argues persuasively that the Wara Sheh were the dominant suzerains among Ethiopia's provincial princes, but their peacemaking reveals their insecurity and their keen awareness of their weakness. Their aim was to stay in power. To that end, they diluted punitive conditions that could be incorporated into the

41 Translation found in Rubenson, *Survival*, 94.

honor and shaming ceremony because they felt being too harsh would only exacerbate resistance. A central part of restorative justice is that the actions that the recipient of forgiveness demonstrates are vital as a sign of his atonement, a sign of his wanting and needing to be forgiven in order to be reconciled into the body politic. Penitence or atonement figured prominently in biblical conceptions of forgiveness for without a reciprocal promise, forgiveness is meaningless. The meaninglessness embodied in forgiveness without atonement expressed itself in "forgive and forget." And this is exactly what the Wara Sheh chose.

Dejazmach Wube thrice defeated was able to resume his position, reassert his patrimony over his provincial lands, levy taxes on his peasants, use his tribute to buy firearms, rally his subjects, and fight three wars (1830, 1831, and 1842) to topple Yimam, Marye, and Ali II in order to assume the imperial throne. The concept of *irq* – Ethiopians' ability to perceive contradictions and comprehend human transgression, often embodied in the multiple layers of meaning of *qiné*, when administering justice, allowed Ethiopians to be more open to negotiation and compromise. The point Wube's experiences make is that the persistence of war during the *Zemene Mesafint* was a result of the ease and ineffectiveness of the restorative justice modalities employed at that time. The Wara Sheh *chilot* was only one court offering restorative justice; many other provincial courts who perceived themselves nearly equal to the Yejju offered their own terms and in the marketplace for clemency, perpetrators had extra incentive to go and seek amnesty elsewhere. Like a storekeeper, when competitors lower their price, a merchant matches or beats the price to attract customers. The relative decentralization of the *Zemene Mesafint* meant that there were multiple memory-keepers tasked with remembering the agreed upon terms under which clemency was granted. As Wube's cooptation of *Abuna* Salama demonstrates when church leadership was splintered, the one institution that gave juridical consistency could, itself, exacerbate the misapplication of justice. When restorative justice was too freely given, without conditions to prescribe what shape and action atonement was to look like, it became toothless and, without bite, Wube's promises of fidelity through acts of submission were meaningless. Not to be forgotten was the fact that being considered magnanimous elevated perceptions of power, and the Yejju rulers sought all appearances of power.

Subsequent rulers learned their lesson and added strict conditions to forgiveness, if those conditions were not met then more punitive terms were added. The era of forgive and forget by fiat that typified the *Zemene Mesafint* ended when *Dejazmach* Kassa Haylu anointed himself Emperor Tewodros in 1855.

3

Conditional Forgiveness: Restorative Justice Done Right

This short chapter features restorative justice at its peak when the monarch controlled the provinces, and the authority of the emperor ensured that there was but one set of memory-keepers to ensure that those who challenged the state and were defeated were brought to justice according to spelled-out principles. The *Zemene Mesafint* had shown the faults of "forgive and forget." Going back to the Bible, restorative justice was revamped in such a way that forgiveness was realigned with the understanding that forgiveness involves both the forgiver, empowered to set the conditions upon which forgiveness is given, and the forgiven who agrees to abide by those conditions to show their contrition. "Conditional forgiveness" increased the chances for durable peace and reconciliation between rival parties because it unequivocally announced the winner and the loser; moreover, it communicated consequences for either living according to the stipulations which could mean lenient revision of the terms, or more punitive terms added if they were abused.

Using the honor and shaming ceremonies of Menilek, before he became emperor, and that of *Ras* Alula, this chapter gives historical weight to Ethiopian traditions of restorative justice described in detail in Chapter 1. In short, the years 1868, after Emperor Tewodros's death, to 1896 and the Battle of Adwa was the period in which restorative justice worked smoothly. However, the analysis picks up in 1855 where the administration of justice veers to an extreme during the reign of Tewodros II, before settling upon its reasonable middle course.

Vengeance & Retribution

Kassa Haylu brought a swift and inexorable end to the *Zemene Mesafint*. In 1853 he took on *Ras Bitwedded* Ali II, head of the Wara Sheh Mesfenate and sovereign over most of Ethiopia. Ali brought most of his vassals and their armies to battle but Kassa prevailed.

Kassa Haylu was related to *Dejazmach* Maru and was raised in Qwara, northwest of Gondar, however, untimely deaths and less-advantageous political alliances all but closed the door for him inheriting the title and *gult* befitting an aristocrat. He was one of the aristocracy that descended the wobbly social ladder. Feeling humiliated, Kassa chose a path less traveled to secure power and prestige – banditry. As a *shifta*, Kassa's bandits overpowered established lords throughout Qwara.[1] His time as a rebel leader taught him lessons in military warfare that would stay with him to the end, for example, cultivating *esprit de corps* by living with his troops sharing similar food and demonstrating to his followers that they should show respect for peasants by plowing fields and sowing seeds in lands in which they billeted. He had a little of Robin Hood in him, redistributing money and booty to his followers making them tremendously loyal and motivated.[2] In addition, in confrontations with Egyptian forces near the border of Sudan early in his career, Kassa became aware of the advantages of military discipline and modern artillery. Charisma, strategic genius, and military experience garnered him victories and with each victory more provincial lords either joined him or were forced to submit before him.[3] His fame spread in step with perceptions of his ruthlessness. To avert deploying an army to put him down, Ali II resorted to wedding his daughter, Tewabech, to Kassa and promoting him to *dejazmach*. Yet even with entry to the highest reaches of power, cemented in marriage and title, Kassa quickly took umbrage at the disdain in which he perceived others cast upon him in the Wara Sheh *chilot* and left the court to resume being a *shifta*, ranging further and further afield causing dynastic instability in many provincial houses.[4]

By the 1850s *Dejazmach* Kassa Haylu, both bandit and ruler, had dispatched all in his path with only the edifice of the Wara Sheh Mesfenate remaining to finally topple. In April 1853, Kassa defeated four of Ali's trusted vassals. In June of that year Ali and Kassa fought their inevitable war and once again Kassa's military genius plus disciplined, battle-hardened soldiers routed Ali's forces at the Battle of Ayshal. The defeat signaled the end of the *Zemene Mesafint*. There was only one holdout preventing Kassa from assuming an undisputed claim to the imperial throne: *Dejazmach* Wube Hayle Maryam.[5] The same *Dejazmach* Wube who had thrice challenged the Yejju rulers for the throne, the same supplicant who had begged for forgiveness three times and had been granted unconditional pardons along with incomprehensibly generous rewards for his reluctant obeisance. And yet, Ali's magnanimity appeared to have paid off for Wube remained loyal beyond the demise of the Mesfenate.

1 Fernyhough, "Social Mobility and Dissident Elites" and Donald Crummey, "Banditry and Resistance."
2 Bahru Zewde, *Modern Ethiopia*, 28.
3 Bahru Zewde, *Modern Ethiopia*, 27.
4 Bahru Zewde, *Modern Ethiopia*, 28–30.
5 Rubenson, *Survival*, 136–40.

Dejazmach Wube was soundly defeated at the Battle of Deresge in February 1855 but unlike past post-conflict protocols, Kassa demanded unconditional surrender that humiliated the defeated Wube and denied his reentry into Ethiopia's socio-political order. Kassa's justice was unforgiving. Capitalizing on cruel symbolism, Kassa had *Abuna* Salama, Wube's handpicked Archbishop, anoint him Emperor Tewodros II. To communicate that humiliation and shaming were no longer to be a choreographed first act in the restorative justice ceremony, Emperor Tewodros strategically chose Darasge Maryam as the location for his crowning, the very church that *Dejazmach* Wube had endowed, in order to humiliate Wube further.[6] Finally, to squelch any notion of forgiveness, Wube was imprisoned at Maqdala until his death in 1867. According to Aleqa Tekle-Iyuesus, one of Tewodros's chroniclers, the imprisoned Wube lamented to the Virgin Mary, "I thought that you would have mercy on my flesh and my soul, but my donations to your church seem to have been in vain!"[7]

In his early career Tewodros often acted with restraint: "Emperor Tewodros gathered the captives, and those who were not professional soldiers but were found to be conscripts he pardoned."[8] Much of his restraint had to do with preventing his roving army from pillaging peasant producers. "Ordinary cruelties" included plundering the agricultural produce still in the fields, emptying grain bins, raiding farms and taking anything of value "oxen, sheep, goats, butter, honey and every other requisite for subsistence,"[9] and burning houses. Knowing that feudal society rested on the peasantry, *Dejazmach* Kassa showed magnanimity towards those at the bottom of the social economic scale. If his own soldiers were caught looting, they were dealt with severely, sometimes by having their right hand cut off.[10] For aristocrats he was increasingly intolerant.

In accordance with the pendulum theory of revolution, forgive and forget was accepted procedure during the *Zemene Mesafint*. Basically, war resolved nothing simply because peacemaking protocols returned

---

6 Crummey, *Land and Society*, 160–1.

7 Reidulf Molvaer, "The Achievement of Emperor Tewodros II of Ethiopia (1855–1868): From an Unpublished Manuscript by Aleqa Tekle-Iyuesus ('Aleqa Tekle') of Gojjam," *Northeast African Studies* (New Series), 5:3 (1998): 23.

8 Molvaer, "Achievement of Emperor Tewodros," 35. As previously quoted, Henry Dufton also noted Tewodros's acts of magnanimity early in his career: "He exercised the utmost clemency towards the vanquished, treating them rather as his friends than his enemies," *Journey through Abyssinia*, 134.

9 Walter Chichele Plowden, *Travels in Abyssinia and the Galla Country* (London: Longmans, 1868), 138.

10 Donald Crummey, "The Violence of Téwodros," *Journal of Ethiopian Studies*, 9:2 (July 1971): 111; Molvaer, "Achievement of Emperor Tewodros," 33.

everything to the status quo that existed beforehand. Fighting was of little consequence: victory gave the victor a fleeting sense of superiority; defeat only resulted in the temporary humiliation of the honor and shaming ceremony. Months later the animus that led to war was rekindled and with the powerbases of victor and foe intact, fighting resumed. Intuiting these limitations, Emperor Tewodros swung the pendulum far to the right. For him defeated rivals were shunted away to prison or killed. For those who chose to submit they had to acknowledge that this new submission agreement meant essentially disassembling their patrimony. This involved paying high taxes and allowing Emperor Tewodros to enlist the defeated adversary's warriors into his own army. Under Tewodros, brave fighters were actively recruited into what he sought to build which was a national army. The implication of these early policies was to undercut the patronage in the provinces by demanding tribute and severing existing patron-client relationships.

After his coronation, Emperor Tewodros became ever more ruthless. When Wollo rebels looted his camp and killed a few guards during the night, Tewodros gave his army permission to ransack the region depriving the peasantry of their livelihood.[11] His increasing cruelty also manifested itself on his own soldiers for insubordination.[12] Tewodros's rule began with grandiose ambitions and the energy to realize them; however, as his modernizing policies became increasingly compromised by internal rebellion, his impulsive, vindictive nature asserted itself. Supporters and even relatives appointed to governorates ran afoul of his demands. Colonial ambitions by Egypt turned Tewodros's attention towards Mitsiwa because of Khedivian designs to annex the coastline of the Red Sea. To stem Egyptian advances with his relatively well-equipped army he requisitioned more tax money and conscripted more soldiers. In this patronage vacuum, as his eyes were fixed eastward, regional lords built their own powerhouses and challenged Tewodros. It was war all over again. Incessant war spread throughout the country, except there was no compromise on Tewodros's part following battles, and retribution reigned. Bloodbaths began to compromise peasant production.

> When he had left the place and was at Debre-Tabor, Téwodros invaded the area from Ribb to Afrïqa Berr, and he caught everyone, those who were ploughing and digging the soil and those who were just walking along the road, and he put 6,700 persons into houses in the town of Yifag and set them on fire.[13]

---

11 Crummey, "Violence of Téwodros," 111–12.
12 Bahru Zewde, *Modern Ethiopia*, 33.
13 Molvaer, "Achievement of Emperor Tewodros," 49.

Donald Crummey equates Tewodros's violence to terror, the systemic violence waged on subjects comparable to Robespierre's reign of terror. His "erratic and intemperate personality" became increasingly volatile and he "began to beat the common people who came to seek his justice."[14]

Tewodros's growing paranoia towards European missionaries, political emissaries, and assorted adventurers resulted in him imprisoning many of them at Maqdala.[15] Naturally this incensed Europeans, especially the British, who organized the Napier Expedition to free the captives. As the British were marching towards Maqdala, the country was in rebellion. Rivals openly assisted the British and Tewodros was largely confined to his hilltop refuge with a force of less than four thousand. The man who sought to unite Ethiopia, create a professional army, abolish slavery and usher in manufacturing was, in the end, a victim of his own ruthlessness, rejected by the aristocracy because he did not rule according to accepted principles, the clergy because of his attempt to redistribute church land and the people because of his increasing ruthlessness.[16] Using field glasses, Tewodros watched his troops slaughtered by a British expeditionary force that featured disciplined rifle-fire and practiced bayonet in hand-to-hand combat on the plains below Maqdala. Wisely Tewodros released the European prisoners, yet that did not stop the British attacking his fortress.[17] When all was lost, perhaps fittingly, Tewodros put a pistol – tradition says the same one Queen Victoria sent him years before as a gift of goodwill[18] – into his mouth and pulled the trigger as opposed to facing the humiliation of defeat to the British and submission to his own subjects afterwards. Self-awareness was not his strong point, but Aleqa Tekle-Iyuesus attributes Tewodros saying "'Please, have mercy (*igzï'o*)!' and the King heard it and felt compassion, and he said, 'My Creator, what is this! You have made my mind ruthless! Either kill me and save your people or let my mind be compassionate!'"[19]

After Emperor Tewodros's death in 1868, the *mekwanint* yearned for the sanity, decorum, and deliberations associated with restorative justice. Vengeance and retribution, they observed, only led to the dismemberment of Ethiopia's body politic. Reviving restorative justice modalities, however, required some ingenious modification.

---

14 Crummey, "Violence of Téwodros," 113, 119.

15 A significant number of the imprisoned Europeans capitalized on their notoriety and published accounts of their ordeals. For more context, see Darrell Bates, *The Abyssinian Difficulty: The Emperor Theodorus and the Magdala Campaign, 1867–68* (Oxford: Oxford University Press, 1979).

16 Molvaer, "Achievement of Emperor Tewodros," 59; Crummey, "Violence of Téwodros," 123; Bahru Zewde, *Modern Ethiopia*, 40.

17 Trevenen Holland and Henry Hozier, *Record of the Expedition to Abyssinia* (London: 1870), vol. 1, 43.

18 Prouty, *Empress Taytu*, 11.

19 Molvaer, "Achievement of Emperor Tewodros," 49.

Restorative Justice Reformed

Restorative justice under the *Zemene Mesafint* had been too lenient. Moreover, it tended to be one-and-done, meaning that the lenient terms decided upon before the honor and shaming ceremony was it – a single agreement tied to forgive and forget. It meant that there was no mechanism to revise the terms outside of going back to war and recalibrating peace afterwards. The post-1855 *mekwanint* altered restorative justice by gauging the sincerity of an offender's penitence, in other words, his willingness to live under the terms of forgiveness, and if those conditions were not met then they reserved the right to add more punitive terms. To an extent they were returning to a biblical understanding of forgiveness and atonement, for theology insinuated a symbiotic relationship between the forgiver and the person seeking forgiveness. Christianity stressed that forgiveness could not be granted without a commitment by the offender to show remorse and amend his ways. The Old Testament provided examples of recidivists and how harsher punishments were given to those who faked contrition. In other words, one-and-done was thrown out the window and in its place "conditional forgiveness" was established whereby, if the supplicant broke the terms of his submission, his rights to govern, tax, and mobilize soldiers were incrementally denied in accordance with the gravity of the infraction. The more truculent the supplicant's actions, the more severe a punishment was administered.

Conditional forgiveness became a hallmark of Ethiopian restorative justice from this time forward. There were many instances of conditional forgiveness resulting in more punitive terms being added later on; less frequently there were also examples of more lenient conditions being deemed appropriate in recognition of true penitence. Two examples, Menilek and *Ras* Alula, both prominent historical figures of the nineteenth century, may suffice to illustrate how "conditional restorative justice" worked and how it reduced rebellion.

Menilek's submission

Menilek, grandson of *Negus* Sahle Selassie, experienced all facets of justice. At eleven years old Menilek was captured during Tewodros's campaign to overthrow this father, *Negus* Haile Malakot, and pacify Shewa.

Taken captive by Emperor Tewodros, Menilek remained at Maqdala until July 1865 when Germame Wolde Hawaryat, an aristocrat loyal to the Shewan dynastic line, sprung Menilek and whisked him away in the dead of night.[20] His time in captivity was more like house arrest.

20 Guébrè Sellassié, *Chronique*, vol. 1, 99–102; Harold Marcus, *The Life and*

Tewodros took great interest in Menilek, provided him with the best church education, ensured he was instructed in martial and equestrian art – in which he excelled – and allowed him to observe the political and juridical deliberations of the court. As a side note, Menilek appears to have embraced Tewodros's attraction to modern technologies for both were fascinated with machines and weapons. Tewodros had tried to "ensnare" Menilek to remain at his court by giving his daughter, Alitash, in marriage, yet a few years later Menilek abandoned her to make his escape. While at court, Menilek made lasting friendships with other notables, specifically *Lij* Wale, brother of his future wife, Taytu. Menilek also had the advantage of watching Tewodros's "descent into madness"[21] and the ramifications of his terror campaign, which resulted in his loss of legitimacy and spurred widespread rebellions. On his journey back to Shewa, after escaping from Maqdala, thousands of supporters rallied around Menilek. Blocking his hereditary claim to the throne was *Ato* Bezzabih, Tewodros's representative in Shewa. Despite having a significantly smaller army, seeing Menilek's bravery and military leadership convinced many of Bezzabih's forces to defect to Menilek compelling the usurper to flee for his life.[22]

Shortly after their battle Bezzabih sent a message to Menilek begging pardon. With support from the clergy and some quarters of the Shewan *mekwanint*, Menilek was persuaded to offer Bezzabih conditional forgiveness. Bezzabih's shaming ceremony required the obligatory *shemma* wound around the waist, shouldering of a mill stone and the kissing the ground, but from there it deviated from the past for strict conditions were added. Although, Bezzabih "was given the large fief of Abba Motti,"[23] the *gult* lands that he had access to were significantly curtailed, greatly reducing his revenue stream. Still the understanding was that Bezzabih would pay regular taxes, serve Menilek when called upon and refrain from further rebellion.[24] As a conciliatory gesture, Menilek forgave those who had worked for Bezzabih and thereby Emperor Tewodros against the rightful heir to the Shewan throne. Quoting Guglielmo Massaja, Harold Marcus states, "Menelik revoked many of Tewodros's reforms and reverted to the 'mild and paternal laws' by which his forebears had governed Shoa."[25]

Times of Menelik II: Ethiopia 1844–1913 (Oxford: Oxford University Press, 1975), 24; Prouty, *Empress Taytu*, 6–8.

21 Marcus, *Life and Times*, 25.

22 Guébrè Sellassié, *Chronique*, vol. 1, 103–4; Marcus, *Life and Times*, 26.

23 Guébrè Sellassié, *Chronique du règne de Ménélik*, vol. 1, 105; Marcus, *Life and Times*, 26.

24 Guébrè Sellassié, *Chronique du règne de Ménélik*, vol. 1, 104.

25 Guglielmo Massaja, *I miei trentacinque anni di missione nell'alta Etiopia*, Vol. 9 (Tivoli: Stabilimento tipografico Mantero, 1928), 28 quoted in Marcus, *Life and Times*, 27.

Bezzabih, however, may have assumed that Menilek's forgiveness was the one-and-done variety of the *Zemene Mesafint* and quickly resumed acting like a king, stopped tribute payments, allied himself with disgruntled Oromos and plotted insurrection. When the evidence was insurmountable, Menilek called Bezzabih to court to respond to charges against him. Bezzabih heeded the summons but refused to disband his army as demanded. Standing before his *chilot*, Menilek was reputed to have said:

> I have three complaints against Bezabeh: 1, he attacked me when, upon my return from exile, he refused to return to me the *alga* [throne] of my father; 2, after I had pardoned him for the love of God, it was discovered that he plotted against my *alga* in my city where he remained; 3, in agreement with his people, he now refuses to abandon my *amba* and he has killed my soldiers. And now wise men and chiefs, examine his case and judge between him and me.[26]

The verdict for this second infraction was severe. Some claim he was shot; Aleqa Tekle-Iyuesus writes "Minïlik wrapped *Ato* Bezzabbih in a wax cloth [*sic.*] and burnt him up."[27] Following his execution, his troops were invited to join Menilek's army and his lands were distributed among loyalists.

How was this example of conditional restorative justice markedly different? First, the terms for reconciliation were clearly spelled out beforehand. Second, it appears that Menilek's *chilot* functioned as the memory-keeper recording exactly how Bezzabih was to demonstrate his penitence; there was no prevarication as to the terms and no marketplace to go to for better terms. Third, forgive and forget was replaced with conditional forgiveness such that the recidivist could be called back to court instead of resorting to combat. Fourth, the Shewan *mekwanint*, which Menilek had won over to his side, acted as judge and jury. Instead of an autocratic decree, like Tewodros declared that could vary from clemency to capital punishment depending on his mood, the *chilot* heard claims from both sides and deliberated based on the evidence. That the court recommended execution does not undercut the basis of Ethiopia's tradition of restorative justice, just the opposite. It makes the case that the conditions under which forgiveness was granted could be revoked and more punitive terms could be administered, depending on the severity of the infraction, up to and including capital punishment.

Switching sides, ten years later in 1878, Menilek was the supplicant and Emperor Yohannes the judge. Emperor Yohannes's reign was beset with difficulties; there was always war, famine, and pestilence but compounding internal problems were threats to Ethiopian sovereignty

26 Guébrè Sellassié, *Chronique du règne de Ménélik*, vol. 1, 106, translation by Marcus, *Life and Times*, 27.
27 Molvaer, "Achievement of Emperor Tewodros," 46.

posed by Khedivian Egypt, Mahdist Sudan, and Italy. In addition, there were two rivals to the throne who required constant attention, Takla-Haymanot of Gojjam and Menilek of Shewa. To foil Menilek's designs, the emperor invaded Shewa via Manz and in a few smaller skirmishes forced Menilek to retreat towards his tent-capital at Leche.[28] Perceiving his weakness and the advantage of reconciliation, Menilek entered into negotiations using church officials to make the initial contacts. The negotiations lasted two months, January through March 1878, and centered on how acts of fealty were to be performed.[29] Through intermediaries, Yohannes insisted upon the whole ritualized honor and shaming ceremony connoting subservience. Menilek argued more for a meeting of near equals. Yohannes got his way.[30] The result was the Wadara Agreement (alternately known as the Leche Agreement), an intricate example of conditional restorative justice.[31]

Naked to the waist, carrying the stone of penitence on his shoulders, Menilek prostrated himself before Emperor Yohannes in submission. Before walking to the emperor's *addarash* (receiving tent), Menilek appeared downcast and in countenance and posture projected remorse and repentance as prescribed in the ethos of atonement. The shaming was memorialized in *azmaris*' songs about Yohannes's compassion and Menilek's subservience.[32] During the ceremony, "the *echege* rose, bowed to Yohannes, and placed a cross before Menelik; he kissed it, and on it took his oath of fealty to Yohannes."[33] But besides the humiliation of the ceremony itself, everything else was carefully orchestrated and agreed upon beforehand with plenty of high officials and court attendants present to act as memory-keepers familiar with the terms to ensure they were followed. And they were.

The next day, to dampen the humiliation, Emperor Yohannes conferred the title *Negus* or King of Shewa on Menilek in a ceremony conducted with great respect and dignity in the imperial tent. Afterwards the coronation was feted with cannon and rifle salvoes before a

28 Zewde Gabre-Sellassie, *Yohannes IV of Ethiopia: A Political Biography* (1975; reprint, Trenton: Red Sea Press, 2014), 131–3.

29 Orlowska in "Re-imagining Empire" describes the negotiations is detail from grand issues of sovereignty to the size of Yohannes's and Menilek's thrones, their placement and what clothes were to be worn, 230–7.

30 Zewde Gabre-Sellassie, *Yohannes IV*, 133, argues that Yohannes always held the upper hand and showed exceptional generosity towards Menilek. This appears to contradict other chronicles, specifically Guébrè Sellassié, *Chronique du règne de Ménélik*, vol. 1, 105, who assert that Menilek drove a hard bargain from a position of power.

31 Guébrè Sellassié, *Chronique du règne de Ménélik*, vol. 1, 145 ft. 3; Orlowska, "Re-imagining Empire," 230–7; Marcus, *Life and Times*, 52–4.

32 Guébrè Sellassié, *Chronique du règne de Ménélik*, vol. 1, 145–6.

33 Marcus, *Life and Times*, 56.

large feast. The reconciliation was further incentivized with presents consisting of "four cannons, several hundred Remington rifles, and corresponding ammunition"[34] given to Menilek by Yohannes. Most consequential were terms of dynastic succession. His promotion to *negus* essentially awarded the imperial throne to Menilek over Yohannes's own son. The terms were carefully negotiated, the rank of *negus* entitled "the Shewan kings [Menilek] to the ownership of the land of the Kingdom," an important distinction to that of a mere *ras*, which also gave Menilek authority over lands he conquered.[35] Patience was on Menilek's side. By heeding the conditions of his forgiveness, Menilek's army remained intact, his patrimony unspoiled and his conquest of southern Ethiopia given a green light.

In return, Menilek agreed to recognize Yohannes as *Neguse Negest* (King of Kings or Emperor). Menilek sent Yohannes a *yewerq wember* (golden seal) as a sign of his obeisance. Additionally, Menilek had to provision the emperor's army while in Shewa, relinquish hegemony over Wollo, pay regular tribute in amounts that dwarfed past vassals' payments (which he did), send troops when called upon, allow Yohannes's army free passage through Shewa to Debre Libanos, and expel all missionaries, for Yohannes could not fathom European Christians proselytizing to Christian Ethiopians in the hope of converting them to a European divinity.[36] Indeed those terms were met, although some with more urgency than others.

Alula's submission

Ras Alula Engeda exemplifies the other extreme of this new understanding of conditional forgiveness where restorative justice could resort to a big stick. Alula had a glorious career, maligned by other aristocrats because of his common origins, but after he proved himself again and again on the battlefield, he rose to a level of respect only exceeded by the emperors. As stated, nineteenth-century Ethiopia was threatened by Khedivian Egypt, Mahdist Sudan, and Italy. Khedive Ismail Pasha gained control of Mitsiwa and extended Egyptian control along most of the Red Sea littoral and into the hinterland; after dredging the Suez Canal, British and French interest in the Red Sea naturally increased and both came into conflict with Egyptian brigades. With the decline of Egyptian hegemony in the region, impecunious Britain ceded Mitsiwa and its hinterlands to Italy to foil France and to save its own treasury. Italy, delighted with this colonial foothold, determined to extend its territory into the highlands of Ethiopia and join the scramble for Africa. Compounding pressures on Ethiopian sovereignty,

34 Marcus, *Life and Times*, 56.
35 Darkwah, *Shewa, Menilek and the Ethiopian Empire*, 113–14.
36 Prouty, *Empress Taytu*, 22–3.

Egyptian occupation of Sudan incited the Sudanese to resist. Led by the Mahdi, "the well guided one" (née Muhammad Ahmad, a Sufi scholar), his followers fought Egypt to a standstill, forcing Egypt to seek British support resulting in the creation of the Anglo-Egyptian Condominium that ruled over Sudan some years later. But the Mahdists' vision was expansionary, and they sought to redeem Islam by conquering and converting Christian Ethiopia.[37] In all these confrontations, Alula fought to preserve Ethiopian independence.

Alula attached himself to the rise of *Dejazmach* Kassa Mercha, a fellow Tigrean, who, as mentioned above, took the coronation name Yohannes IV in 1871. As a "king's man," Alula led Yohannes's battles against the Egyptians at Gundat (1875) and Gura (1876). Recognized for his fearlessness and brilliant military strategy, Alula was promoted to *ras* and henceforth functioned as both supreme military commander and trusted political councilor. Soon Emperor Yohannes appointed him governor over the Marab Mellash, literally "beyond the Marab River," most often referred to as Hamasen or the Eritrean highlands, overlooking Mitsiwa and where Alula established Asmara as his capital.[38] Alula was the first line of defense against the Egyptians and Italians both trying to advance from the East, and the Mahdists from the West. Indeed, Alula defeated the Mahdists at Kufit in 1885 on the border of Sudan.[39] Two years later he crushed the Italians at the Battle of Dogali nearby Mitsiwa, momentarily stopping Italy's colonial ambitions.[40] More than anyone, Alula defended Ethiopian sovereignty but with a decidedly Tigrean ethnic bias, even beyond that of his benefactor Emperor Yohannes. Being of humble birth Alula was not steeped in the "wax and gold" polysemic nature of *qiné* and may not have been able to fathom the discursive reasoning, foresight, and circumspection that enabled well-educated Ethiopians to envision alternate consequences

37 The history of Emperor Yohannes's travails with Egypt, Great Britain, Italy, and the Madhists fills tomes. The scholar most adept in unraveling the alliances and misalliances, conflicts and peace-brokering, promises, and treacheries is Sven Rubenson in *The Survival of Ethiopian Independence.* Based on years in British, French, Italian, German, Egyptian, and even Turkish government archives, his map through the vicissitudes of these complex times is likely the most accurate. Reconciling reliance on foreign diplomatic accounts with Ethiopian chroniclers to give a more Ethio-centric account, see Zewde Gabre-Sellassie, *Yohannes IV.*

38 Wolbert Smidt, "Hamasen" in *Encyclopaedia Aethiopica.*

39 Haggai Erlich, *The Cross and the River: Ethiopia, Egypt and the Nile* (Boulder: Lynne Rienner Publishers, 2002), 59–78.

40 The Battle of Dogali is best commemorated and historicized in the twenty articles published in Taddesse Beyene, Tadesse Tamrat, and Richard Pankhurst, eds., *The Centenary of Dogali: Proceedings of the International Symposium, Addis Ababa-Asmara, January 24–25, 1987* (Addis Ababa: Institute of Ethiopian Studies, 1988).

of certain actions. His loyalty and ideology were firm, perhaps too firm. Unable to compromise, Alula incurred the enmity of many rulers and, perhaps for military support, perhaps to lure him away from Asmara and placate the Italians, Yohannes recruited Alula to fight alongside him at Matamma in March 1889 against the Mahdists. On the brink of victory a stray bullet killed Emperor Yohannes and the Mahdists claimed their victory after a reassembled detachment overtook the funeral cortege, killed a number of elderly, Ethiopian notables, severed their heads and paraded them along with Yohannes's head around Sudan.[41] With Ethiopia in disarray, dynastic trouble brewing and Alula absent from Asmara, the Italians advanced into the highlands, took Asmara and proclaimed their new colony of Eritrea in January 1890 without firing a shot.

Alula remained loyal to Yohannes's heir, *Ras* Mengesha Yohannes, but more so to Tigrean hegemony. Tigray, however, was racked with drought and famine. *Ras* Mengesha, surrounded by the Italians in Eritrea, the Mahdists in Sudan to the west, and Menilek in Shewa to the south, knew that his people were war-weary and undernourished, and that he did not have the resources to contest the throne. Upon Menilek's coronation as *Neguse Negest*, *Ras* Mengesha agreed to travel to Addis Ababa and formally submit. *Ras* Alula, Yohannes's elder statesman and victorious general, had considerable influence over *Ras* Mengesha and did everything in his power to prevent Mengesha from submitting to the Emperor. As hateful of the Italians as he was, Alula went so far as to conclude a tentative treaty condoning Italy's takeover of Eritrea in exchange for Italian support against Menilek. Alula remained truculent, sometimes backing *Ras* Mengesha for all the right reasons, other times going against Mengesha's will expressly to cause the king to divert his attention away from Shewa to squelch internal rivalries in Tigray, which, of course, Alula had started. Unbowed, Alula "reacted furiously and performed the traditional war dances, inciting everyone to shout anti-Shoan slogans."[42] One time Alula absconded with 400 rifles destined for Menilek and when reprimanded only returned 200, saying that the others were necessary to defend the homeland when in fact he used them against Menilek's Tigrean allies. Another time he suggested *Ras* Mengesha's overthrow if he submitted to Menilek.[43] Added together these incidents meant that Alula could be indicted for high treason.[44]

41 For a detailed account of the flukiness of the Battle of Matamma see Zewde Gabre-Sellassie, *Yohannes IV*, 297-300.

42 Haggai Erlich, *Ras Alula and the Scramble for Africa* (Trenton: Red Sea Press, 1996), 179.

43 Erlich, *Ras Alula*, 179.

44 Marcus, *Life and Times*, 144–5.

But circumstances changed and three things led to Alula's change of heart. First was when Menilek realized Italian treachery in the Treaty of Wechale that made Ethiopia a protectorate of Italy. Second was when Italian colonial designs became apparent after they took Alula's lands in Marab Mellash. Third was when Menilek began to act as sovereign of all Ethiopians against Italian aggression. With a change of heart Alula accompanied *Ras* Mengesha to Addis Ababa in June 1894 to submit. The conditions of Alula's forgiveness were telling.

Arriving in Addis Ababa, a retinue of 6,000 men accompanied the Tigrean contingent of *Ras*es Mengesha, Alula, Hagos, and Wolde Mikael. To demonstrate superiority, Emperor Menilek mobilized 12,000 soldiers to meet them; moreover, he ordered that all firearms be seized from merchants for he did not want them sold to the Tigreans. After setting up camp, the Tigrean *ras*es along with the clergy of St. Mary's of Aksum proceeded to Menilek's *addarash* located on the promontory where he had constructed his new *gebbi* (palace). In front was Menilek, wearing his crown and seated on his throne. Around him were his jury of *mekwanint* standing beside him on each side in descending rank, all assembled to witness the honor and shaming ceremony. Mengesha, Alula, Hagos, and Wolde Mikael each carrying a stone on their bare shoulders, prostrated themselves and asked for forgiveness. Uttering one word, Menilek granted it. To dignify the occasion all five sat in silence for approximately fifteen minutes while rifle and cannon fire saluted the submission. Finally, the *Neguse Negest* and the four *ras*es kissed the cross as a sign of peace. Conditional forgiveness, however, was still to be conferred. After three days of banquets and meetings Menilek finally presented his terms as "a sign of loyalty: a) that Salamiti, hitherto governed by *Ras* Hagos, be transferred to Empress Tāytu; b) that the *neburā'ed*, the chief of the holy city of Aksum, be nominated by the emperor; c) that the revenue of Tigre be paid to the imperial treasury; and d) that Zawditu's *gult* rights over Enderta be renewed." [45]

The terms were severe. Essentially, many hereditary lands were dispossessed and given to the two most powerful women in Ethiopia with kinship ties to Tigray – Empress Taytu and future Empress Zawditu. Menilek, henceforth, controlled the church by controlling the ecclesiastics of Aksum thereby the ideology of Tigrean separateness was undercut. Most consequential, the very basis of the old feudal system of patrimony that enabled a ruler to keep tribute in cash or kind was severed. Tigray was now a province whose revenue supported the treasury of the Shewan emperor thus significantly enhancing his hegemonic power over his Tigrean rivals.

Alula's terms were even harsher. As Marab Mellash had been taken over by Italy, Alula had no patrimonial lands to demand tribute from in

45 Erlich, *Ras Alula*, 187.

Eritrea. (He was able to retain some of his *gult* lands in Tigray itself, but these were negligible). His aim by submitting was to lure the emperor to go to war with Italy to retrieve those lost territories. Yet the conditions of his forgiveness for treasonous acts were quite unique; they were to blindly follow Emperor Menilek's decisions regarding the Marab Mellash. Alula had no choice. He was reconciled into the body politic as a "king's man" once again, but this time more like a "salary man" given a stipend by the emperor to be ordered here and there at will. And *Ras* Alula complied. As a test of his loyalty Menilek ordered Alula to take part in the Wallamo expedition and gave the great victor of Gundat, Gura, Kufit, and Dogali 200 men to lead. Humiliation writ large! Yet, as his obedient servant, Alula accepted Shewan hegemony and earned the trust of Menilek such that he became a close military adviser leading up to and during the 1896 Battle of Adwa where he served with distinction.

These two examples demonstrate how conditions could be negotiated as in Menilek's case or dictated as in Alula's. Circumstances were considered to determine how lenient or severe the conditions were to be. Emperor Yohannes incentivized Menilek to adhere to the conditions by giving him more than he thought possible. Menilek was made *negus*, King of Shewa, and inheritor of the realm in the event that Emperor Yohannes passed away, all this for promising loyalty to the crown. But even more remunerative were all the issues that were left out of the conditional agreement like conquering the Oromo lands to the south which generated revenue with which to build his own military in preparation for his ascension to the throne. By the time of Emperor Yohannes's untimely death, Menilek had built his army sufficiently to preempt opposition to him, as *Ras* Mengesha Yohannes understood.

Ras Alula's case differed in that it emphasized the punitive aspects of conditional forgiveness. *Ras* Alula's reputation as a warrior and general were never in doubt, nor was his Tigrean chauvinism, nor his capacity to manipulate or influence politics as he demonstrated after Emperor Yohannes's death. In other words, his willingness to disrupt was well known and believed to be incorrigible. The conditions for his reentry into the good graces of the imperial order were harsh and construed to prevent him from returning to his powerbase, with all its potential to muster an army and challenge the state. Instead, Emperor Menilek demoted Alula and tested his military prowess in small campaigns in the south before Adwa.

4

The Battle of Adwa: Justice Misinterpreted

About the Battle of Adwa, the *New York Times* reported on "Italy's Terrible Defeat."[1] From Rome to Paris, New York to London headlines decried Italy's humiliating defeat at the hands of Ethiopian savages. Conversely, *The Daily Gleaner* published in Kingston, Jamaica acclaimed "Abyssinia Defeats Italian Attack."[2] From Harlem to Port-au-Prince, Dakar to Cape Town blacks celebrated Africa's victory over European imperialists. The Battle of Adwa, bar none, is Ethiopia's signature event. No Ethiopian historical episode before or after has so affected world history. Emperor Menilek's victory damaged the aura of European invincibility. It gave hope to the world's oppressed populations. It spawned the creation of Ethiopic churches where Jesus Christ assumed a dark complexion and Christian theology appropriated aspects of African Traditional Religion. It compelled Taj Weekes to call his reggae band Adowa a hundred years later.

The battle was of short duration, its aftermaths lengthy and consequential. In part the prolonged aftershocks had everything to do with misperceptions of justice: Italians not understanding Ethiopia's weighted traditions of restorative justice wherein sentences could vary from amnesty to execution; Ethiopians not comprehending Western law nor the manner in which the court of public opinion swayed politics and racialized perceptions of what was considered just. This chapter attempts to unpack competing views of justice, their collision course and a bifurcated outcome whereby Ethiopia tried to meld European and Ethiopian jurisprudence. The first section addresses the Battle of Adwa, what instigated colonial aggression, war preparations and the battle itself. The second, post-conflict, section assesses the prevailing interpretations on how magnanimity or punishments were administered to different actors. The third section looks at the contradictory conceptions of justice, how the plurality of restorative justice modalities were misunderstood by Europeans, and how European terms of extraterritoriality and maritime law were nearly indecipherable to Menilek and his court. It also traces Ethiopia's puerile attempt to accommodate these two contravening legal systems. The chapter concludes by returning to

1 "Italy's Terrible Defeat," *New York Times* (March 4, 1896).
2 "Abyssinia Defeats Italian Attack," *The Daily Gleaner* (March 6, 1896).

restorative justice and considers what reconciliation means between an aggressive colonial nation and a traditional African state.

The Battle of Adwa

The Battle of Adwa started around midnight February 29, leap day, and ended by noon on March 1, 1896 – a scant twelve-hour battle, though bloody to an extreme.[3] The Italians lost 4,000 men including about 50 percent of their officer corps; over 2,000 *askaris* (Eritrean recruits from both lowlands and highlands of Hamasen, Eritrea) died; 1,500 wounded, and 3,000 prisoners. This was out of a force of around 18,000, meaning a casualty ratio of nearly 1:3. For their part, Ethiopian casualties were considerably higher and although a reliable count was not taken, estimates range from 4,000 to 6,000 killed, and 8,000 wounded.[4]

While the clash of troops was short, the conflict extended back to the Treaty of Wechale of 1889.[5] Menilek had been playing a risky game with the Italians by signing away political and trade concessions with them to pincer Emperor Yohannes and facilitate his pathway to the throne.[6] After Yohannes's sudden death, the Treaty of Wechale was rushed through in the euphoria following Menilek's coronation, giving preference to Italy in commerce and diplomacy, but soon it became apparent that there was a significant translation error. The Italian interpretation of Article XVII stipulated "an obligation of the Emperor to conduct

---

3 For contemporary sources see George Berkeley, *The Campaign of Adowa and the Rise of Menelik* (Westminster: Archibald Constable, 1902); and Oreste Baratieri, *Mémoires d'Afrique, 1892–1896* (Paris: Delagrave, 1899). Berkeley's account provides exceptional detail. For a more recent account of the Battle of Adwa and perhaps the best in accessing Italian archives to provide a decidedly Eurocentric view see, Raymond Jonas, *The Battle of Adwa: African Victory in the Age of Empire* (Cambridge: Belknap Press, 2011). For a volume that highlights the Ethiopian perspective see Abdussamad H. Ahmad and Richard Pankhurst, eds., *Adwa Victory Centenary Conference* (Addis Ababa: Institute of Ethiopian Studies, 1998). A more polemical, self-published book that highlights many Ethiopian sources is Abebe Haile Melekot's *The Victory of Adowa and What We Owe to Our Heroes* (Addis Ababa: 1998). Pierre Pétridès, *Le Héros d'Adoua* (Paris: Plon, 1963) provides a meticulous account of the strategy and number of troops involved in the battle.

4 Erlich, "Battle of Adwa" in *Encyclopaedia Aethiopica.* These numbers differ from those supplied in Marcus's earlier work, *Life and Times*, 172–3.

5 Italian imperial designs on Ethiopia went back to the mid-eighteenth century, see Robert L. Hess, "Italian Imperialism in Its Ethiopian Context," *International Journal of African Historical Studies* 6:1 (1973): 94–109.

6 One of the more comprehensive, though rather disjointed assessments of the Treaty of Wichalē is found in Ernest Work, *Ethiopia, a Pawn in European Diplomacy* (New York: Macmillan Co., 1935), 51–156.

his foreign affairs through Italian channels,"[7] thus reducing Ethiopia to little more than an Italian protectorate. The Amharic version said Ethiopia could avail itself of Italian representation if it chose. "Italy's Chicanery" provoked six years of diplomat disputes. Time and again Menilek requested that the Treaty of Wechale be amended. The famine of the early 1890s was one reason the spat did not detonate into war sooner, for the famine, mixed with epidemics, devastated northern and central Ethiopia, causing an untold number of deaths and millions of internally displaced peoples.[8] In response, Menilek ordered his soldiers to assist peasants to plow and seed fields.[9] Not coincidently, at this time the Italians moved up into the highlands of Eritrea taking all of *Ras* Alula's province of Marab Mellash as far as the Marab River and declaring it their colony – this was in blatant disregard of Article III of the Treaty. Italy's next subversive move was to try to lure Tigrean *ras*es, including at one time or another both Mengesha and Alula, to their side against Menilek and thus acquire a foothold in Tigray. Yet when *Ras*es Mengesha and Alula submitted to Menilek, that strategy too failed. The only recourse was to resort to military conquest.

In October 1895 the Italians crossed the Marab River and occupied Adigrat. Ethiopians interpreted this as a declaration of war. Menilek mobilized over 100,000 soldiers from all over Ethiopia, including Oromo and other southern peoples he had conquered.[10] The logistics were not overly complicated. Augustus Wylde observed: "The Abyssinian hordes [troops] are the same as locust, they live on what they can get from the surrounding country; when they have devoured everything, they have to move on to another place where supplies are procurable."[11]

Patriotism united various ethnic, language, and religious groups against a European nation. Accompanying the column north was Empress Taytu along with her court women and her own force of 5,000 troops. Soldiers were often attended by wives and retainers tasked to carry provisions, make meals and provide comfort;[12] thus, the forced

7 Sven Rubenson, *Wichale XVII: The Attempt to Establish a Protectorate Over Ethiopia* (Addis Ababa: Haile Sellassie I University Department of History, 1964), 59.

8 Pankhurst, "The Great Ethiopian Famine of 1888–1892."

9 Marcus, *Life and Times*, 136.

10 For the brutality and social transformation brought about by Menilek's southern expeditions and the effects of the Battle of Adwa, see Etana Habte, "Adwa Victory, Menilek's Power and Local Autonomy in Wallagga Territory of Ethiopia: The Case of Leeqaa-Naqamtee and Leeqaa-Qellem (1896–1941)" in *Territorial Conquest, Central Power and Local Autonomy in Ethiopia 1880s–1941* (Quezon City, Philippines: Flipside Digital, 2011).

11 Augustus Wylde, *Modern Abyssinia* (London: Methuen, 1901), 216.

12 Tsegaye Tegenu provides an exceptionally detained analysis of how Menilek's army was provisioned, see "The Logistic Base and Military Strategy of the Ethiopian Army" in proceedings of the *Adwa Victory Centenary Conference*, 99–128.

march north was more like a mass human migration accompanied by an equally large auxiliary of horses, donkeys, sheep, and goats. Since supply lines were nonexistent, this huge population lived off the land, decimating the agricultural produce of the regions it passed through; what foodstuff was not picked by humans was nibbled by livestock. Every time the caravan stopped the circle of devastation expanded leaving hunger in its wake.

Seeing little resistance, the Italians struck south erecting fortifications at Mekele and sent a battalion, under Major Toselli, to occupy the high ground of Amba Alage another seventy kilometers further south. Italian intelligence knew Menilek's army was moving north but totally misrepresented the numbers reporting two forces, each of around 12,000. Looking out over *Ras* Mekonnen's advanced guard of nearly 40,000,[13] Major Toselli could see with his "own eyes the monster they had conjured."[14] Surrounding the mount, Mekonnen, Menilek's peace-broker, sent a message to Toselli offering safe passage in the hope of perhaps negotiating a way out of hostilities. Toselli, fully understanding the numerical imbalance, stood his ground for pride of country. On December 7, 1895 the Ethiopians attacked. Because of the high ground and ample time to dig trenches and set up their artillery, the Italians fought hard, causing many fatalities. But with wave after wave of Ethiopians surging from every vantage point, the Italians could not redirect their fire quickly enough and the force of two thousand was overrun by noon. Toselli sounded a retreat to Mekele, their only hope. Yet the retreat turned into a massacre for two reasons.[15] First, most of Toselli's forces were Eritrean *askaris*, ethnically, linguistically, and religiously akin to *Ras*es Wele, Mengesha and Alula's Tigrean forces. Moreover, another 700 of the Italian force were Tigray-speakers fighting for *Ras* Sebhat and Sheik Thala, who had their own grievances with Menilek and chose to side with Italy. The sense of betrayal was overpowering, it centered around the fact that Blacks chose to fight Blacks for White man's gain. Second, as some of the Italian forces managed to outrun their pursuers, and the fact that fortified Mekele was still seventy kilometers away, local villagers harassed them and fell upon the weak to express their anti-foreign hatred.

By January 1896, Mekele was in Menilek's sights and again Menilek offered peace, which was rejected a second time. Italian resistance was well orchestrated for they had refortified the ramparts after Amba Alage. Five Ethiopian surges were repelled. Resorting to a blockade,

---

13 Jonas, *Battle of Adwa*, 125. Pétridès estimates *Ras* Makonnen's own army at 25,000, *Le Héros d'Adoua*, 156f, but under his command were the troops of *Ras*es Wele, Mengesha, and Alula, and *Fitawrari* Gabayyahu whose valor in leading the final uphill charge is generally recognized as the deciding thrust, Bahru Zewde, *Modern Ethiopia*, 77.

14 Jonas, *Battle of Adwa*, 124.

15 Jonas, *Battle of Adwa*, 127, 129–30.

the Ethiopians laid siege to the city for forty-five days, cutting off reinforcements, provisions, and most importantly its water supply. By January 17th soldiers were drinking muddy, insect-infested water. Menilek had them cornered, yet, in a "magnanimous gesture" that provoked many Ethiopians to question his leadership, he was merciful and allowed the Italians to evacuate and rejoin their compatriots in Adwa.[16] "After they came out, there was none who would offer them water to drink without the permission of the His Majesty. His Majesty granted permission and they drank."[17] They were even provided with camels and mules to transport weapons, ammunition, and the commissariat out of the fortress "between two parallel columns of Ethiopian soldiers."[18] The Italian commander "Gallino, too, was given a mule with a richly ornamented saddle"[19] as a sign of respect for the vanquished. *The Lagos Weekly Record* elaborated, "Ras Makonnen escorted the garrison force to General Oreste Baratieri's camp near Adigrat, and defended them from angry attacks of the people. This was certainly an act of magnamity unknown even among civilized nations and shows that the Abyssinians are as honourable and merciful as they are courageous."[20]

Relief and celebration that Italy's sons were spared further bloodshed blazoned headlines all over Italy, but politics in Rome precluded an amicable resolution. Prime Minister Francesco Crispi was under tremendous pressure to redress two humiliating defeats by Ethiopian "savages" – Dogali and Amba Alage. Directives to General Balatieri, supreme commander of Italian forces in Eritrea and Ethiopia, were to double down and zealously pursue the conquest from their foothold near Adwa. War was inevitable.

By Pierre Pétridès's count there were 131,000 Ethiopian troops bivouacked in and around Adwa,[21] excluding wives and retainers. Environmental pressure was extreme. The northern advance had turned into a "*sitzkrieg*," a phony war where the two sides merely postured in front of one another. By the end of February 1896, food was scarce, and people resorted to eating grasses and leaves. Everyone felt hunger pangs. The countryside was stripped of firewood. On the day of the battle some of

16 The depth of this "magnanimous gesture" is probed by Negussay Ayele, "Adwa 1896: Who Was Civilized and Who Was Savage?" in *The Battle of Adwa: Reflections on Ethiopia's Historic Victory Over European Colonialism*, ed. Paulos Milkias and Getachew Metaferia (New York: Algora, 2005), 163.

17 Letter 152, "Yosēf Negusē to Alfred Ilg and Léon Chefneux, Maqalē 31 March 1896" in Bairu Tafla, *Ethiopian Records of the Menilek Era: Selected Amharic Documents from Nachlab of Alfred Ilg 1884–1900* (Wiesbaden: Harrassowitz Verlag, 2000), 458.

18 Jonas, *Battle of Adwa*, 145.

19 Letter 152, "Yosēf Negusē to Alfred Ilg and Léon Chefneux, 458.

20 "The Italians and Abyssinia," *The Lagos Weekly Record* (March 7, 1896), 4.

21 Pétridès, *Le Héros d'Adoua*, 156f.

the Ethiopian soldiers were many kilometers away in Aksum "attending church and picking up food requisitioned from resentful clerics there."[22] In contrast, Italian supply lines from Mitsiwa provisioned General Balatieri's camp followers quite well, the Italian-born troops washed down pasta with wine brought from home. With hunger so serious, Emperor Menilek and his war council were forced to contemplate demobilizing the army and advising everyone to return home as they were able.

And then chauvinist pride compelled General Balatieri to order his troops to advance on the moonless night of leap day with orders for his four generals to set up an offensive line on the high ground closer to Menilek's forces. The battle had commenced.

For calamitous reasons, the generals never formed Balatieri's offensive line. The acrimony among General Matteo Albertone, the machismo, General Guiseppe Arimondi, the careerist, General Vittorio Dabormida, the haughty aristocrat, and General Giuseppe Ellena, the defensive-minded strategist, was palpable yet even more venom was reserved for Balatieri. Albertone, perhaps relying on faulty maps, ordered his advanced guard of *askaris* to what he thought was Kidane Mihret Mountain thus overshooting Balatieri's deployment line. Albertone's whole army marched into no man's land. At four in the morning Major Turitto's *askaris* ran into Menilek's sentries. A courier raced into the tent where the emperor and empress were up and, as was custom, were saying morning prayers, along with *Ras*es Mekonnen and Mikael, and "threw himself on the ground before the emperor" warning them of the *askari* incursion. "The emperor shrugged off the warning and continued his prayers." Only when the third and fourth courier arrived did Menilek and his *ras*es order the drummers to sound the alarm, then they "took holy communion. The green-yellow-red flags were dipped before the crucifix. The communicants bowed, beseeching the God of Combat, St. George, to help the country, the emperor and the faith." [23] That Ethiopian leaders bothered to take communion and ask for absolution during this Sunday mass at the moment of attack, speaks volumes about the sacerdotal connection between church and state. Another version of events says that *Ras* Alula, always leery of Italian intentions, sent two spies to Sauria and they observed the Italian departure and ran back and informed *Ras* Alula who in turn notified Emperor Menilek.[24]

---

22 Prouty, *Empress Taytu*, 156; Abebe Haile Melekot, *The Victory of Adowa*, 141.

23 Prouty attributes this account of the battle to an unknown Ethiopian author. Remarkable is the reverence shown to decorum and the divine when there was likely pandemonium all around, *Empress Taytu*, 155.

24 Wylde, *Modern Abyssinia*, 204.

By daylight fighting had begun. Albertone hearing that Turitto's *askaris* were under fire moved closer. The element of surprise and the delay to muster the Ethiopian army gave Albertone the initial advantage. Ethiopian troops appeared confused and hesitant. Seeing the setback, Empress Taytu "cried to them with all her strength. 'Courage! Victory is ours! Strike!' The Soldiers ... could not run away when encouraged by a woman and [returned to the fray]. Taytu shed her femininity and became a valiant warrior ... her cannoneers to her right of where she stood fired so continuously that they succeeded in breaking the center of the enemy army."[25] Yosef Neguse, another eyewitness in a letter to Alfred Ilg and Léon Chefneux recounted,

> the heroine queen of Ethiopia, Empress Tāytu, however, began to play the role of heroes. In order to be an example to people who are devoid of love for a home country and religion, she went down on foot having arrayed the artillerymen in the front and the riflemen on the left and right, ordering the banner of the *Tābot* of Zion to be carried, priests follow. Seeing the cannons being loaded, she took up position, and as the position became a target for cannon shots, she moved to a fortified position from where she had shots directed across and, hence, they were defeated.[26]

The battle, in fact, was more complex and multipronged than some contemporary chroniclers depicted.[27] Every Ethiopian ruler deployed his forces against Italy's three columns. Albertone bore the brunt of the early fighting. Communicating back to Balatieri, Albertone requested reinforcements. Balatieri ordered Dabormida to veer left to come to Albertone's aid. Dabormida veered right. Two columns were pinned down – north and south – miles from each other by huge armies of well-armed Ethiopians, and far in front of Arimondi's center column that sheltered Ellena's reserves and Balatieri's headquarters behind Raio Mountain. It was only a matter of time before Menilek's forces stormed the gap and overwhelmed Arimondi and pressed down upon Ellena and Balatieri.[28]

The fighting was fierce. Ethiopians outnumbered Italians by nearly five to one. Like Amba Alage, Ethiopia riflemen targeted Italian officers. David Chapple states: "Both Ethiopian troops and *askaris*, in my

---

25 Empress Taytu's actions are feted by Guébrè Sellassié, *Chronique du règne de Ménélik*, vol. 2, 441–2. The English translation is taken from Prouty, *Empress Taytu*, 156–7.

26 Letter 152, "Yosēf Negusē to Alfred Ilg and Léon Chefneux," 461.

27 Guébrè Sellassié, *Chronique du règne de Ménélik*, vol. 2, 435–48.

28 Arguably for the most detailed account of the battle see Richard Caulk, *"Between the Jaws of Hyenas:" A Diplomatic History of Ethiopia (1876–1896)* (Wiesbaden: Harrassowitz Verlag, 2002), 483–564. Shorter analyses can be found in Assefa Abreha, "The Battle of Adwa: Victory and its Outcome" in proceedings of the *Adwa Victory Centenary Conference*, 129–81; and Jonas, *Battle of Adwa*, 173–207.

opinion, shot better than most European troops."[29] There was little firepower advantage between the two armies. The *askaris*' artillery batteries were rather obsolete; nevertheless, in terms of numbers, placement and rapidity of fire they were effective. Ethiopian Hotchkiss machine guns, however, neutralized Italy's artillery advantage by being highly mobile. Both sides used a wide array of single-shoot, falling-block guns as well as bolt-action repeater rifles from the finest arms manufacturers in Europe and America. What is surprising is the ammo. According to Chapple, Menilek's forces used better ammunition and had more of it. Italian ammo often misfired.[30] While most colonial wars featured an asymmetric technological advantage favoring the European metropole, there was near parity at the Battle of Adwa thanks, in part, to Emperor Menilek's captivity at Maqdala where he caught Tewodros's abiding passion for all things modern and mechanical and later set about brokering trade agreements to fill his armory with the latest weapons and munitions.

Barbarities existed on both sides. Italians wrought devastation with volleys of gunfire from their battlements and bayonets in close quarters. Writing shortly after the battle Augustus Wylde claims Ethiopian casualties were 5,000 to 6,000 dead and "8,000 badly wounded, of whom perhaps a quarter died." Cuts and concussions were not counted, only those "actually disabled." He goes on to write that when he visited the environs some months later "nearly all of these [wounded] would be cripples for life, the bones of the arms and legs being shattered."[31] Ethiopians were equally cruel. Moreover, there were highly sexual provocations from Taytu's women-followers as well as other wives throughout the camps who questioned the manliness of their Ethiopian soldiers and challenged them by crying, "Kill! Kill! The brave man will bring me a trophy [genitalia of a victim]."[32] Castration played a huge part in Italy's memorialization of the battle, for it justified their bringing civilization to the savages.[33]

After the Hotchkiss machine guns silenced Albertone's artillery and the Ethiopian army led by Emperor Menilek turned both flanks to gain the high ground and rain down small-arms fire into the midst of his army, Albertone, wounded in battle, surrendered at around 11:00 a.m. to "save what few men that there were left alive."[34] The fatal turn to the right and the sluggishness of Dabormida's redeployment gave *Ras*es

---

29 David Chapple, "The Firearms of Adwa" in proceedings of the *Adwa Victory Centenary Conference*, 69.

30 Chapple, "Firearms of Adwa," 47–78.

31 Wylde, *Modern Abyssinia*, 212–13.

32 Prouty, *Empress Taytu*, 157.

33 Harold Marcus, "Racist Discourse about Ethiopia and Ethiopians Before and After the Battle" in proceedings of the *Adwa Victory Centenary Conference*, 391–402.

34 Wylde, *Modern Abyssinia*, 207.

Alula and Mengasha, along with other Tigrean troops, ample time to mobilize and pinned down Dabormida. Sources agree that Dabormida's forces put up effective resistance repulsing four Ethiopian surges. These involved bayonets against spears with blood spilling everywhere. Sources diverge over how Dabormida was killed, one stating that he was shot by his own "Turk-basha" (*askaris*).[35]

Observing the opening between Albertone and Dabormida, *Ras*es Mekonnen, Wele, and Mikael along with the Oromo cavalry shot the gap straight at Arimondi's defensive line on Raio Mountain. Once sheer numbers overwhelmed Arimondi, killing him and decimating his line, Balatieri called a general retreat asking Ellena to secure the withdrawal, but the rout was on. The destination was Adigrat, the last Italian stronghold in Tigray. The Oromo cavalry, with speedy steeds and adept use of swords and spears, turned the retreat into a rout. George Berkeley remarks "the great strength of their army lies in the fact that every man is a warrior trained from childhood to use the sword, shield and spear."[36] As a mopping up operation, the Oromo cavalry doubled back and attacked Dabormida from the rear sealing the utter destruction of the Italian army. By 4:30 p.m. the battle was over.

Magnanimity and Punishment

While magnanimity was a spanner in the toolbox of peacebuilding, punishment was a saw alongside it. In the aftermath of the Battle of Adwa both tools were used. By evening Ethiopia's dead and wounded were returning on stretchers carried by wives and retainers, and on the backs of horses and donkeys. Mixed amongst the carnage were Italian and *askari* prisoners and wounded. Anger provoked revenge.

Oromo cavalrymen, astride their horses, brandishing swords or spears, wearing lion's mane headdresses and often depicted barechested imprinted a visual image that Italian artists commemorated in sketches and paintings. The rationale for such images was to justify the original attack and press for Italy to avenge their defeat.[37] The Oromo cavalry's slaughter of hundreds of fleeing Italians and *askaris* only perpetuated the image, as reported by Italian survivors. Retribution was also waged by local people all the way through Tigray to the Marab River and even into the Hamasen (Eritrea) in retaliation for abuses per-

35 Abebe Haile Melekot, *The Victory of Adowa*, 166–7. Wylde claims he interviewed the Ethiopian assailant who killed Dabormida during the battle, *Modern Abyssinia*, 220.

36 Berkeley, *Campaign of Adowa*, 7.

37 Silvana Palma, "The Italian Iconography of Adwa: A Domesticated Memory" in proceedings of the *Adwa Victory Centenary Conference*, 491–500; see "Galla Cavalry" reproduction, 500D.

petrated by Baratieri's forces in occupying Tigray in the first place.[38] Describing their anger Augustus Wylde states, "The survivors from the centre were then attacked by the Agamé population and many cruel massacres took place, the bodies of the slain being mutilated and their heads cut off and put on the rocks that lined the sides of the road."[39] Typical of all battles, soldiers, wives, and others in the vicinity combed through the dead bodies looking for loved ones and taking booty from enemies who had perished. Nikolai Leontiev, the Russian ally of Menilek's who did not witness the battle but arrived within weeks heading the Russian medical team dispatched to assist in the evacuation of the wounded to their makeshift hospital back in Addis Ababa, wrote:

> The women who carried jugs of water to the soldiers, set their burdens on the ground and helped take prisoners. The dead lay in heaps ... streams of blood turned to rivers ... and the enormous field of killing looked like some horrible chess board where fate, with a merciless hand, had interfered in a terrible endgame. The intoxicated conquerors began to loot. Clothes were taken from the dead. The Abyssinians set fire to the grass and the flames spread, in their fiery glow could be seen in outline, shadows rising from the earth. These were unfortunate Italians, some wounded, some lying as if dead to avoid capture. They were compelled into resurrection to save themselves from being burned. They were seized and led to the emperor with the triumphant cry, "Sing, black vultures, sing ... here is human flesh for you to eat."[40]

Burning the grassy battlefields to flush out prisoners from among the dead was a vindictive move; however, whether as a sign of divine disapproval or mere chance, it began to rain late in the afternoon squelching the fires and this inferno. Prized booty were weapons, then coins, then clothes, and then scrota from stripped bodies. Ethiopians castrated some Italians. Raymond Jonas, after a long discursive based on Italian archival embellishments confides: "Most castration likely occurred among the dead."[41] Genitalia were a trophy, a sign of valor steeped in Ethiopian history, as in other times and cultures.[42] Emasculation desexualized men. Edmond Combes and Maurice Tamisier wrote that Oromo women of castrated warriors were widows forced to live with breathing men incapable of reproduction.[43] Conversely scrota acquired

---

38 Wylde, *Modern Abyssinia*, 219.

39 Wylde, *Modern Abyssinia*, 209.

40 Translation by Chris Prouty of Yu Elets (pseudonym for Nikolai Leontiev), *Emperor Menelik and His War with Italy* (St. Petersburg: 1898). See Prouty, *Empress Taytu*, 158.

41 Jonas, *Battle of Adwa*, 227.

42 Margaret Sewall Ball, "Grim Commerce: Scalps, Bounties, and the Transformation of Trophy-Taking in the Early American Northeast, 1450–1770" Ph.D. dissertation, Department of History, University of Colorado (2013), 67–130.

43 E. Combes and M. Tamisier, *Voyage en Abyssinie, dans les pays des Galla, de*

a talismanic quality that demonstrated a man's prowess and to have one or more aided marriage negotiations. Such traditions were hard to stop. "It was this aspect of the practice that Menelik addressed on the eve of [battle]. 'Bring me the man, not the testicles,' ... A prisoner is worth more."[44]

Menilek ordered restraint. "As soon as the *negus* saw he was victorious, he ordered his men not to kill those who gave themselves up."[45] Prisoners were gathered and dispersed to various encampments. Wounded Italians coalesced around Menilek's tent city where his reception tent was converted into a dispensary for Italian medics to attend to injured Italian soldiers. About three weeks later Nikolai Leontiev organized a Russian Red Cross mission up to Adwa, primarily to care for Italian prisoners of war. While many died after the battle and on the long march back to Addis Ababa, the vast majority of prisoners survived to be pawns in the peace process.

The most magnanimous act that historians have puzzled over is Menilek's decision to prematurely halt his victory on March 1, 1896 on the battlefield outside Adwa instead of pursuing the disheveled fragments of Baratieri's army to Adigrat and into Eritrea in order to annihilate them and systematically destroy Italy's military infrastructure all the way to the port of Mitsiwa. *Ras* Alula wanted to run them into the sea and make Hamasen part of Ethiopia again, a sentiment widely shared by many other Tigrean leaders. In all likelihood, Menilek could have exploited the chaos after Adwa to defeat the Italians, for later Baratieri was court martialed for dereliction of duty having quit the battle at 12:30 p.m. and having left no orders for a concerted retreat because he fled and his whereabouts were unknown for three days.[46] Baratieri, after all, was the political and military Commander-in-Chief of Eritrea, until relieved of his duties by General Baldissera, who not coincidently arrived in Asmara on March 6th[47] – perhaps a motive for Baratieri to attack in the first place knowing he was to be dismissed. Considering the lack of leadership, panic-stricken soldiers in full retreat, brazen Ethiopian cavalry and well-armed foot soldiers capable of outwalking their Italian adversaries, few loyal European settlers in Eritrea, and an Eritrean population with questionable political allegiances, it was feasible that Menilek could have liberated Eritrea. However, Harold Marcus's six-fold explanation for why Menilek erred on the side of caution and did not follow up his victory to reclaim Eritrea continues to resonate.

Choa et d'Ifat (Paris: Louis Desessart, 1836), 2: 322–3.

44 Jonas, *Battle of Adwa*, 228.

45 Translation by Prouty, *Empress Taytu*, 158.

46 Berkeley, *Campaign of Adowa*, 366–7.

47 Berkeley, *Campaign of Adowa*, 351.

> If he had pressed the Italians too hard, national pride might have compelled Rome to mount a larger military effort. Also, Menelik knew from experience that his army could not easily overcome the heavily fortified position into which the Italians retired; he did not wish to risk his reputation as an astute military leader and his army's hard-won prestige. He had no desire to lead his army, short of rations as it now was, through the poor and already ravaged country south of Eritrea, particularly in view of the imminence of the short rainy season. His men had now been in the field for a longer period of time than usual, and were becoming restive; in addition to being soldiers, they were farmers and had to return to their homes to plough and sow. Menelik may have felt that his incorporation of more Tigres [*sic.*] into the empire would strengthen the position of Ras Mengesha, whose loyalty to the Crown remained opportunist. Finally, the essential object of the war had been won, and another generation and a half of independence guaranteed for Ethiopia.[48]

Without doubt this act paved the way for separate identities to be forged and histories to be written that have polarized relations between the peoples and states of Ethiopia and Eritrea.

Estimates of the numbers of prisoners that were taken by Menilek's army vary but all are within reason considering the lack of reliable statistics. One authority writing soon after the battle claimed that around 4,000 Italian and *askari* prisoners were taken;[49] another estimate was decidedly lower at 1,865 Italian and 1,000 *askari*.[50] A consensus appears to have emerged among contemporary historians claiming 1,900 Italian and as many as 1,500 *askari* prisoners were captured.[51] More important, however, is the way they were treated for it demonstrates how conditional forgiveness was manifest on the continuum between amnesty and execution.

Historians generally concede that the Italian prisoners were treated with kid gloves in comparison to the *askaris*. Menilek, everyone agrees, used them as pawns in the bickering over repealing the Treaty of Wechale and to compel the Italians to sign a new treaty guaranteeing Ethiopian sovereignty. After considerable delay in Tigray, partly owing to the fact that Menilek was able to feed his troops with food supplies taken from the Italians, the withdrawal to Shewa got underway during the *belg* (little rainy season), which made conditions miserable.

48 Marcus, *Life and Times*, 176–7. Paulos Milkias provides a different view on the rationale for Menilek's decision, "The Battle of Adwa: The Historic Victory of Ethiopia Over European Colonialism" in *The Battle of Adwa*, ed. Milkias and Metaferia, 64.

49 Wylde, *Modern Abyssinia*, 212.

50 Berkeley's discursive footnote shows the statistics he used to come up with his guestimates, *Campaign of Adowa*, 346.

51 Prouty, *Empress Taytu*, 165; Jonas, *Battle of Adwa*, 233.

Additionally, there was little by way of food and firewood to be salvaged from the ravaged countryside that bore the burden of the northern march six months earlier. Many of the most severely wounded Italians died en route to Shewa.[52] The strong were, as typical of Ethiopian warfare, parceled out to various Ethiopian *ras*es. Their treatment pretty much aligned with their views on Menilek's magnanimous gesture to let Eritrea go, those in favor of restraint generally treated their Italian prisoners well; those opposed treated them harshly. That many Italians fell ill had more to do with exposure and dietary issues. "The best-natured of their captors fed them just as they fed themselves, – which meant (except in the case of the greatest chieftains), that they lived on small portions of *enjera* and sour milk; sometimes roasted beans, sometimes meat; sometimes *tegg* (the native beverage) to drink."[53] Despite eating traditional Ethiopian food with all its spices, amoebic dysentery or other parasites causing diarrhea mostly came from tainted water.

Once in Addis Ababa "the prisoners were to enjoy the warmth of Menelik's paternal embrace and the full measure of Ethiopian bounty in a banquet that surpassed anything they had yet seen."[54] The Russian Red Cross team's first order was to treat Italian prisoners, some were even medevaced, if travel by caravan could be called that, to Harar where an Italian medical unit was stationed.[55] As it took eight months to agree to sign the new treaty, most of the Italians were housed among the Ethiopian population. Prisoners of rank were treated particularly well; General Albertone was given private quarters along with servants. All Italian prisoners were given free visitation rights by anybody. After a sixteen-point list of generous acts, Negussay Ayele concludes, "Menelik's civility and humanity toward captive Italian soldiers was truly astounding."[56] At the end between 1,587 and 1,759 Italians were repatriated back to Italy. While the former may be more accurate considering those who died of wounds, that number out of a total of approximately 1,900 prisoners demonstrates the care they were afforded.

The situation for the *askaris* was far worse. Scholars depict their treatment as one of the dark chapters of Ethiopian history. The wounded were largely left to die either of their wounds, thirst, exposure, or a combination of all three. Of the approximate 1,500 who were captured a debate ensued over an appropriate punishment. Primary sources generally concur that the argument coalesced over geography: those *ras*es from Tigray – Alula and Mengasha, and even those who recently allied

52 Jonas, "The Long March" *Battle of Adwa*, 238–49.
53 Berkeley, *Campaign of Adowa*, 349.
54 Jonas, *Battle of Adwa*, 247.
55 Marcus, *Life and Times*, 177.
56 Negussay Ayele, "Who Was Civilized and Who Was Savage?" 172–3.

with the Italians like Sebhat Aregawi and Hagos Tafari – whose lands had been invaded, sought the harshest punishment including amputation and/or execution; the emperor and others, like *ras*es Mekonnen, Wele, and Mikael from the south, never wanted to exonerate the *askari* but were in favor of some less punitive measures.[57] Menilek's wife, Empress Taytu, advocated severe punishment. Knowing it was impossible to appease both sides, Menilek put the decision to "the Egyptian Archbishop, Abune Matewos, head of the Ethiopian Orthodox Church, who, quoting the Fetha-Negest (Laws of the Kings), also of Egyptian origin, passed the sentence."[58] In the end, Menilek concurred. Sources claim that for between 400 and 800 of the 1,500 *askaris* the "sentence was mutilation – that is, the cutting off the right hand and left foot – [which was] the customary punishment for the offences of theft, sacrilege and treason."[59] Menilek was castigated with ownership of the harsh punishment by European media and biographers: "of the Ascari, 406 were turned loose after having had their right hand and left foot cut off by his command, or at all events with his consent, – a fact that will live in history to his disgrace."[60] Augustus Wylde says that after the wrists and ankles were sliced and the "hands and feet put in a pile ... the stumps [were] plunged into boiling fat to stop hæmorrhage."[61] After severing their limbs, the amputees were free to return to their homes in Eritrea. Many, of course, died on the way; others returned, received severance pay from the Italian authorities and reintegrated back into their villages without the stigma of treason, as they were viewed by the Italians as heroes. The number of amputees in and around Asmara and other population centers initially may have caused notice, but seeing amputees, either due to an accident or because of punishment, was relatively commonplace.

The Western press, however, fixated on *askari* amputations as a clear sign of Ethiopian savagery. Yet even those Europeans writing soon after the battle recognized that amputation "was perfectly just,"[62] a legitimate form of punishment according to the laws of not only Ethiopia but all lands bordering the whole Red Sea littoral from Egypt to the tip of the Arabian Peninsula. What the records do not address is what happened to the half to three-quarters of the *askari* whose limbs were not amputated. Were they released, and if so under what conditions?

57 Wylde, *Modern Abyssinia*, 212–13; Berkeley, *Campaign of Adowa*, 347.
58 Milkias and Metaferia, "Battle of Adwa," 65.
59 Wylde, *Modern Abyssinia*, 213.
60 Berkeley, *Campaign of Adowa*, 347.
61 Wylde, *Modern Abyssinia*, 213.
62 Wylde, *Modern Abyssinia*, 213.

Justice and Cultural Divides

This section assesses how Europeans misread Ethiopia's restorative justice modalities, and how Ethiopians misinterpreted European rules of war, commercial and maritime law, and extraterritoriality both *de jure* and *de facto*. It also traces Ethiopia's early attempts to accommodate these two contradictory legal systems. To address these issues the sequence will be reversed: first *askari* amputations through the lens of Ethiopian restorative justice will be assessed, followed by the compassionate treatment of Italian prisoners, and finally the more complex issue of building peace between states.

Defiance and punishment

Although the amputation of the left foot and right hand was harsh and could be perceived to contradict the interpretation that magnanimity characterized Ethiopian actions after the Battle of Adwa, within the prevailing cultural and religious paradigms they are nevertheless comprehensible and coherent. Retribution was a last resort within restorative justice. Again, the contradiction can be understood from a biblical perspective. Restorative justice implies both blanket amnesties and penalties but, in all, "forgiveness" figures prominently. Forgiveness assumes obligation, for although the power to be merciful lies with the forgiver, the one seeking forgiveness is obligated to show contriteness and to be accountable for future actions, in other words, to correct their criminal or, in this case, treasonous ways. Accountability is one of the components of forgiveness and, if the accounting does not measure up, forgiveness does not mean forgetfulness. Rather, in cases of recalcitrance there is a component of punishment tied into the biblical understanding of forgiveness. Certainly, Ethiopian priests and high officials understood Romans 13:4 implicitly, which states: "It is the servant of God to execute wrath on the wrongdoer." In cases of recalcitrance, punishment was the stick implied in the symbiotic understanding of forgiveness. In the case of the *askaris* the situation, from the Ethiopian perspective, was one of treason. Time and again Menilek's forces had warned the *askaris* that if they continued to fight on the side of the Italians they would be viewed as traitors. Augustus Wylde noted, "Those soldiers who had served at the defense of Macalle had been warned of what punishment they would receive if they were again found in arms against Abyssinia."[63] As early as the Battle of Dogali (1887) the lines of enmity between Ethiopians and Italians and their *askaris* had been drawn;[64] thus, Menilek, under pressure from his court and with approval of Abune Matewos, found the *askaris* were unworthy of forgiveness, for

63 Wylde, *Modern Abyssinia*, 213.
64 Erlich, *Ras Alula*, 103–6.

they had wilfully fought against their Ethiopian brothers and showed no remorse for their treasonous ways.

Another matter needs scrutiny. Penance assumes a person will change his ways, but when that person is part of a larger group and there is no indication the group is interested in change, then it becomes increasingly difficult to believe the individual will reform. Ethiopians observed this with the *askaris*. After the battle there was no mass defection of the *askaris* to the Ethiopian side. Nor was there the sense of comradery between victor and vanquished as Arnauld d'Abbadie noted after battles in the 1840s.[65] The *askaris* either fled with the Italian forces, aiding the foreigners' retreat, or were taken prisoner like their Italian masters. In traditional warfare a defeated soldier had the autonomy to ask for clemency to return to his domicile or join the victor's army. There was no indication that *askaris* sought to join Menilek's forces. Furthermore, Ethiopian intelligence knew there were many *askari* brigades in Adigrat and Eritrea firmly committed to Italian suzerainty. In the relief of Adigrat, which took place well after the Battle of Adwa, 140 *askaris* were sent out on recognizance and the majority of the troops at Adigrat were *askari*. Moreover, General Baldissera, the new Commander-in-Chief of Eritrea, deployed a force that "consisted of only 16,717 men" most of whom were *askari*, and "occupied Adi Caje on April 12th"[66] in preparation to relieve Adigrat. Between Adwa and Adigrat, Berkeley notes: "The relieving force [in battle with the Dervishes at Kassala] consisted of the reorganized 3rd, 6th, 7th and 8th Native Battalions, (they were considered better suited to the climate of the Kassala region at that time of year than Italian troops) the same that had fought at Adowa."[67]

Based on what Ethiopians believed to be treasonous acts years before the Battle of Adwa and in the months immediately after, Menilek had ample evidence to suspect the *askari* prisoners would continue to fight against their Ethiopian brethren. Using a saw in the toolbox of restorative justice the Ethiopians sought to neutralize defiant *askari* by cutting off limbs. As noted, the tools of restorative justice ran the gamut from clemency to severe punishment and, depending on circumstance, the best option was selected to promote peace and reconciliation. This was the definition of Ethiopia's reformist understanding of restorative justice that had added conditions to forgiveness after the *Zemene Mesafint*. Amputating the right hand and the left foot effectively incapacitated the *askari* from ever taking up arms again. Recall they had been warned many times, the last during the evacuation of Mekele. A left foot was essential for placing a foot in a stirrup to mount a horse. A right hand was essential for brandishing a sword or throwing a spear.

65 d'Abbadie, *Douze ans*, 455.
66 Berkeley, *Campaign of Adowa*, 362.
67 Berkeley, *Campaign of Adowa*, 359.

Figure 3 Eritrean askari amputees; photo taken in 1896 at a field hospital in Massawa, Eritrea. Attribution: Luigi Naretti, public domain, The National Museums of World Culture – The Museum of Ethnology, Stockholm.

Granted this archaic rationale was based on traditional warfare but it just as effectively neutralized an infantryman by preventing him from walking and squeezing the trigger of a gun. Ethiopians rationalized amputations could promote peace as they would decommission a few of the *askari* and send a gruesome message to others to terminate fighting on behalf of Italians. Once neutralized, the *askaris* were allowed to return to their homes and reintegrate themselves into the social fabric of Ethiopian or Eritrean society, thus, conforming to their understanding of restorative justice.

Pawns of peace

Italian archives support the idea that Ethiopians treated Italian prisoners unjustly by using them as pawns to negotiate a peace accord. However, "unjust" connotes coloniality, whereas holding prisoners was an accepted component of peace negotiations in Ethiopia's past. According to Arnauld d'Abbadie, prisoners, most often aristocrats, were considered booty to be ransomed off to their relatives or districts as war restitution or part of the restorative justice package of traditional Ethiopia.[68]

68 D'Abbadie, *Douze ans*, 454.

Repatriation became an issue when Italians began prevaricating over revoking the Treaty of Wechale and tried to use the negotiation process to turn their military defeat at the Battle of Adwa into a diplomatic victory. Under these circumstances Menilek used the prisoners as leverage until the treaty was revoked and Ethiopian sovereignty recognized. Immediately after a new treaty was negotiated, a convention for the repatriation of prisoners was signed and by late 1896 all the soldiers were allowed to return to Italy or stay in Ethiopia under a general amnesty. Granting amnesty was an idea the Ethiopian people supported, and the judgement to be either harsh or lenient, after counsel of his court, was the emperor's to make, for Menilek was the embodiment of the state.

Historically, on the rare occasions when Ethiopians imprisoned the vanquished, they did so by parceling them out to various victorious *ras*es to be sheltered in aristocratic households throughout the kingdom. The practice of dividing prisoners up went back centuries out of expediency for, after the fall of Gondar, Ethiopia did not have an established capital city and found a roving tent capital more suitable to keep an eye on rebellious lords. Under those conditions there were no fixed prisons; rather, it was more efficient to disperse prisoners to distant regions where they could be watched relatively effectively and at little cost because they were considered outsiders. With white skin, Italians stood out even more and their whereabouts was easy to ascertain. Many of them were treated almost as houseguests. Much of the Western media blitz after the battle reprimanded Ethiopians for barbarous treatment of prisoners. Italian press releases alleged that they were being castrated – sketching a picture of the emasculation of manhood that fit the narrative for Ethiopian barbarity; however, when the Italian press arrived in Addis Ababa they were allowed unfettered access to the prisoners and found that they were fully capable of "the sweetness of fatherhood and family."[69] Menilek understood the propaganda war over prisoners as pawns and actively disseminated a counter-narrative. Using his cadre of foreign advisers, especially his all-purpose Swiss engineer/counselor, Alfred Ilg, and the French orientalist and journalist, Casimir Mondon-Vidailhet, Menilek encouraged them to communicate the "truth" about the conditions of Italian prisoners and accurately chronicle the history of the Italo-Ethiopian conflict correcting the deceit spread by Italian officials and media.[70]

69 Jonas, *Battle of Adwa*, 306.

70 Bairu Tafla, "Menilek's Diplomatic Front: The Role of Alfred Ilg in Events Leading to the Conflict" in proceedings of the *Adwa Victory Centenary Conference*, 27; and Alain Rouaud, "Mondon-Vidailhet et la guerre: un Français défenseur de l'indépendence éthiopienne" in proceedings of the *Adwa Victory Centenary Conference*, 39–44.

Other foreign travelers provided a more objective assessment of their treatment.[71] The Frenchman, La Jonquière, claims prisoners were "treated with humanity."[72] The Englishman, Powell-Cotton agreed that while some Italians "had a rough time of it they were not unkindly treated" and that "if a prisoner complained with good reason of the man he was billeted on, the latter was punished."[73] When Wylde finally arrived in Addis Ababa months after the battle he noted, "that the peasantry went out of the way to do them little kindnesses and would give them all sorts of little things, such as eggs and bread, and never dream of asking payment in return."[74]

Prisoners were paid as laborers or, if they possessed special skills, were employed as supervisors because of their technical expertise. By 1896 Addis Ababa was taking shape as a quasi-modern capital demanding masons and carpenters to construct its infrastructure. With these construction projects in mind, skilled Italian prisoners were settled on the western side of Addis Ababa in a neighborhood that became known as *Talian Safar* (Italian Quarters). For these projects, they were given significant freedom and authority over hundreds of Ethiopian unskilled laborers in a reversal of who was ordering whom around. To the chagrin of the Italian statesmen who tried to vilify Ethiopia's treatment of their prisoners, some of these POWs chose to stay in Ethiopia for the duration of their lives.

Concerning prisoners as pawns, initially the Italians conducted negotiations after the Battle of Adwa as if the outcome of the war was meaningless. The Italian government even used Pope Leo XIII to ask for the immediate release of the Italian prisoners in the name of Christian brotherhood.[75] Infuriated Menilek refused to "sacrifice the sole guarantee of peace that I have with me."[76] The audacity of the Italian diplomatic effort likely had never been encountered before in Ethiopian political history. In defeating a European country for the first time, Ethiopia was exposed to new rules of war whereby metropolitan interests disregarded the humiliation of defeat to try diplomacy, once again, to achieve the desired colonial objectives by simply recycling slightly altered syntax. Italy was clearly interested in receiving international

---

71 A thorough compilation of sources on the treatment of Italian prisoners is provided by Richard Pankhurst, "Menilek and the Utilisation of Foreign Skills in Ethiopia," *Journal of Ethiopian Studies*, 5:1 (1967): 44–7.

72 C. de la Jonquière, *Les Italiens en Erythrée* (Paris: H. Charles-Lavauzelle, 1897), 336.

73 P. H. G. Powell-Cotton, *A Sporting Trip through Abyssinia* (London: Rowland Ward, 1902), 399.

74 Wylde, *Modern Abyssinia*, 402–3.

75 Abebe Haile Melekot, *Victory of Adowa*, 185–8.

76 Translation of Carlo Rossetti, *Storia diplomatica dell'Etiopia durante il regno di Menelik II* (Turin: 1910), 196, found in Bahru Zewde, *Modern Ethiopia*, 83.

recognition for dominion status over Ethiopia regardless of the outcome of the war. Menilek, for his part, realized that if constant pressure were not applied sovereignty would be lost. In this case, then, the release of Italian prisoners was conditioned on Italy's playing by an old set of rules that recognized military victory. But beneath political expediency, Menilek's acts of magnanimity point to restorative justice with a major proviso – forgive but never forget.

Legal misunderstandings

On March 11, 1896 Major Tomasso Salsa arrived at Menilek's camp to begin peace negotiations. Instead of feigning contrition, as in an honor and shaming ceremony where the defeated party demonstrates submission by shouldering a stone, Salsa had the effrontery to demand concessions that were tantamount to the original gains Italy sought in the Treaty of Wechale.[77] Right away Ethiopian conceptions of restorative justice were upended. And it was not simply Salsa's bravado, for after Salsa was put under house arrest, Italian negotiators continued to remonstrate that the new treaty give Italy most favored status. African sovereignty was bucking European imperialist ideology and the pressure on Italy to pursue colonial expansion forced her to defy accepted diplomatic protocol and follow a legal strategy, shaped into a treaty that changed rules of war especially concerning surrender. Only after Menilek's determination to hold the prisoners indefinitely did Italy dispatch Dr. Nerazzini to unconditionally abrogate the Treaty of Wechale and sign the Peace Treaty of October 1896 that guaranteed Ethiopian sovereignty for at least another two generations.[78]

But the diplomatic overtures to claim legal jurisdiction in Ethiopia were not new. Sven Rubenson's *The Survival of Ethiopian Independence* historicizes all the attempts by the British, French, and Italians in the nineteenth century to conclude advantageous agreements and treaties that would grant concessions or cede portions of Ethiopian sovereignty to European imperialists. In 1841, Major H. Cornwallis Harris managed to conclude a commercial treaty with *Negus* Sahle Selassie of Shewa giving Britain "free and unrestricted commercial intercourse." Not to be outdone, Rochet d'Héricourt, out of his own patriotic fervor and with little support from Paris, also negotiated a treaty with Shewa "to guarantee the advantages" of trade with France in 1843.[79] This was only the beginning of colonial incursions. Though late, Italy was even more aggressive. Count Pietro Antonelli spearheaded Italian encroachment from Mitsawa onto the highlands of Hamasen – Eritrea. Unsurprisingly, Antonelli authored the trickery of the Treaty of Wechale. The

77 Caulk, *"Between the Jaws of Hyenas,"* 586–9; Prouty, *Empress Taytu*, 162–3.
78 Guébrè Sellassié, *Chronique du règne de Ménélik*, vol. 2, 455–6.
79 Rubenson, *Survival*, 152, 159.

lesson Ethiopians learned was that agreements, treaties, and laws were one-sided and subject to manipulation in favor of European agents. If, on the other hand, Ethiopia sought to challenge those same agreements, treaties, and laws – which were held to be inviolable and the empire subject to prosecution – loyal European counselors were needed to assist them through the legal and quasi-legal tangles.

In the nineteenth century the Imperial Court was only vaguely aware of Western legal practices. As trade increased and European nations dispatched representatives to Addis Ababa, Emperor Menilek was obliged to engage foreign advisers to counsel him on an array of legal issues mostly dealing with treaties, maritime law, commercial law and the perplexing extraterritorial claims of foreign merchants who insisted on obtaining legal recourse in their own nation's Consular Courts instead of Ethiopian courts, which they feared.

Maritime law affected Ethiopia and particularly Menilek's natal province, Shewa, directly as the abolition of slavery was packaged in ordinances defining appropriate ship cargo. Transporting human chattel had been deemed illegal at the beginning of the nineteenth century and Great Britain's fleet policed the seas, boarding any ship or dhow suspected of carrying slaves. Aleu Amba, halfway down the escapement from Ankober – Shewa's old capital – to the Afar desert, the gateway to the sea, was arguably the largest slave market in all of Ethiopia. Menilek and his forefathers benefited enormously from the slave trade. Slavery supplemented Ethiopia's treasury. However, the money earned often was unacceptable to European governments for the purchase of arms because it was tainted by the slave trade.[80] The impasse forced Menilek to take steps to eradicate the trade and was perhaps his first concession to the preeminence of international law.

In terms of commerce, the nineteenth century was replete with European adventurers and inchoate diplomats coming to Ethiopia to dupe Ethiopians and leave with vast fortunes. That this rarely happened had much to do with lack of valuable primary and agricultural commodities, logistics, and the guile of their Ethiopian counterparts who saw through their veiled greed. Poet and fortune-seeker, Arthur Rimbaud's business ventures in Ethiopia illustrate the complexity of commercial and maritime law. He apprenticed with Bardey Company in Aden to learn the intricacies of trading in the Red Sea's silver-based economy where arbitrage ruled. In the mid-1880s he moved to Harar as it transitioned from Egyptian to Ethiopian rule. First and foremost, he was an arms dealer selling Fuse Gras and other French-made arms to eager Ethiopian clients both legally and illegally.[81] Imperial rivalries sometimes impeded legal import of arms; other times European metro-

80 Marcus, *Life and Times*, 73.

81 Charles Nicoll, *Somebody Else, Arthur Rimbaud in Africa 1880–1891* (London: Jonathan Cape, 1997).

poles facilitated illicit arms shipments. Interstate commerce appeared arbitrary. To Ethiopians, rules were made and repealed for the sake of foreign profits. But colonial trade restrictions were further complicated by the insistence on monetized payments. These payments involved converting merchandise into Maria Theresa thalers in an environment where the coin's value was also subject to arbitrage. These realities were troublesome to Ethiopian merchants, as they were for Rimbaud who ended up bankrupt. International business law, itself in embryonic form at the time, superimposed capitalist exchange upon a barter economy that baffled all, except Banyans (Indian merchants from Gujarat).[82]

Extraterritoriality in the form of Consular Courts and the territorial sovereignty that European legations claimed for the land beneath embassies confused Menilek and Ethiopia's traditional elites, for how could European law supersede the laws of a sovereign state?

Puerile attempts to accommodate European legal systems

Discrepancies between Ethiopian and European legal understandings pushed Menilek to accommodate those two contravening legal systems. In the years after the Battle of Adwa, Menilek took baby steps to blunt European imperialism and bolster Ethiopian statehood. The following long aside sets the historical context for the marginalization of restorative justice practices in Ethiopia and provides the background for Ethiopia's eventual adoption of Western legal codes.

Peace negotiations after the Battle of Adwa conveyed two lessons: first, that treaties – therefore law – were malleable and that there was no power disparity between delegates of the victor and vanquished, for when one was a European power even defeated delegates came to the table acting as equals; second, that all players could use any and every tool available to mold new rules. Menilek and Ethiopia took years to realize the second lesson.

Menilek's experiences with Major Salsa and Dr. Nerazzini only reinforced the insidious nature of European colonialism. Alfred Ilg, Léon Chefneux, Casimir Mondon-Vidailhet, and Nikolai Leontiev had served well prior to and through the war but their limitations became ever more apparent as Ethiopia emerged as an independent nation in the eyes of the world. To counter its isolation Menilek employed a coterie of loyal European experts to mediate between Ethiopia and the rest of the world. Ilg stayed on but there was an uptick in the foreign counselor corps employed by Menilek, partly because of the increased number of foreign legations present in Addis Ababa. To meet these diplomatic obligations Menilek needed foreign language skills to ensure that he would never be deceived again. Also, to safeguard against hidden

[82] Charles Schaefer, "Enclavistic Capitalism in Ethiopia, 1906–1936: A Study of Currency, Banking, and Informal Credit Networks" (Ph.D. dissertation, University of Chicago, 1990), 66–134.

agendas by his counselors, he employed representatives from disparate countries: Serkis Terzian, an Armenian of proven loyalty who often functioned as translator, Athanas Sourvis a Greek who was reported to be Menilek's private secretary, and E. V. Senigov a gifted Russian linguist, reputedly more trustworthy than Leontiev, were some of the more noteworthy. As Ethiopia marched into the twentieth century this counselor corps expanded significantly and their tasks multiplied in part to keep abreast of expanding diplomatic, commercial, banking, and philanthropic activities. For example, while the British and French managed to establish their own Consular Courts to resolve mostly commercial and financial disputes between their subjects conducting business in Ethiopia, Menilek's government wanted to know what took place in those court cases, for the disputes revealed much about fraudulent commercial practices taking place in Ethiopia; therefore, he sent foreigners to sit in and report back to him.[83] Article 7 of what is widely recognized as the Klobukowski Treaty between France and Ethiopia, signed in 1908, ensured that: "If the accused is an Abyssinian he is judged according to Abyssinian law; if a foreigner, according to the law of his own country."[84]

Addis Ababa was in a construction boom: housing, infrastructure, bridges, roads all needed skilled workers especially after the majority of Italian prisoners were repatriated. To fill the gap architects and artisans from all over the world were invited to Ethiopia. Each project required contracts, purchase receipts, shipping manifests, and bank transfers to ensure speedy delivery of building materials. More money was spent on military training and arms acquisitions. Hospitals and medical clinics were established. A postal service was developed.[85] Every one of those initiatives required paperwork that had to conform to international standards. The bureaucratic expertise necessary to deal with the red tape required to adhere to commercial laws and international banking regulations superseded Ethiopians' skill set.

The construction of the Djibouti-Addis railway demonstrated the legal hitches Ethiopia had to overcome. France's benevolent gesture to construct the railway challenged the sovereignty of Ethiopia by blending financial pressures involving loan repayment and profits, with issues over extraterritorial claims to the railway line at least up to Dire Dawa.[86] Modernity tried its best to run roughshod over Ethiopia.

---

83 Interviews with Avedis Terzian, son of Serkis Terzian, Addis Ababa, 11 May 1987; and J. J. Kothari, 17 March 1987.

84 General Virgin, *The Abyssinia I Knew* (London: Macmillan, 1936), 126–7.

85 A reliable inventory of early developments in Ethiopia was compiled by Adrien Zervos, *L'empire d'Éthiopie: le miroir de l' Éthiopie moderne, 1906–1935* (Athens: Bibliothèque Nationale d'Athènes, 1936).

86 T. Lennox Gilmour, *Abyssinia: The Ethiopian Railway and the Powers* (London: Alston Rivers, 1906); and Shiferaw Bekele, "The Railway, Trade and

From 1896 to 1906, the year that symbolized the end of Menilek's political consolidation, life in the Imperial Court was less about balancing aristocratic ambitions in one province versus another, and more about acceding to the expectations of the world economy. Contractual agreements ruled. If there were lapses, the first batch of plenipotentiaries were sure to visit the *gebbi* (palace) for an audience with Menilek to protest those contractual infractions. Modernity required the emperor to adopt a parallel legal system initially confined to the economic sector of Ethiopian society.

To wrest trade and finance away from the private Indian firms that manipulated currency supply, like G. M. Mohamedally & Company, and assume control of the economy, Menilek needed to establish a bank that would comply with all the legal rules and regulations imposed on international commerce. Concession granting was a shortcut to development and Menilek came to terms with the National Bank of Egypt to establish the Bank of Abyssinia in 1905 through which to funnel international transactions. The bank's history was fraught with problems, not the least of which was: whom did it serve? The British Legation view was that the British staff's primary allegiance was to promote British interests. Ethiopian officials thought their purpose was to push Ethiopian interests.[87] Eventually, by the 1920s, the politics was straightened out and the Governor of the Bank functioned more as Ethiopia's intermediary to the world economy writing hundreds of letters to order mints to issue currency, foreign banks to expedite exchanges, investment banks for development loans, chambers of commerce, and private companies for all sorts of issues. The fledgling Bank of Abyssinia was Ethiopia's window into the rules-based and litigious world of international commerce.

The disconnect between tradition and modernity sparked debate amongst Ethiopia's intellectuals and political elites. Gebra Heywat Baykadagn, in his *Government and Public Administration*, best articulates the views of progressives, stating that Ethiopia must cast aside traditional practices and adopt Western education and technology, and model itself after Japan.[88] Those who subscribed to his views were

---

Politics: A Historical Survey, 1896–1935 (M.A. Thesis, Department of History, Addis Ababa University, 1982).

[87] Schaefer, "Politics of Banking: The Bank of Abyssinia, 1906–1931," *International Journal of African Historical Studies,* 25:2 (1992): 361–89.

[88] Gäbrä Heywät Baykädgn, *Mängəstənna yähəzb astädadär "Government and Public Administration"* (Addis Ababa: 1953). His book was translated by Tenkir Bonger and published under the title *The State & Economy in Early 20th Century Ethiopia* (London: Karnak House, 1995). Gäbrä Heywät Baykädgn's reformist views have been analyzed by Ethiopia's noted historians, see Shiferaw Bekele, "Gäbrä-Heywät Baykädan and the Emergence of a Modern Intellectual Discourse," *Sociology Ethnology Bulletin,* 1:3 (1994): 106–20; and Bahru Zewde,

known as the Japanizers. Adopting the ideology of the Meiji Restoration, the Japanizers understood the threat technology posed and proposed to speedily appropriate Western ways to ensure Ethiopia's independence. To their minds this included law.

Restorative Justice Sidelined

Restorative Justice at the outset of the twentieth century moved from the central method of dealing with challenges to the state to a restricted mode to resolve domestic disputes. Up to 1906 Menilek still had to contend with ambitious rivals in north and central Ethiopia. Expansion to the south raised other challenges with local rulers, restive populations and the *neftenya* (northern soldier-settlers) who seized upon the opportunity for self-aggrandizement to challenge government-appointed governors and sub-governors. In many of these cases the *zufan chilot* or *shaleqa* courts deliberated on the best method to resolve the political issue and decided to employ restorative justice mechanisms. This often would involve some form of submission and expectation of atonement; in important cases elaborate honor and shaming ceremonies were enacted. Appropriate remedy, that is what the deliberative body of *mekwanint* that constituted the *chilot* determined was proper, could range anywhere along the continuum from clemency to corporal punishment. Increasingly, though, appropriate remedy involved *gizot* (demotion) or administrative transfer from the center of politics and influence to a peripheral area, usually where the individual had few or no connections and thus no patron-client relations to fall back upon.

Modernity sidelined restorative justice though its mechanisms were thought appropriate to adjudicate issues within the state, but sorely inadequate to settle interstate disputes. Monetary transactions demanded convertible currency, which required adherence to international exchange mechanisms. Well before the end of the nineteenth century the world economy had invented procedures backed by law and written into legal documents that had to be signed. Those contracts could not be ignored.[89] The less formal reliance on Indian, Greek, Armenian, and Yemeni traders to satisfy Ethiopia's hunger for manufactured goods had reach its limits; forging bilateral trade agreements with Western nations that possessed legal standing was the sign of the times.

Pioneers of Change in Ethiopia: The Reformist Intellectuals of the Early Twentieth Century (Addis Ababa: Addis Ababa University Press, 2002), 49–52, 111–16.

89 Heinrich Scholler, "The Special Court of Ethiopia 1922–1936: Mixed Jurisdiction as an Instrument of Legal Development" in *Proceedings of the Seventh International Conference of Ethiopian Studies*, ed. Sven Rubenson (Uppsala: Scandinavian Institute of African Studies, 1984), 381–92.

Menilek's empire bumbled its way through this transition. Rapidly, it became evident that imports and exports were subject to international regulations. Non-compliance could mean a trade embargo. To engage in global commerce and international geo-politics, Ethiopia developed a layered legal system adopting western mechanisms for transnational issues and traditional law, including restorative justice modalities, for domestic affairs.

5

The Battle of Segale: Justice and Legitimacy

Interpretations surrounding the Battle of Segale fall into a deep sinkhole in Ethiopian historiography. Briefly stated, the Battle of Segale marks the beginning of *Ras* Tafari/Emperor Haile Selassie's fifty-eight years at the helm of the Ethiopian state, and, not coincidentally, the end of *Lij* Iyasu's brief interregnum. A coup d'état by the leading dignitaries including *Lij* Iyasu's second cousin, *Ras* Tafari, brought him down but not without a fight. For decades historiography reflected *Ras* Tafari/Emperor Haile Selassie's triumphalism arguing that *Lij* Iyasu's indiscretions, administrative mismanagement, and apostasy justified regime change. As new primary sources are unearthed, a reappraisal of *Lij* Iyasu's politics and administration sketches a different picture, one in which he assiduously pursued modern tax and customs reforms to ensure a solvent national treasury as well as attempts to sever the religious tie between church and state in order to bring about reconciliation between Christians and Muslims.[1] Through a twenty-first century lens those pursuits appear prescient. The fault line separating the pro-*Lij* Iyasu camp from the pro-Tafari camp centers on a reassessment of the coup d'état, the Battle of Segale and *Lij* Iyasu's treatment afterwards. This chapter treads on firmer ground focusing on measures the coup-makers took to validate their rule by conforming to conventional political practices, ensuring economic stability and following accepted restorative justice modalities.

One further issue, the Battle of Segale was the last time the Ethiopian government resorted to using traditional forms of restorative justice exclusively to settle a dispute that easily could have torn the country apart. As Chapters 6 and 7 will demonstrate, in subsequent decades appropriated Western legal systems were used to administer justice at the expense of socio-political reconciliation.

1 Éloi Ficquet and Wolbert Smidt, eds., *The Life and Times of Lij Iyasu of Ethiopia* (Zurich: Lit Verlag, 2012) demonstrates the multiple prongs scholars have pursued in reassessing *Lij* Iyasu's life and work.

Succession, Menilek to *Lij* Iyasu

Emperor Menilek, the victor of Adowa, the savior of Ethiopian sovereignty, and the worldwide model of colored resistance to colonial oppression, suffered a stroke in 1906. Before his ailment incapacitated him, *Aleqa* Gebre-Igzibiher Elyas inventoried Menilek's accomplishments "on the road to civilization/progress" and came up with twenty-six initiatives that transformed Ethiopia. These ranged from infrastructure such as hospitals, a postal service and the Bank of Abyssinia to educational undertakings such as establishing a printing press to publish *Aimro* ("Mind, Intelligence, Knowledge"), and scholarships for the brightest to study abroad.[2] Yet by1908 "the chief public concern and worry ... was the news of Emperor Menilek's illness."[3] Knowing Ethiopian history, Menilek offered paternal advice to his nation in the form of a proclamation warning his subjects about the bloodshed and chaos following Emperors Tewodros's and Yohannes's death and admonished them to accept his succession decree. In it Menilek declared his grandson Iyasu Mikael, son of *Negus* Mikael Ali of Wollo and his daughter Shewaragga, heir apparent. To add gravitas to the proclamation, Menilek concluded, "May he who contravenes these words be cursed both in Heaven and on earth!"[4]

Acknowledging his infirmity, Menilek summoned many of the nation's dignitaries to his bedside and reaffirmed *Lij* Iyasu Mikael as Crown Prince and his trusted confidant, *Ras* Tesemma Nadew, as Regent until *Lij* Iyasu came of age. Between 1909 and 1913, Emperor Menilek continued to deteriorate and progressively fell into a vegetative state, shunning imperial duties and increasingly shunned by courtiers and foreign emissaries. His strong-willed wife, Empress Taytu, wilfully stepped into the vacuum, making government appointments and commanding allegiance while often countermanding her husband's previous decrees. By 1910 *Ras* Tesemma and other leaders had had enough of her conniving and blatant favoritism of her kin and northern allies and removed her from power, telling her to either retreat to a convent or take better care of her ailing husband. She chose the latter.[5]

Lij Iyasu was a child. In 1907 at age ten, his grandfather invited him to Addis Ababa to attend his new palace school along with the sons of top

2 Gebre-Igzibiher Elyas, *Prowess, Piety and Politics: The Chronicle of Abeto Iyasu and Empress Zewditu of Ethiopia (1909–1930)* ed. and trans. Reidulf Molvaer (Koln: Verlag, 1994), 307–9.

3 Mers'é Hazen Wolde Qirqos, *Of What I Saw and Heard: The Last Years of Emperor Menelik II & the Brief Rule of Iyassu* (Addis Ababa: Centre Français de Études Éthiopiennes & Zamra Publishers, 2004), 47.

4 Mers'é Hazen Wolde Qirqos, *Of What I Saw and Heard*, 52.

5 Prouty, *Empress Taytu*, 305–48.

aristocrats including Tafari Makonnen. As described in Chapter 1, their education was comprehensive with lessons on the Gospels, Psalms, and Biblical interpretation, the *Kibre Negest* and *Fitha Negest*. The privileged scions were instructed in horsemanship, fencing, and war strategy. To prepare for diplomatic ventures these elites were taught foreign languages, first and foremost French. Rounding out their schooling, they were taught jurisprudence including perceiving unforeseen consequences best articulated in *qiné*. To cement the lessons, "experiential learning" was mandated. In his early teens, *Lij* Iyasu "presided over court hearings on Wednesdays and Fridays and heard cases brought to him by the people;" likewise Tafari Makonnen dispensed justice from an exceptionally tender age. Ras Makonnen appointed his son ruler of Garamullata near Harar at age thirteen and gave him the title *Dejazmach* Tafari. Later attending the Menilek Lyceum, after his father died, Tafari was also appointed governor over Salele, a district north of Addis Ababa, where he safeguarded law and order. In other words, these elite students could bring legal questions raised in their own courts to the classroom for critique by their instructors who were well versed on matters of justice. What separated them was not their theoretical and practical understanding of justice, but each student's temperament.

Lij Iyasu's temperament was radically different from the those of Tafari Makonnen, Imru Haile Selassie, and Zewde and Getachew Abate, sons of *Ras* Gobena, who all more or less comported to the Ethiopian penchant to be reserved and cerebral.[6] *Lij* Iyasu, on the other hand, was impulsive, disinclined towards study, loved physical exertion, hunting, and the carnal pleasures of living in the city with its *azmari bets* and brothels. In 1911 *Ras* Tesemma died suddenly. Some say he suffered a stroke; others claim he was poisoned.[7] "After Ras Bitwodded Tesemma died, Lij Iyasu took the whole business of governing in his [own] hands, and he became greatly feared."[8] He had the backing of his father, *Ras* Mikael. With a revered but vegetative emperor confined to his bed, a smart, ambitious empress sequestered to the emperor's care, a teenager attempting to mount the throne even though the throne was already occupied, a powerful and disgruntled father, and an aristocracy that yearned for decorum, political savvy and stability, it was a time of marked instability.

Foreign influence was a political and economic fact. The French, British, and Italian legations asserted jurisdiction over their subjects through their Consular Courts, steered economic penetration ensuring an open market to all foreign powers, and contemplated carving up Ethiopia into spheres of influence in the eventuality that Menilek's empire

6 Angelo Del Boca, *The Negus: The Life and Death of the Last King of Kings* (Addis Ababa: Arada Books, 2015), 55.
7 Jon Abbink, "Täsämma Nadäw" in *Encyclopaedia Aethiopica.*
8 Gebre-Igzibiher Elyas, *Prowess, Piety and Politics*, 321.

should crumble, the latter clearly articulated in the Tripartite Treaty of December 1906.[9] To an extent, all the prominent figures in Ethiopian history from this point on were very aware of Ethiopia's global positioning, spoke one or more European languages and were educated in Western thought and technology, *Lij* Iyasu and Tafari most prominent among them.

A sense of doom pervaded the capital upon Menilek's death in 1913. *Lij* Iyasu's youth, impulsiveness and radicalism alarmed conservative elites. Addis Ababa felt as if it had been overrun by foreigners. Concessionaires, some invited others not, sought to pocket Ethiopia's riches. A small import/export sector, superimposed above the dominant subsistence economy, controlled money supply and thus development. Sovereignty guaranteed on paper appeared to be in doubt. Most egregious was the perception that law and order had evaporated. Without Menilek, the monolith at the center, the monarchy dissolved into regional rivalries reminiscent of the *Zemene Mesafint*. Into the fracas, a new political faction emerged best represented by *Neggadras* Hayle Giyorgis. Hayle Giyorgis built his reputation on bureaucratic reform.[10] As *neggadras* (lit. head merchant) of Addis Ababa and Dire Dawa, the epicenters of enclavistic capitalism, Hayle Giyorgis championed tax reform and customs collection on imports and exports to fund Ethiopian entrepreneurship, but in reality his reforms resembled crony-capitalism intent on benefiting one quadrant of the court – himself, *Lij* Iyasu, and their allies. Later he was elevated to *bitwedded* as Minister of Foreign Affairs and Commerce and *de facto* Prime Minister during *Lij* Iyasu's reign.[11] *Neggadras* Hayle Giyorgis's reforms were Western oriented, inspired by Hasib Ydlibi, a London-educated Syrian, who was among the earliest wave of twentieth-century concession seekers to operate in Ethiopia.[12]

Granting concessions was the modus operandi for peripheral development in the early twentieth century, but controlling concessionaires was nearly impossible.[13] The Bank of Abyssinia, a concession to the National Bank of Egypt, was created to facilitate Ethiopia's financial exchanges with the world economy. From inception in 1905 to around 1920 the bank rarely did that. As noted above, conflict over whom it was to serve characterized its first years. The Bank of Abyssinia succeeded

9 The objectives of the Tripartite Treaty are spelled out in a letter from Paul Cambon, French Ambassador to Britain, to the Marquess of Lansdowne, January 9, 1905 [British Foreign Office, hencforth F.O. 401/8 No.8].

10 Gebre-Igzibiher Elyas, *Prowess, Piety and Politics*, 323.

11 Bahru Zewde, *Modern Ethiopia*, 126; Mers'é Hazen Wolde Qirqos, *Of What I Saw and Heard*, 151.

12 May Ydlidi, *With Ethiopian Rulers: A Biography of Hasib Ydlibi* (Addis Ababa: Addis Ababa University Press, 2006).

13 Octave Collat, *L'Abyssinie actuelle* (Paris: Comité de l'Afrique Française, 1906), 70–6.

between 1909 and 1916 as a foreign concession because it was nothing more than a front for money laundering.[14]

Miles Backhouse, already the third Bank of Abyssinia Governor by 1909, aligned the bank with *Neggadras* Hayle Giyorgis and *Lij* Iyasu, as they were reputedly setting the economy on a new path.[15] On this path, the Bank of Abyssinia became a storefront for shady businesses. In 1910 the bank partnered with Hasib Ydlibi's rubber concessions and became "intermediaries in rubber export" such that its Merchandise Accounts ledger increased by 400 percent.[16] Using its connections with Hayle Giyorgis, a pathway was created to bypass currency exchange regulations, ineffectual as they were, and maximize profits for Ethiopia's crony capitalists. These lessons were applied to other commodity exports including ivory. J. Yardley, a British military officer stationed in southern Sudan, commented on the bank's business with Henry Darley, a notorious fortune-seeker:

> A special legalized trade sprang up between Maji and Mbale in donkeys, mules and ivory. This no doubt attracted the riff-raff of what is now Kenya, the Swahili's, Buluchi's and the rest, who arriving in Maji were employed by Abyssinians, and especially the Bank of Abyssinia, to hunt ivory, for them at rates of interest which could never be paid off and plunged them deeper and deeper into servitude.[17]

Lij Iyasu went elephant hunting too, but only as a tertiary activity during his slave raiding expeditions to the southwest.[18] Bahru Zewde notes that during *Lij* Iyasu's "notorious campaign of 1912 ... about 40,000 Dizi ... were uprooted from their homes and dragged across the country to the capital ... Similar tales of dislocation exist about the provinces of Kafa and Maji."[19] While there is no evidence the Bank of Abyssinia

---

14 Schaefer, "Politics of Banking," 361–89.

15 After dismissal as Governor of the Bank of Abyssinia, Miles Backhouse remained in Ethiopia as in-country concession-seeker for the Ramsden-Backhouse group, a syndicate of primarily British investors working closely with Hasib Ydlibi, *Neggadras* Hayle Giyorgis, and *Lij* Iyasu to procure gold mining concessions in Wallega among other concessions, Alemseged Debele, "A History of Mining in Wallagga, Western Ethiopia, 1899–1991" (Ph.D. dissertation, Addis Ababa University, 2020), 90–2.

16 Merchandise Accounts notation in Bank Notes Store Books, Bank of Abyssinia, 1914–1930.

17 J. Yardley, quoted in Ian Parker and Mohammed Amin, *Ivory Crisis* (London: Chatto & Windus, 1983), 114–15.

18 Leonard Mosley, *Haile Selassie: The Conquering Lion* (London: Weidenfeld and Nicolson, 1964), 72. For an economic assessment see Jon Edwards, "Slavery, the Slave Trade and the Economic Reorganization of Ethiopia, 1916–1935," *African Economic History,* 11 (1982): 3–14.

19 Bahru Zewde, *Modern Ethiopia*, 93; Mers'é Hazen Wolde Qirqos, *Of What I Saw and Heard*, 117–18.

participated in the "thriving business selling victims,"[20] *Lij* Iyasu used the same informal credit networks that constituted the basis of commodity/currency exchange dominated by Indian (Banyan) traders to aid the sale of slaves. Currency speculation engendered a corrupt system, one that either flooded or drained Ethiopia of wealth and thus its solvency. At times *Lij* Iyasu wallowed in Maria Theresa thalers and lavishly endowed churches and mosques and gave cash generously to supplicants or hosted splendid banquets.[21] On other occasions his treasury was empty. In one instance soldiers had not been paid and were near rebellion prompting *Lij* Iyasu to try to borrow from the Bank of Abyssinia which he found void of cash having forgotten that he had ordered its reserves be spent purchasing Japanese rifles.[22] To pay the soldiers, *Lij* Iyasu ended up seizing Menilek and Taytu's treasury in the final year of the emperor's life.[23]

In fairness, *Lij* Iyasu was well aware of corruption in the capital and within every provincial administration associated with Ethiopia's extractive tributary system. His reforms were intended to correct methods of surplus extraction and incentivize peasant producers.[24] In the interest of fiscal responsibility, *Lij* Iyasu ordered a government inventory of assets and an accounting of loans and other rents to the aristocracy and churches. This did not go down too well and was quietly abandoned.[25] Yet it raised questions. Why was the monarchy curtailing long-standing methods of wealth accumulation that were tied to peasant production? Why was *Lij* Iyasu's government redeeming "loans" that all others assumed were "gifts"? Why was the new capitalist system it championed so corrupt and damaging?

The point of this rather long excursive is to return to the political economy circa 1916 in order to focus on the underlying conditions that led to the conspiracy to overthrow *Lij* Iyasu. In the disputed historiography of this period, shockingly, all sorts of other rationales – administrative ineptitude, flagrant disrespect for social norms, promiscuousness, religious apostasy – were weighed to validate or repudiate the coup

20 Mosley, *Haile Selassie*, 72.

21 Gebre-Igzibiher Elyas, *Prowess, Piety and Politics*, 316, 325–7, 337–8; Mers'é Hazen Wolde Qirqos, *Of What I Saw and Heard*, 117.

22 Mosley, *Haile Selassie*, 71.

23 Mosley, *Haile Selassie*, 71.

24 Through oral sources from Wallega, Alula Pankhurst and Ezekiel Gebissa present a conciliatory view of *Lij* Iyasu and how he favored local Oromo producers by evicting the Gondare or *neftenya* who had been exploiting them and openly stealing from them at the Thursday markets, "Ledj Eyasu's Visit and Removal of the 'Gondare' from Laqamte," *Ya'ityopyã tenãtoč mashét*, 8–9 (1987–1988): 82–93.

25 Mers'é Hazen Wolde Qirqos, *Of What I Saw and Heard*, 124–5, 161. For a sympathetic view of this initiative, see Ydlidi, *With Ethiopian Rulers*, 273–4.

d'état. Yet in reality it was *Lij* Iyasu's economic ineptitude that galvanized his opposition. Tafari confiding to Major Dobbs, British Consul in Harar, observed: "Never have our courts been so busy. Every soldier, every chief, every trader is tired of the condition of the country. Trade has diminished, prices have increased, revenue has decreased and there is no security." Through Tafari's eyes *Lij* Iyasu was an "idler" and Hayle Giyorgis "a man with one thought, to fill his pockets, with not a thought for the good of the country."[26] A partisan view, indeed, but Tafari's assessment of the political economy points to the fact that Ethiopians were feeling the instability at the center in their own purses.[27]

Much research has been devoted to the role of the French, British, and Italian legations in galvanizing opposition to *Lij* Iyasu because of their fear that he supported Turkey and Germany.[28] In the midst of World War I when the world was being sectioned off into either allies or enemies, the legations' concerns were justifiable. May Ydlibi blames the coup on the French minister, Monsieur Brice, who, like a puppeteer maneuvered Ethiopian figureheads to his bidding, cajoling Wilfred Thesiger and Count Colli, ambassadors of the British and Italian legations, to follow his lead, and asserted direct control over foreign concessions as if Ethiopia were a colony.[29] The problem with her Euro-focus was it negated the agency of Ethiopian political actors.

Orchestrating the coup d'état did involve counting *Lij* Iyasu's wives, concubines, and wives of fellow aristocrats with whom he had relationships.[30] It did involve considering his surly behavior that was apparent to all: "He would go around brothels in the city at night accompanied by one or two persons. Sometimes, he would be involved in a shoot-out

26 Mosley, *Haile Selassie*, 83. It is noteworthy that in his own autobiography Haile Selassie launches into *Lij* Iyasu's corruption as the number one reason for the 'rancour' between the two, Haile Sellassie, *My Life and Ethiopia's Progress*, ed. and trans. Edward Ullendorff as the *Autobiography of Emperor Haile Sellassie I, "My Life and Ethiopia's Progress," 1892–1937* (Oxford: Oxford University Press, 1976), 43–4.

27 Harold Marcus provides a relatively objective description of *Lij* Iyasu's strengths and weaknesses. The weaknesses he identified included his misguided policies, his philandering, his long absences, his hatred for administration, ending with the main accusation being the way he allowed corruption to proliferate, *Haile Sellassie I: The Formative Years* 1892–1936 (Lawrenceville: Red Sea Press, 1995), 13–14.

28 Tebibe Eshete, "A Reassessment of Lij Iyasu's Political Career" in *Personality and Political Culture in Modern Africa: Studies Presented to Professor Harold G. Marcus*, eds. Melvin E. Page, Stephanie F. Beswick, Tim Carmichael, Jay Spaulding (Boston: African Studies Center, 1998), 173–7.

29 May Ydlibi, *With Ethiopian Rulers: A Biography of Hasib Ydlibi* (Addis Ababa: Addis Ababa University Press, 2006), 263.

30 Gebre-Igzibiher Elyas, *Prowess, Piety and Politics*, 358–9; and Paul Mérab, *Impressions d'Ethiopie* (Paris: H. Libert, 1921), vol. 2, 249.

with city guards at night."[31] His father, guardians, and churchmen were incapable of reining him in. It did involve acknowledging his lack of sustained attention to the affairs of state. His interest in governing was episodic: at times passionate, at other times distracted. It did involve counting his long absences from the capital where he remained incommunicado on issues that needed his stamp of approval. It did involve verifying allegations that *Lij* Iyasu leaned towards a Turko-German alliance, something the Triple Entente legations could not tolerate. It did involve confirming claims of barbarism not only towards subdued populations and captured slaves, but to defeated adversaries. This was in contradistinction to accepted methods of bringing an end to battle and dealing magnanimously with rivals and their soldiers – issues described at length in preceding chapters. On a personal level, it did involve reflecting upon *Lij* Iyasu's lack of respect and decorum shown to peers. Shortly after *Ras* Tesemma died, *Lij* Iyasu went to live with *Fitawrari* Habte Giorgis, yet in one celebrated instance when meeting Habte Giorgis while riding in Addis Ababa, *Lij* Iyasu made old, rheumatic Habte Giorgis dismount saying: "How dare you address me while you are still on horseback?"[32] This was an exceptionally disrespectful slight that embarrassed Habte Giorgis in front of his retainers and people on the street, certainly one that would be remembered. He referred to Menilek's courtiers as "sheep because they were fat."[33] Finally, it did involve awareness of the fiscal corruption inherent in *Lij* Iyasu's economic "reforms" that privileged a small cohort at the expense of traditional elites. Yet all these were not enough to justify the overthrow of *Lij* Iyasu.

The *mekwanint* had sworn fealty to *Lij* Iyasu per Emperor Menilek's instructions. Unseating Menilek's hereditary successor was considered unfitting, despite the fact that Ethiopian history is an account of plots, sub-plots, and wars to topple the sovereign as *Dejazmach* Wube's machinations attest. To break their vow of loyalty, a ruler's transgression had to challenge the essence of the state. The trouble was, all those issues listed above were offenses deemed pardonable in the past. Menilek's *zemetchas* (slave raids) were grisly affairs. Relations with women married or otherwise, were symptomatic of loose marriage and divorce arrangements. Corruption was endemic. For a

31 Mers'é Hazen Wolde Qirqos, *Of What I Saw and Heard*, 162.

32 Asfa-Wossen Asserate, *King of Kings: The Triumph and Tragedy of Emperor Haile Selassie I of Ethiopia* (London: Haus Publishing, 2015), 22. Fitawrari technically means 'commander of the vanguard,' but essentially is a military title of high esteem that confers admittance into the aristocratic ranks.

33 Avedis Terzian provides other accounts of how *Lij* Iyasu deliberately humiliated *Fitawrari* Habte Giorgis and other courtiers, see Richard Pankhurst, "The Reign of *Lij* Iyasu – As Avedis Terzian Saw It" in Ficquet and Smidt, eds., *Life and Times of Lij Iyasu*, 93.

sovereign to denounce the resurrection of Christ, however, was sacrilege and excoriated by every Christian.

The Coup d'État

Conversion to Islam was the cardinal issue contrived to legitimate the conspiracy to overthrow the uncrowned emperor – the economy remained in the background.[34] *Lij* Iyasu's reputed apostasy would absolve the Shewan *mekwanint* of their oath of allegiance to Menilek's grandson under dictates codified in the *Fitha Negest* thus aligning priests and politicians in their determination to bring Ethiopia back to the true religion.[35] All sources acknowledge *Lij* Iyasu's dalliance with the Muslim community in Harar, Jigjiga, Wollo, the Danakil Desert, and places in between.[36] As his hagiographer explained, *Lij* Iyasu sought to reconcile Ethiopia's Hebraic religions,

> My strongest desire is that all natives of Ethiopia should be of one heart and [all together] watch the country's frontiers. Even if we differ with respect to religion, still you must not forget that we absolutely have to unite in love of [our] country ... For the Muslims he had a camel slaughtered and for the Christians an ox, and he made a [common] banquet in [one and the same] hall [for all].[37]

But for apostasy itself, the record is less conclusive.[38] Hasib Ydlibi claims he asked *Lij* Iyasu directly whether he had converted to Islam, to which he replied:

> I would never think of doing so. It is perhaps true that when I am in the country of Muslim subjects I might favour them, but I do the same to the Oromos when I am in their country. They are all my subjects and I believe that they are each entitled to every mark of favour in equal shares, be they Christian, Muslim or even heathen.[39]

---

34 One of the first objective assessments of the coup d'ètat that incorporated Amharic sources is Aby Damesse's "Lij Iyasu: A Perspective Study of the Short Reign" (Addis Ababa: Haile Selassie I University, B.A. thesis, 1964).

35 Paulos Tzadua, trans., *The Fetha Nagast*, 286–8.

36 A measured assessment of *Lij* Iyasu's motives for courting Muslims focuses on Ethiopia's geopolitical position and *Lij* Iyasu's determination to secure access to the Red Sea, Tibebe Eshete, "A Reassessment of Lij Iyasu's Political Career," 169–73.

37 Gebre-Igzibiher Elyas, *Prowess, Piety and Politics*, 352. All insertions added to the translation are by Reidulf Molvaer.

38 Éloi Ficquet, "Understanding *Lij* Iyasu through his Forefathers: The Mammedoch *Imam*-s of Wello" in Ficquet and Smidt, eds., *Life and Times of Lij Iyasu*, 5–29.

39 Ydlidi, *With Ethiopian Rulers*, 250.

The evidence used at the time to assert *Lij* Iyasu's conversion was based on his marriages to Muslim women cementing alliances to powerful Muslim families, photos of him in Muslim garb (later alleged to have been forged by foreigners), accounts of him prostrating himself praying to Allah, endowing the construction of mosques, and forming a relationship with the Mad Mullah – Mohamed Abdullah Hassan, the Somali cleric who instigated the Dervish rebellion to free Somaliland from Britain – by sending him arms and allowing dervishes safe passage through the Ogaden.

From rumors to a plan, the dethronement was not accidental but one that gestated for over a year. Tafari Makonnen appears absent from the original list of conspirators; rather, two conservative stalwarts *Fitawrari* Habte Giorgis led the political-military clique and *Echege* Wolde Giorgis led the religious faction. Soon enough Tafari joined, contributing his savvy and slyness to ridding the country of his cousin *Lij* Iyasu. Tafari's reasons included laudatory motives such as preserving Ethiopian sovereignty and orthodoxy, but also personal payback for insults and *gizot* (demotion) heaped on him, even though *Lij* Iyasu had orchestrated Tafari's marriage to Princess Menen Asfaw, his niece and *Ras* Mikael's granddaughter. Again referring to Heran Sereke-Brhan's dissertation, kinship tied almost everyone together yet rarely was it sufficient to countermand political ambition.[40] Noteworthy are the names of conspirators who at one time or another were confidants and allies of *Lij* Iyasu but took offense over his actions and attitudes and switched sides.

Up to the last moment the plot seemed in doubt. *Lij* Iyasu was away in Harar, all the Shewan *mekwanint* had convened at the palace in Addis Ababa and all that was needed was for *Abuna* Matewos to declare *Lij* Iyasu excommunicated, and yet he demurred.

On September 27, 1916, a symbolically important day as it was Masqal – the commemoration of finding the True Cross, *Abuna* Matewos and *Echege* Wolde Giyorgis, the highest prelates of the Ethiopian Orthodox church, were present at the palace along with most of the elites including a contingent who remained loyal to *Lij* Iyasu, like *Neggadras* Hayle Giyorgis the *de facto* Prime Minister. Charges against *Lij* Iyasu were read out loud and *Abuna* Matewos was expected to accede to the charge of apostasy yet he hesitated, seeking more proof. Finally, the *Echege* forced his hand saying, "have you not heard that he married the daughter of the Muslim Abba Jifar" and then listed other proofs.[41] With the *Echege*'s hand on his shoulder for support, *Abuna* Matewos declared,

40 Throughout their long-lasting hostilities, Menen remained loyal to her husband instead of her uncle and grandfather. Also see Heran Sereke-Brhan, "Building Bridges, Drying Bad Blood."

41 Gebre-Igzibiher Elyas, *Prowess, Piety and Politics*, 360.

Figure 4 Lij Iyasu and Dejazmach Tafari, rivals for the throne. Attribution: Unknown c. 1916, public domain, via Wikimedia Commons.

"From this day forth, oh chiefs ... you are freed from your oath to the apostate Lij Yasu. Let us all take a new oath, to be true to our religion."[42] Still people vacillated. Seeing hesitation, *Ligaba* Beyyene Wendemegenahu, a minor official, filled with fervid indignation waved his sabre and shouted: "Let those who are Muslim stand on one side and we shall see." thus starting a general panic with bullets zinging in every direction. Someone had the presence of mind to beat the war drum, intoning a bass tone to the staccato of rifle fire and returning sanity to the medley. According to Mosley's use of uncited sources, there were upwards of one hundred casualties.[43] According to Gebre-Igzibiher Elyas the shooting was in celebration and those who died, died due to a festive fusillade of stray bullets.[44] Clearly, on the day of the putsch, blood flowed in the Great Hall of Emperor Menilek's palace.

The new government was to be headed by Zawditu, Menilek's daughter, as empress of the realm with *Dejazmach* Tafari Makonnen elevated to *ras* and declared *enderase* or Regent and heir to the throne. To ensure the conservative voice was reflected in imperial decisions *Fitawrari* Habte Giorgis was to make the third partner in the triumvirate.[45] Over a week later, Her Majesty Empress Zawditu delivered a speech in which she justified her ascension to the throne by emphasizing her emotional connection to her father, Menilek, whom she rightly claimed was denied an appropriate burial and mourning period, a sacrilege blamed on *Lij* Iyasu, and her spiritual faith in God who supported her in her years of grieving and banishment. Thus, by tying Iyasu's disrespect for Menilek to the country's veneration for the victor of Adwa along with divine providence, Zawditu claimed, "because of damage to our country and our religion, you placed me on the throne of my father by your knowledge and your will. From now on, you are my joy; otherwise I implore God to fulfill the wishes of Ethiopia's powerful and patriotic people."[46] To officiate Zawditu's enthronement, aristocrats fixed their seals to her coronation.

42 Mosley, *Haile Selassie*, 94–5; and Gebre-Igzibiher Elyas, *Prowess, Piety and Politics*, 360.

43 Mosley, *Haile Selassie*, 95.

44 Gebre-Igzibiher Elyas, *Prowess, Piety and Politics*, 360.

45 Mosley conjectured that the *rases* believed that as long as Empress Zawditu and *Fitawrari* Habte Giorgis "worked together" they could impede the youthful Tafari's modernization plans, *Haile Selassie*, 96.

46 Gebre-Igzibiher Elyas, *Prowess, Piety and Politics*, 362.

The Battle of Segale

The coup d'état did not go unchallenged. Half believing it was untrue after word reached Harar that he had been excommunicated and deposed, *Lij* Iyasu Mikael mobilized his forces and ordered them to march towards Addis Ababa while he initially remained in Harar. On October 6, 1916 near the railroad station at Miesso, *Lij* Iyasu's greatly outnumbered forces were defeated by 15,000 troops led by *Dejazmach* Ayalew Birru, sent down from the capital. Gebre-Igzibiher Elyas depicts it as Muslim against Christian with the latter quickly declaring victory and then "they pursued those who fled and butchered many Somalis with their sabres and daggers."[47] *Lij* Iyasu fled to Dire Dawa to attend to some personal and financial affairs including dispersing a portion of his treasury which he had taken to Harar earlier,[48] and finally to board a train headed for Djibouti only to debark somewhere in the desert and vanish into the Danakil with "his faithful followers."[49] Shiferaw Bekele historicizes this crucial period showing *Lij* Iyasu's "amateurish" decision-making, continual desertions by allies he thought were loyal to him, and the resolve of the plotters to conclude the coup d'état swiftly.[50] In the interval between the coup and the Battle of Segale, *Lij* Iyasu recruited forces among the Afar and made his way towards Wollo to unite with his father.

His father, *Negus* Mikael, opposed his son's dethronement. Rather slowly he mobilized his army of 100,000 men, generally recognized as the most formidable force in the land, to march on Addis Ababa. At the time *Ras* Tafari Makonnen's army numbered 16,000, but alliances quickly concocted bolstered them. The central government recruited or enticed with future favors *Ras*es Seyoum Mengesha, Hailu Giorgis, and Walda Giorgis, rulers of provinces to the north and west of Wollo, to block *Negus* Mikael or, at minimum, ensure his isolation and safeguard their tacit support for Empress Zawditu. To buy time, *Dejazmach* Lulsaggad, a one-time Iyasu loyalist, was dispatched north to block *Negus* Mikael's march on Addis Ababa.

Dejazmach Lulsaggad had no particular affection for *Ras* Tafari and sufficient reason for personal resentment towards all three, for his marriage to Princess Menen Asfaw had been quickly dissolved by *Lij* Iyasu and *Negus* Mikael, Menen's uncle and grandfather, as they thought it more expeditious to marry her to Tafari. Putting aside past marital

47 Gebre-Igzibiher Elyas, *Prowess, Piety and Politics*, 365.
48 Ydlidi, *With Ethiopian Rulers*, 268–71.
49 Ydlidi, *With Ethiopian Rulers*, 271.
50 Shiferaw Bekele, "Dïrré Dawa, Harer and Jigjiga in the Weeks before and after the Overthrow of Iyasu on 27 September 1916" in Ficquet and Smidt, eds., *Life and Times of Lij Iyasu*, 151–63.

anquish, Lulsaggad hastened to Addis Ababa with his army shortly after the coup to pledge allegiance to the new regime. As proof of his loyalty, *Dejazmach* Lulsaggad moved north to block *Negus* Mikael. Arriving at Tora Mask on the plains near Ankober, weary from their long march to Addis and then immediately north, *Dejazmach* Lulsaggad encountered *Negus* Mikael's well-rested army. With superior forces, the Wollo army surrounded Lulsaggad's forces, routed them, killing their commander and mutilating many of the wounded. Around sixty managed to escape and made their way to Addis Ababa to recount the disaster. Tafari's and Mikael's first salvos near Harar and Ankober, respectively, were similar in that they exhibited little magnanimity.

To buy time for the arrivals to swell the ranks of the new regime's army encamped at Segale, its commander, *Fitawrari* Habte Giorgis, sent mediators with cases of ammunition to *Negus* Mikael to sooth his anger and ask for a parley. While the latter did not happen, receipt of bullets – always in short supply – tempered Mikael's restlessness. After delaying his attack, which allowed the Shewan forces to swell and outnumber his 100,000, Mikael decided to attack at night, typically something not done in Ethiopian warfare. Like the Italian battle plan for Adwa, night-time reconnaissance was faulty. Flanking the Shewan camp, a cavalry unit and two companies of Wollo infantrymen got lost in the swamps of the Sendafa plain flushing thousands of ducks and geese roosting in the wetlands. This ruckus alerted Habte Giorgis's guards. War drums sounded and before daylight the fight began.[51]

The Battle of Segale is generally believed to be the bloodiest after Adwa. On October 27, 1916, Mikael faced off in the center against Habte Giorgis, yet the main thrust was led by young, brave *Ras* Ali on the left flank opposite the night's sneak attack. In Leonard Mosley's account, *Ras* Ali's troops advanced straight into *Ras* Kassa Haylu's machine gun volleys – delivered by France in the nick of time – and despite heavy losses finally engaged the enemy in hand-to-hand combat where the Wollo Oromos' spear and sword skills began to turn the tide. Seeing his forces being overrun, *Ras* Tafari steered his cavalry through *Ras* Kassa's lines and into *Ras* Ali's forces. "For a moment the men around the Wollo general faltered and Tafari's horsemen were through. They surrounded *Ras* Ali and battered him to his knees, and he dropped his sword in submission."[52] Simultaneously Habte Giorgis was losing ground to Mikael's forces and then, suddenly, the tide began to shift. Mosley attributes this to the bullets given to Mikael, for using an old merchants' trick many of the bullets had been emptied of gunpowder, refilled with a non-combustible powder and packed at the bottom of the cases. With dud ammunition and reinforcements coming from the wings *Negus* Mikael

51 Mosley, *Haile Selassie*, 104–5.
52 Mosley, *Haile Selassie*, 106.

held firm brandishing his sword until *Ras* Wasaw called upon him to surrender and offered his protection. [53] Gebre-Igzibiher Elyas' account of the battle is more sensory and fierce, more marbled in the assemblage of personalities, more garbed in religious symbolism, less dichotomized "because the soldiers of Shewa and Wello were identical in appearance, in language and in dress ... Shewan killed Shewan and Wello killed Wello. As the passwords given [to help identify friend and foe] were forgotten in the confusion [of the battle]."[54] Yet, like the Battle of Adwa, hostilities ended around 3:30 in the afternoon. Eight thousand Oromos from Wollo and three thousand government soldiers died.[55]

Victorious *Ras* Tafari turned his attention to reconciliation. One version states that after the battle reprisals were few and that Tafari immediately offered amnesty to the defeated warriors provided they pledge loyalty to Empress Zawditu thus allowing them to return to Wollo unmolested.[56] Others contend that many wounded were summarily dispatched; those who fled were pursued on the plains and chased down the escarpment and into the Danakil Desert and still others were mutilated.[57] *Negus* Mikael, *Ras* Ali, and other notables were allowed to submit peacefully. Haile Selassie writes in his autobiography: "We arranged everything benefitting his [*Negus* Mikael] dignity, so that no humiliation whatever should affect him."[58] Cleanup lasted a few days. Mikael's camp was captured almost intact, Tafari ordered money and armaments be accounted for, this against established military practices of seizing booty. *Ras* Tafari in an act of self-awareness recognized, perhaps for the first time in the history of Ethiopian military campaigns, that his soldiers had decimated the countryside ransacking local farmers' granaries and livestock leaving them near starvation for a season or two. He, thus, issued a proclamation: "If a campaigning soldier during the recent ... battle entered your house and plundered your property [or] destroyed your crops, then all of you [to whom that happened] should notify Ligaba Beyyene, and we have arranged that you shall receive [compensation for] the estimated [loss]."[59]

53 Mosley, *Haile Selassie*, 106.
54 Gebre-Igzibiher Elyas, *Prowess, Piety and Politics*, 371.
55 Del Boca, *The Negus*, 67.
56 Marcus, *Haile Sellassie I*, 24.
57 Mosley, *Haile Selassie*, 107.
58 Haile Sellassie, *My Life and Ethiopia's Progress*, 55.
59 Gebre-Igzibiher Elyas, *Prowess, Piety and Politics*, 374.

Justice Conditionally Given

Entering Addis Ababa victorious, the army was lionized with gun-salutes, citizens and soldiers lined the streets, women ululated both in joy upon seeing their loved ones return and in sorrow for their absence, and *Ras* Tafari, in splendid regalia, led his own cavalry to the palace. In the ensuing days one of the hardest tasks was maintaining law and order in a city that wanted to celebrate.

On November 5, 1916, the formal honor and shaming ceremony took place at Jan Meda (the city's parade ground/polo pitch). Huge, open-fronted tents were erected. In the middle of the largest, Empress Zawditu was seated on a dais with all her attending ladies around her. Attired in her finest vestments with embroidered gold and silver filigree, she wore a plain white *netalla* (scarf) over her mouth, only allowing her eyes to show. By rank the *mekwanint* stood on either side. The ceremony was perhaps one of Ethiopia's grandest spectacles. The British Minister to Abyssinia, the Honourable Wilfred Thesiger, in a letter to his mother stated: "It was the most wonderful sight I have ever seen, wild and barbaric to the last degree and the whole thing so wonderfully staged and orderly. Billy and Brian were thrilled and should never forget it"[60] – indeed Billy (née Wilfred) never forgot. The Thesiger family was familiar with "native theatre," for the British Plenipotentiary's brother was no less than the Viceroy of India, yet this ceremony was authentic, unlike the manufactured orientalism of the Dehli Durbars that were more a showcase of British imperialism that his brother, Lord Chelmsford, orchestrated.

Cavalrymen galloped up to the tent shouting about their bravery and brandishing swords, riding horses festooned with ornamental saddlery and with war trophies hung around the horses' necks. Next, wave after wave of foot soldiers ran up to the tent wielding their rifles, yelling and dancing all as acts of fidelity. This was all part of the honor portion of the ceremony. Each lord who took part in the Battle of Segale rode up, descended from his horse, bowed before Empress Zawditu and *Enderase* Tafari Makonnen and then took his rightful place among the *mekwanint* under the tent canopy. Interspersed among them were priests and deacons, who had accompanied their region's lord into battle, carrying crosses, icons, and church banners. Religious symbolism infused every facet. In almost every account the crowning honor, however, went to the surviving son of *Dejazmach* Lulsaggad and the sixty or so survivors of Tora Mask. Wearing the bloodstained clothes that they had fought in, they filed past Ethiopia's governing elite in silence. All war drums stopped beating. In the honor ceremony, like *irq* – which pushes people to comprehend then reconcile good with evil – honor was about

60 Wilfred Thesiger, *The Life of My Choice* (London: Collins, 1987), 55.

boasting as well as mourning, offering loyalty as well as demanding rights. Lulsaggad's soldiers sought respect and remembrance for the thousands slaughtered by Mikael's forces.

The shaming ceremony followed immediately. While sequencing is hazy, sources indicate that *Negus* Mikael was led in front of the empress's tent with silver chains around his wrists and ankles wearing a simple white *shemma* wound tightly around his waist with one shoulder bare and his face exposed. With great dignity he bowed before the empress and was led away to the *gebbi* (palace). Captured Wollo officers and troops followed and finally Mikael's "three principal generals, in chains and dressed like the *Negus*, but each carrying a large stone on his shoulder as a mark of servitude. They came before the tent and prostrated themselves on the ground before following their chief to prison."[61] The public forum allowed all to witness who had been defeated. Perhaps at no other point in subsequent twentieth-century Ethiopian history was the *wurdet* (shaming ceremony) so meticulously planned. It followed the script of prescribed traditions of restorative justice assiduously in order to communicate the legitimacy of the coup-instigators as Ethiopia's legitimate and tradition-bound rulers. The ceremony was imbued with Christian Orthodox symbolism as well as patriotic fervor, the same kind that bound Menilek's allies – as well as his wayward rivals – under the tricolor Ethiopian flag to defend Ethiopia against the Italians at Adwa. The ceremony reputedly lasted three and a half hours. The public spectacle was organized as a media barrage broadcasting to the public that the new triumvirate would conform to political, social, and religious norms, and restore Ethiopian tradition. Magnanimity was shown, not forgive-and-forget, but the conditional forgiveness that the polity had adopted that exhibited generosity yet tempered it with punishment as needed. For *Negus* Mikael this meant "imprisonment on an island in Lake Dendi in Chebo by the hand [order] of Fitawrari Habte-Giorgis,"[62] the senior member of the triumvirate and an agemate of Mikael's.[63]

Why was *Negus* Mikael's punishment of lifetime banishment considered appropriate and not excessive? According to a letter to Viscount Grey, Thesiger writes, "His [*Negus* Mikael's] presence created a great impression. He had fought in the first line and had risked everything for his son, who had not even the courage to support him, and his bearing and conduct were in every way worthy of one who had been the proud-

61 Thesiger, *The Life of My Choice*, 55. Slightly different versions are given by Gebre-Igzibiher Elyas, *Prowess, Piety and Politics*, 374, 376; and Mosley, *Haile Selassie*, 107. Haile Sellassie, by contrast, hardly mentions the ceremony in *My Life and Ethiopia's Progress*, 55.

62 Gebre-Igzibiher Elyas, *Prowess, Piety and Politics*, 376.

63 Asfa-Wossen Asserate, *King of Kings*, 29.

est man in Abyssinia."[64] If anything Mikael should have been shown leniency for his parental love and devotion for his son. Yet the reasons for Mikael's banishment from politics may be deeper seated than simply coming to his son's defense, for the Imperial Court understood a different reality. Wolbert Smidt's assessment of newly discovered primary sources indicate that, after the death of *Ras* Tesemma, Mikael assumed the role of "a defacto co-regent" and "was the key-person behind all crucial government decisions."[65] In another article Smidt argues that *Negus* Mikael was legitimately the heir of Menilek because he took Menilek's crowns to Dessie and wore them at his own coronation in 1914 as *Negus* of Wollo and Tigray. Smidt claims that this represented a power shift from Shewa to Wollo and that the coup of 1916 is really less about *Lij* Iyasu adopting Islam and more about the shift of power back to the north.[66] For the putschists, the animus about the way government was run and the level of corruption was blamed on both father and son. To their minds the father was equally responsible for the realignment of Ethiopian politics; moreover, his determination to shift power to Wollo and to enfranchise the Muslim population as coequals from his position behind the throne signified to the plotters that reform was wasted on him, that the only remedy was a very stiff sentence. Again, his extreme sentence was consistent with Ethiopia's maturing understanding of conditional forgiveness within the modalities of restorative justice. What is also noteworthy is that *Negus* Mikael lived contrite and under detention for the rest of his life, first in Chebo finally at Holeta.

Lij Iyasu and restorative justice, Round 1

Lij Iyasu had ascended the escarpment with mostly Muslim fighters recruited from the eastern lowlands to join his father at the Battle of Segale but they only reached the environs of Ankober. By that time the battle was underway and the outcome increasingly obvious. Instead of sending reinforcements to his father, *Lij* Iyasu chose to retreat into the Danakil with his troops intact. For months he sheltered in the desert slowly making his way to Wollo where *Ras* Yimer and *Fitawrari* Sirah Bizu remained loyal to the Menilek/Iyasu dynastic line and were rebuilding Wollo's army with, among others, soldiers who had been given clemency and free passage back home having sworn loyalty to Empress Zawditu. Maqdala, the same mountaintop fortress from which Emperor Tewodros had tried to repel the British Napier Expedition, was

64 Thesiger to Viscount Grey – November 3, 1916 [F.O. 371/2594].

65 Wolbert Smidt, "The Foreign Politics of Lïj Iyasu in 1915/16 According to Newly Discovered Government Papers" in Ficquet and Smidt, eds., *Life and Times of Lij Iyasu*, 109–11.

66 Wolbert Smidt, "The Coronation of Negus Mika'él: King of Wällo and Tegray, in May 1914, New Findings," *Annales d'Éthiopie*, XXIII (2007–2008): 413–34.

selected to headquarter *Lij* Iyasu's growing army. After causing terrible problems for the fragile governate of *Ras* Abate, the central government dispatched *Fitawrari* Habte Giorgis to Maqdala.[67] Seeing how impenetrable it was *Fitawrari* Habte Giorgis decided to lay a siege that lasted months. The problem was Iyasu's forces had stockpiled resources by devastating the farming communities for miles around; as a consequence, Habte Giorgis had to send provisioning brigades further afield for food to sustain his own troops. Knowing how shorthanded he was, *Lij* Iyasu ordered *Ras* Yimer and *Fitawrari* Sirah Bizu to attack on August 27, 1917, in the midst of the rainy season. The battle was fierce, fatalities were in the thousands on both sides. *Fitawrari* Habte Giorgis along with *Ras* Kassa Hailu and other Shewan notables finally prevailed capturing both generals, although Sirah Bizu died of wounds about a week later. *Lij* Iyasu again slipped away into the Danakil Desert.[68]

This time the form of restorative justice was harsher. *Ras* Yimer, some of his lieutenants and warriors were marched back to Addis Ababa for yet another honor and shaming ceremony at Jan Meda, feting *Fitawrari* Habte Giorgis's exploits and defaming *Ras* Yimer and his supporters. But not all the captured soldiers were so fortunate. Many of the "prisoners taken [were] mutilated, with the loss of a hand or a foot or worse – for having fought again after being previously pardoned for fighting with Ras Mikael."[69] Like the *askaris*' mutilation after the Battle of Adwa, maiming was the saw in the toolbox of restorative justice to be used for repeated acts of treason. By disobeying their pledge to the Empress Zawditu, their right hand and left foot were cut off to ensure they would never mount a horse, throw another spear or brandish a sword. According to the *Fitha Negest*, it was justice severed and served.

Lij Iyasu remained at large, confined to the desert, disrespected by his former Muslim allies whom he abandoned at Maqdala, and gravely ill with syphilis causing dementia and partial paralysis, making him utter nonsense and foam at the mouth – according to the admittedly biased British Foreign Office interpretation that openly championed the putschists.[70] Through meticulous archival research and interviews with Afar, Aramis Houmed Soulé offers a revisionist history, one where *Lij* Iyasu capitalizes upon his inclusive political strategy, cultivated during his years in power, to incorporate the Afar into his realm by seeking asylum in Awsa under the protection of Sultan Yayyo Mohammad. The deposed ruler was even given a compound atop a hill

67 Thesiger Report from Addis Ababa to Balfour of Foreign Office, London, February 27, 1917 [F.O. 371/2854].

68 Gebre-Igzibiher Elyas, *Prowess, Piety and Politics*, 385–7.

69 Mosley, *Haile Selassie*, 122.

70 Leonard Mosley relies heavily on communications between the British Consulate in Addis and the Foreign Office in London and their championing of *Ras* Tafari. This involved demonizing *Lij* Iyasu, see *Haile Selassie*, 122.

near Aysayta, eponymously call "Iyasu Gora" (Iyasu's hill). From there *Lij* Iyasu sought to reconnect with Oromo, Somali, and other Muslim groups to counter *Ras* Tafari's growing influence. But, alas, the political and military costs of keeping him in Awsa were too high; that and the fact that *Lij* Iyasu wanted to return to the highlands to negotiate some rapprochement with *Ras* Seyoum Mengesha, his brother-in-law, led to his departure in 1919. Orchestrated by the Afar network, *Lij* Iyasu was brought to Tigray and lived under Seyoum's protection for about two years. After negotiations broke down between *Ras* Seyoum and Empress Zawditu's court, *Lij* Iyasu was apprehended by *Ras* Gugsa Araya who personally delivered him to *Ras* Tafari in Dessie on 21 May, 1921, rather peacefully it should be noted.[71]

Empress Zawditu and others at court were terribly suspicious of Tafari and what he would do to the former ruler. To leave the administration of justice to him, they thought, would err on the side of retribution unbecoming of an ex-emperor. Too severe a punishment would be an indication that the putschists did not represent the compassionate and just leadership of an idealized ruler who was supposed to exhibit charity, mercy, and understanding. The first question then, was who would be charged with administering justice? *Ras* Hailu Tekle Haymanot of Gojjam actively sought to be made custodian as his daughter Seble Wengel Hailu was *Lij* Iyasu's first official wife,[72] but Hailu's imperial ambitions were well-known. A compromise was devised; *Lij* Iyasu would be entrusted to *Ras* Kassa Hailu, an aristocrat of the highest lineage who was dutiful, loyal, and content with his patrimony – a rare combination.

Round 1 of *Lij* Iyasu's incarceration exemplifies the fine line between forgive-and-forget and conditional forgiveness, for it demonstrates the limits of leniency accommodated within Ethiopian traditions of restorative justice.

Lij Iyasu was brought before the *zufan chilot* (Imperial Court) manacled in gold chains around wrists and ankles as befitting an ex-emperor, and handed over to *Ras* Kassa to jail at Fiche, northwest of Addis Ababa. Once there he was pampered. The most insightful account is written by Asfa-Wossen Asserate, grandson of *Ras* Kassa, the details of which were family lore passed down by his father, *Ras* Asserate Kassa and other family members. Asfa-Wossen writes,

> *Ras* Kassa took *Lij* Iyasu to Fiche, the capital of his province. There, in a house specially constructed for him, the royal internee had several rooms and even a balcony at his disposal. My father ... told me that

71 Aramis Houmed Soulé, "Lïj Iyasu and the 'Afar,'" in Ficquet and Smidt, eds., *Life and Times of Lij Iyasu*, 171–6.

72 Zuzanna Augustyniak, "Lïj Iyasu's Marriages as a Reflection of his Domestic Policy" in Ficquet and Smidt, eds., *Life and Times of Lij Iyasu*, 39–47.

> my grandfather was punctilious about treating *Lij* Iyasu in a manner befitting a former emperor. Whenever he entered the room where Iyasu happened to be, *Ras* Kassa would remove his shoes, take off his cloak (*kabba*) and bow three times before addressing the prisoner ... For fear that the resident cook might be bribed to put poison in the former emperor's food, *Lij* Iyasu's meals were all personally prepared by *Ras* Kassa's wife, Princess Tsige Mariam Beshah ... [and] were placed inside a wooden box with a padlock, to which only the princess herself and *Lij* Iyasu had a key.[73]

Many sources recount that *Lij* Iyasu became obese with food and drink. *Ras* Kassa had even sent for an Italian physician in Axum who made the journey to treat *Lij* Iyasu's syphilis.[74] Empress Zawditu, Iyasu's aunt, was sympathetic towards him and perhaps feeling a tinge of guilt showered him with gifts, all of which were approved by the Regent. Gebre-Igzibiher Elyas, chronicler of both Zawditu and Iyasu, provides more detail:

> they sent him a golden [gilded] bed and golden [gilded] chair, golden tassels [for the canopy], a silk canopy, different kinds of velvet carpets, and silk [bed and armchair] covers, clothes appropriate for royalty, and all kinds of furniture. The Gospels and Psalms bound in gold were given to him. A monk was assigned to stay with him and explain the meaning of the [religious] books [given to him]. They granted him [permission] that a woman of his choice ... could help him.[75]

Other sources indicate not one but a steady stream of young women were sent to his bedchamber.[76] For eleven years *Lij* Iyasu languished in opulent surroundings nevertheless in detention, prohibited from networking but not altogether ignorant of the affairs of state.

Lij Iyasu and restorative justice, Round 2

In 1932, well after *Negus* Tafari became emperor and took the coronation name Haile Selassie, *Lij* Iyasu was offered the opportunity to escape. *Ras* Hailu sent an emissary to Iyasu, the plan was to lavish the jailers with revelry and booze, bribe other guards, steal away in the middle of the night, escort Iyasu to Gojjam, meet up with *Ras* Hailu's forces and with the help of other aggrieved *ras*es descend upon Addis Ababa to restore Ethiopia's rightful ruler. All went well, in fact, *Ras* Kassa was

---

73 Asfa-Wossen Asserate, *King of Kings*, 32.

74 Mosley, *Haile Selassie*, 179.

75 Gebre-Igzibiher Elyas, *Prowess, Piety and Politics*, 417.

76 Leonard Mosley states, "Ras Kassa, was a God-fearing and church-going chieftain but was not inclined, such being Ethiopian broad-mindedness, to see any conflict between his own religiousness and the satisfying of the sexual needs which his hostage soon indicated were clamant ... Kassa kept him plentifully supplied with female comforts," *Haile Selassie*, 179.

absent attending the Crown Prince's wedding when word reached the wedding party that *Lij* Iyasu had escaped. Problems arose when the predicted groundswell of disaffected lords did not join the rebellion. *Ras* Kassa filled with shame for allowing his charge to escape submitted to Haile Selassie. Haile Selassie magnanimously overlooked the infraction and deputized Kassa to apprehend Hailu. Perceiving his plot was foiled, *Ras* Hailu came to a palaver arranged by *Ras* Kassa near Fiche during which the Imperial forces descended from the highland, captured Hailu and led him off to the capital to face the emperor. He was later to be imprisoned and relieved of his title and lands. Haile Selassie's autobiography includes many pages about *Ras* Hailu's intrigue and few about Lij Iyasu's escape. For the emperor the main threat was the unveiling of a scheme between Hailu and the Italians to overthrow Haile Selassie, with Iyasu merely an appendage. Plot foiled, Hailu captured, the *zufan chilot* (Imperial Court) condemned him to death, but Haile Selassie, the ultimate and benevolent judge, "commuted the sentence of death" and sentenced him "with his property confiscated, in confinement at a specified place."[77]

Lij Iyasu and some bodyguards, were caught about four days later having crossed the Blue Nile where "the people of Gojjam seized him and handed him over to *Dejazmach* Dasta Damtaw."[78] Apprehended a second time, "the golden chain was looped around his neck once more, and he was taken in an old Chevrolet bus to Addis Ababa."[79] This time there were no lords willing to intercede on *Lij* Iyasu's behalf to request leniency. Haile Selassie could take his revenge.

Gold chains removed and with rusty shackles fixed to wrists and ankles, *Lij* Iyasu was sent to prison in Gara Mulleta, Hararge province, which was Haile Selassie's titular seat of power and where the captive would find few allies. The prison was crude and basic, gone were the lavish trappings of Fiche. Kept in miserable conditions, the more accepted ending states that *Lij* Iyasu died or was killed there in the autumn of 1935 in the midst of the Italian invasion on the premise that the imperial court feared Mussolini would restore the ill, out-of-touch former ruler to the throne as a puppet to moderate Ethiopian resistance to Fascist occupation.[80] But another version exists, far less substantiated but nevertheless persistent. It claims that *Lij* Iyasu was taken from Gara Mulleta to Addis Ababa and interned, some say, in the

77 Haile Sellassie, *My Life and Ethiopia's Progress*, 205.
78 Haile Sellassie, *My Life and Ethiopia's Progress*, 206.
79 Mosley, *Haile Selassie*, 182.
80 Bahru Zewde, "Iyasu" in *Encyclopaedia Aethiopica*; Wolbert Smidt, "Glossary of Terms and Events of the Lïj Iyasu Period: Controversial and Non-Controversial Facts and Interpretations" in Ficquet and Smidt, eds., *Life and Times of Lij Iyasu*, 184.

basement of Haile Selassie's palace at Sidist Kilo to die or be killed in close proximity to the throne.[81]

How does Round 2 reflect Ethiopian concepts of restorative justice? *Lij* Iyasu's submission required him to abide by the term of his conditional forgiveness which was to stay out of politics for the rest of his life. Harsh punishment, no doubt, but mollified by the lavish quarters with both culinary and carnal comforts provided him at Fiche and the respect conferred by *Ras* Kassa bowing three times before addressing him. Implied was that *Lij* Iyasu would be penitent. Atonement was understood as both short-term contriteness as well as lifelong redress.

To escape, to plot with another imperial aspirant, to symbolically challenge the supremacy of Emperor Haile Selassie was a violation of *Lij* Iyasu's sentence. One of the duties of the *zufan chilot* was to be the nation's memory-keeper, to recall the circumstances under which justice was served and its verdict given. There was no doubt about *Lij* Iyasu's guilt in Round 2. Another aspect of conditional forgiveness was that when the terms of the indictment were abused, the accused was not remanded to the Imperial Court but could be re-sentenced, swiftly, silently by the judge, in this case, Haile Selassie, to a harsher punishment along the continuum between clemency and vengeance. To imprison *Lij* Iyasu at Gara Mulleta in primal, unsanitary conditions devoid of royal trappings was well within Ethiopian traditions of restorative justice.

One more issue needs to be addressed before closing the chapter on *Lij* Iyasu, and it pertains to his death. Whether he died at Gara Mulleta or in Haile Selassie's palace in Addis Ababa is debatable; what is of consequence is whether he died of natural causes or was killed. Asfa-Wossen Asserate relates two scenarios that appear to indicate that Empress Menen and Emperor Haile Selassie genuinely mourned his death: "the empress was officially notified of the death of *Lij* Iyasu, and a session of lamentation was held at the royal palace," and in the other scene, as *Dejazmach* Belay Ali, a close relative of *Lij* Iyasu "entered the Great Throne Room, Haile Selassie came towards them wailing and crying, with his burnouse worn inside-out – a traditional sign of mourning – and informed them that *Lij* Iyasu was dead."[82] Their mourning could indicate that he died of natural causes; however, others have argued that Haile Selassie was capable of feigning grief which could be in character with his duplicitous, politically-all-consuming nature. Reidulf Molvaer, in his postscript to Gebre-Igzibiher Elyas's chronicle which he translated, assembled a startlingly comprehensive collection of accounts about *Lij* Iyasu's death from reputable oral sources including Endalkatchew Makonnen who states he had been killed. Possible assas-

81 Asfa-Wossen Asserate, *King of Kings*, 34.
82 Asfa-Wossen Asserate, *King of Kings*, 34–5.

sins are named, yet sufficient contradictions remain. Complicating the picture, Molvaer notes that upon *Lij* Iyasu's death Haile Selassie ordered priests to provide him with a Christian burial mass even though they objected on grounds that *Lij* Iyasu had apostatized.[83]

But even if *Lij* Iyasu was killed on Haile Selassie's orders it would, in itself, conform within the continuum between vengence and forgiveness.[84] Capital punishment was condoned under extreme circumstances in the Old Testament and the *Fitha Negest*,[85] and therefore could be resorted to within the framework of restorative justice. The case of *Ras* Hailu demonstrates this: The Imperial Court condemned him to death only to have the emperor commute his sentence to life in prison because execution was considered bad form. Emperor Tewodros lost support of the *mekwanint* because he was too ruthless and ordered too many of his adversaries killed. Haile Selassie was nothing but cautious. As his diatribe on the conspiracy between Ras Hailu and the Italians in 1932 demonstrates, he was well aware of Fascist designs on Ethiopia and their calculation that promoting *Lij* Iyasu's claim to the throne as their lackey would undermine Ethiopian independence.[86] The circumstances were dire, for around the time of *Lij* Iyasu's death, Haile Selassie departed for the front to fight the Italians at Maychew. Already Italy's military superiority was acknowledged, and the emperor's participation was more to delay the inevitable; nevertheless, the emperor was already thinking about the implications for Ethiopian sovereignty following military defeat. The idea of restoring *Lij* Iyasu to the throne certainly was frightening, for if *Lij* Iyasu had acted irrationally before, what was to ensure he did not accept Italy's offer to be their Ethiopian figurehead? Perhaps *Lij* Iyasu was killed upon Haile Selassie's orders in which case an analysis of a Round 3 in the meting out of Ethiopian restorative justice should be undertaken.

Another wrinkle needs to be considered, although merely introduced here. Shortly after his coronation, Haile Selassie expedited passage of the 1930 Penal Code. These statutory laws emphasized punishments along continental lines for they were modeled after French penal codes "adapted for use in Asia ... [specifically it] might have naturally been inspired by the Code of (French) Indochina."[87] The 1930 Penal Code's emphasis on retribution did not negate the *Fitha Negest*; rather,

83 Gebre-Igzibiher Elyas, *Prowess, Piety and Politics*, 566–9.

84 Kathleen Daly in "Restorative Justice: The Real Story," *Punishment and Society*, 4:1 (2002): 58–61 takes issue with the idea that restorative and retributive justice are opposites. She argues that the restorative (good) / retributive (bad) binary on "empirical and normative grounds" is "neither accurate nor defensible," for punishment blurs the lines.

85 Paulos Tzadua, trans., *The Fetha Nagast*, 287.

86 Del Boca, *The Negus*, 156–8.

87 Aberra Jembere, *Legal History of Ethiopia*, 11.

it inserted into Ethiopian legal discourse the Napoleonic notion that started from the presumption of guilt and reasoned that offenders were to be punished for the injury they caused to individuals or society if they could not prove themselves innocent. The French viewed ambiguity as an anathema to justice. Clear, fixed verdicts were sought. How much influence the 1930 Penal Code had on Haile Selassie's purported ordering of the execution of *Lij* Iyasu Mikael is unclear but pushing into the realm of conjecture and bordering closely on counter-factual history, perhaps French retributive penalties which sanctioned capital punishment in cases of treason, factored into Haile Selassie's thinking.

Assessing Legitimacy

After the Battle of Segale why did the *zufan chilot* opt to use traditional methods of justice as opposed to considering international legal norms? After the Battle of Adwa, Menilek and his court became aware that international law pandered to political expediency. Certainly, Italy argued that the results of Adwa should be legally overturned and that Italy's protection over Ethiopia, falsely codified in the Treaty of Wechale, should remain in effect. Menilek's court took an accelerated course in the capricious nature of European justice and learning how to politicize prisoner exchange in order to maintain Ethiopian sovereignty. The Consular Courts that sprang up in Ethiopia, the result of signing the Klubukowski Treaty in 1908, allowed Ethiopian jurists and politicians frustrated by their rulings to conclude two things about international legal standards: first, there were no standards; second, law was all about gaining an advantage and codifying it. In many ways, European "law of war" and "just war theory" – as loose and inarticulate as these were in 1916 – attempted to regulate declarations of war, ensure proportionality and safeguard terms of surrender, but principally they favored the victor; they justified the assumption or resumption of power. In many ways, if the successful coup had rejected Ethiopian traditions of restorative justice and adopted European victor's justice, they would have been quickly recognized by the international community. By contrast, the putschists' power-grab would have likely been rejected by the Ethiopian public.

Politically, Ethiopia's modernization embraced elements of colonialism; more accurately Ethiopia used the armaments and architecture of modernization to halt colonial encroachment. Economically, modernization promoted laissez-faire capitalism yet viewed from the periphery represented corruption and favoritism of the few over the many. Neither were attractive, ergo very little else from Europe was viewed favorably by Ethiopian elites or peasants, least of all European jurisprudence. Ethiopia's encounter with European legal systems always put

Ethiopia at a disadvantage. Nor had European justice been recognized as just: Blindfolded Lady Justice, holding her balance, strictly followed the letter of the law but European laws were written by the enfranchised, systemically overweighting one side of the balance.

It was critical that the putschists gain legitimacy with their adversaries. The way to do this was by applying to a shared, historically grounded, religiously endorsed code to bring about peace to the nation and reconciliation with the new regime. Justice was arbitrated by an anonymous, covered face with eyes wide open to appraise the social and political implications of the verdict in order to best serve the state and the people.

6

Italians, Collaborators, and the Indifferent: Muddled Justice

This chapter assesses the chaos Italy caused Ethiopia and efforts to rebuild the Ethiopian state after liberation in 1941. It begins with the Italian invasion, the rationale for creating *spacio vitale* ("living space") in which to settle Italy's impoverished population, the brutality of occupation and the degree to which Italians imposed their own political, economic, and judicial institutions on Ethiopia. To balance the analysis, a summary of Italy's reputed positive contributions will be gauged and shown to be harmful to Ethiopia's autochthonous development. Yet despite their negative effects, Italy's re-engineering of Ethiopia's infrastructure accelerated Ethiopia's push towards modern development afterwards. The focus of the chapter, of course, is the liberation of Ethiopia by British forces fighting alongside Ethiopian Patriots. After the defeat of *Africa Orientale Italiana* (Italian East Africa) in 1941, a reckoning was in order. While traditional forms of restorative justice had been deemed superior for bringing about peace and reconciliation, in post-liberation Ethiopia international understandings of "rules of war" determined how the Italian army and *askaris* were to be treated. A confusing mixture of Western legal systems was used to administer justice for Italian civilians and Ethiopian collaborators. Almost forgotten were the indigenous juridic mechanisms previously discussed. This chapter attempts to explain why restorative justice was overlooked and only resorted to in a few cases in which European legal solutions were thought inadequate.

After liberation the task of administering justice split the Ethiopian population down the middle: Patriots versus collaborators, and the indifferent were forced to assert that they had always been on the winning side, surreptitiously aiding the Patriots by supplying food and shelter or through a million other micro-actions. Naturally the ranks of the collaborators shrunk and shrunk again until only a small number were deemed traitors worthy to stand trial. But here is where legal procedures became muddled and misdirected. By 1941/42 the whole legal basis for the administration of justice was confused. Ethiopia's traditions of restorative justice lived on in the national memory, but Emperor Haile Selassie had initiated both civil and penal reforms based on hybridized European models in the early 1930s. Moreover, Italy had introduced its own courts thus isolating the Ethiopian public even more from traditional forms of restorative justice. Finally, British military officials acted very much like a colonial regime which meant asserting British military law, yet a third layer of European jurisprudence to confuse legal procedures.

The Italian Wreck

Italian colonial designs on Ethiopia were longstanding. Giulio Baravelli lists political slights and violent skirmishes from the Battle of Adwa to 1935, always with Italians as victims of Ethiopian treachery.[1] With Ethiopians characterized as illiterate xenophobes resistant to modern ways, Baravelli justifies conquest comparing the land mass of England to its colonies which were ninety times greater, while Italy's were only five times greater. This prompted Baravelli to conclude: "The Italy of Mussolini will no longer submit to the impositions which mortified and humiliated the Italy of former days who had not awoken to the conscience of her history."[2] Justified, Italy invaded.

By 1936 Italy had eviscerated Ethiopia.[3] Superior armaments, use of illegal weaponry (dumdum bullets deemed illegal for military use according to the Hague Convention of 1899), yperite (mustard gas equally illegal), poisoning of lakes and waterways, armored transport, and air domination allowed the Italian army to overrun Ethiopia's proud but poorly provisioned forces.[4] Use of gas was to figure prominently a decade later as Ethiopia tried to prosecute Italy for war crimes.[5] There was nothing to stop the Italian offensive as they broke out of their Eritrean citadel and marched on Addis Ababa.[6] Their passage literally

1 Giulio Cesare Baravelli, *The Last Stronghold of Slavery: What Abyssinia Is* (Rome: Societa Editrice di "novissima," 1935), 57–67.

2 Baravelli, *The Last Stronghold of Slavery*, 87, 89.

3 Alberto Sbacchi, *Legacy of Bitterness: Ethiopia and Fascist Italy, 1935–1941* (Lawrenceville: Red Sea Press, 1997).

4 Norman Angel, "The Politics and Morals of Mustard Gas," *Time and Tide*, (1936); Jeff Pearce, *Prevail: The Inspiring Story of Ethiopia's Victory over Mussolini's Invasion* (New York: Skyhorse Publishing, 2014), 229–47. The most comprehensive analysis can be found in the edited volume Angelo Del Boca, *I gas di Mussolini: Il fascismo e la Guerra d'Ethiopia* (Rome: Editori Riuniti, 1996).

5 Perhaps accentuating the tragedy, Ethiopia's Ministry of the Press and Information published a compendium of fascist telegrams ordering the use of yperite in Ethiopia, see ICC Legal Tools Database, *La civilization de l'Italie fasciste en Ethiopie*, Database Record Number: 239108 (2024 [1948]).

6 The standard account remains Angelo Del Boca, *The Ethiopian War 1935–1941* (Chicago: University of Chicago Press, 1965).

scorched the earth and decimated Ethiopia's political establishment, leaving the country leaderless, or almost.

Emperor Haile Selassie knew war clouds hung low over his country and tried to use diplomacy and the League of Nations to halt Mussolini's advance, but his faith in collective security was misplaced. Battles began in October 1935; Ethiopians initially slowed the Italian advance such that Mussolini became impatient and replaced General De Bono with the superior tactician, General Pietro Badoglio. Within a matter of months Badoglio had halted, pincered, and routed many of the Ethiopian *rases*' armies. As preparations for the Battle of Maychew began, Haile Selassie was essentially alone. The armies of *Ras* Kassa and *Ras* Seyoum had been reduced to a few hundred, *Ras* Imru, perhaps the most capable and inspirational leader, was far away near the Tekeze River trying to extricate his troops after the Battle at Shire and was never able to join his cousin, the emperor, at Maychew.[7] The intention was to attack the advanced guard of the Italian army causing disruption and perhaps delaying them to allow the little rains to do what the Russian winter did for Russia against Napoleon and the Kaiser's Germany, slow the Italian advance and allow Haile Selassie to regroup and rearm his forces. But Seyoum's and Kassa's reluctance to engage after their humiliating losses convinced the emperor to delay for days. This gave Italian air reconnaissance sufficient time to pinpoint the Ethiopian buildup and deploy reinforcements. Ethiopian forces attacked at dawn on March 31, 1936. The battle lasted all day during which both sides ran out of ammunition on various fronts and soldiers resorted to hand-to-hand combat using bayonets and spears. Ensuring victory, the Italian air force dropped bombs on the Ethiopian lines and strafed troops with machine gun fire scattering them in all directions. At Maychew Haile Selassie asserted his warrior instincts – his machismo, a personality trait in stark contrast with the effete statesman and loving father-of-the-nation personas he so assiduously cultivated. Colonel Konovaloff extolled Haile Selassie's bravery tinged with foolishness: "He was always in the zone of artillery fire and continually exposed himself to danger. In the end he went down into the plain and machine-gunned the enemy himself with terrific effect. Low flying aircraft could not hit him."[8] But the outcome was preordained. Ethiopia lost 8,000 men, Italy lost 400 Italians and 873 Eritrean *askaris*.[9]

The finale came during the retreat to Korem where Ethiopians were caught in the open plains around Lake Ashange and bombarded by wave

7 *Ras* Imru's own story was recorded by George Steer, *Caesar in Abyssinia* (Boston: Little, Brown and Company, 1937), 272–6.

8 Theodore Konovaloff was military adviser to the emperor and afterwards recounted his observation to George Steer, *Caesar in Abyssinia*, 316.

9 Del Boca, *The Negus*, 170.

after wave of Italian fighter planes firing machine guns, and bombers dropping incendiary bombs and poison gas.

> It was pointless to try to protect your body from the corrosive liquid. Calico cloaks rapidly soaked it up ... And when there was only motionless bodies stretched out on the ground, then the airplanes dared to fly lower to strafe those in whom there was still even a breath of life.[10]

To make matters worse the Azebo Oromos of Wollo allied with Italy and, led by Captain De Sarno, rained bullets down on the fleeing Ethiopian troops. The dead were stripped of their rifles, cartridges, and clothes, and castrated.[11]

The irony should not be lost, for after the Battle of Adwa the Italian press chastised Menilek's forces for the barbarity of genital mutilation. Now when the tables were turned and Ethiopian troops were in disorderly retreat, the Azebo Oromos, ostensibly under Italian orders, also emasculated the dead and wounded, a fact history overlooks. Italian writers and journalists applauded Mussolini's foreign adventure and conjured up the old colonial reasoning about bringing civilization to savages. Luca dei Sabelli went on to rationalize "the invasion as 'a mission of justice' against 'an island of barbarism'"[12] and yet even emasculation of Ethiopian soldiers by those in the pay of Italian fascists paled when compared to the supreme barbarism, pummeling Ethiopian troops and civilians with mustard gas causing severe blistering, permanent eye damage as well as likely death as it burned the soldiers' mouths, throats, and lungs causing pulmonary edema.

Military resistance was over. Haile Selassie retreated to Addis Ababa and after much consultation with the *mekwanint* left Ethiopia to plead his case to the League of Nations in Geneva. The decision was not easy or lightly taken. Empress Menen and *Ras* Kassa were the most forceful advocates for exile. As George Steer wrote: "The Empress had made up her mind that the Emperor should come with her ... she would take the Emperor to Jerusalem, the Sacred City, where the aid of heaven would be invoked before the aid of Geneva."[13] The royal family boarded a ship at Djibouti and were received with honors in British Palestine and housed at the famous King David Hotel. During his stay Haile Selassie visited Golgotha, the Lord's Tomb and, of course, the Ethiopian Orthodox monastery where he attended Mass in Ge'ez.[14] Leaving his wife and part of his family he proceeded to London, reconnected with some

---

10 Quoted in Del Boca, *The Negus*, 173.

11 Del Boca, *The Negus*, 173; Mosley, *Haile Selassie*, 227.

12 Giampaolo Calchi Novati, "Italian Relations during the 19th–20th centuries" in *Encyclopaedia Aethiopica*.

13 Steer, *Caesar*, 362. Perhaps the most accurate account of these deliberations is found in Richard Pankhurst, "Emperor Haile Selassie's Autobiography, and an Unpublished Draft" *Northeast African Studies* 3:3 (New Series, 1996): 80–101.

14 Haile Sellassie, *My Life and Ethiopia's Progress*, 295.

of his young, European-educated technocrats plus foreign advisers, such as the Americans Everett Colson and John Spencer, and penned his address to the League of Nations. The central point was to serve justice by calling on League members to collectively confront Italian aggression. With regal bearing Haile Selassie addressed members of the League of Nations reminding them of the treaty they had all signed, how Ethiopian pleas for financial and military aid had been ignored and at the end the emperor posed the question: "What, then is the meaning of Article 16 and the Covenant and of collective security?"[15] It appeared that God and the League both ignored his appeals.

The issue for League members became: Did the *de facto* conquest of Ethiopia become *de jure* thus removing even their tepid acknowledgement that the treaty obliged them to sanction Italy or punish her in some way? Members' inaction implied that it had.[16] Legally, however, Emperor Haile Selassie still claimed to be sovereign and tried to maintain the prerogatives of government while in exile in Bath, England. Because of poor communications, Haile Selassie had almost no say over armed resistance nor domestic governance. His efforts were confined to foreign affairs but even in this arena he was essentially talking to a mirror. When appeasement failed and Hitler and Mussolini were clearly seen as a threat to world peace, the Ethiopian government in exile was finally taken seriously or at least seriously enough to become a pawn on Great Britain's military chessboard. Yet between 1936 and 1940 Italy wrecked Ethiopia.

The socio-political implications of occupation

It is fundamental to understand that Italian occupation was limited to the spiderweb of a garrison state. The web included all larger towns and cities and the connecting roads between them. Italy never conquered Ethiopia entirely. Because of its geography much of the countryside remained inaccessible, a landscape into which Ethiopian Patriots could vanish. Writing for the *Christian Science Monitor*, Edmond Stevens traveled through Ethiopia and noted:

> Although [our] route lay through the most populous and wealthiest parts of Gojjam, we failed to discover the slightest trace of Italian influence or penetration beyond the occasional empty bottle in native use. There was no Italian merchandise of any description in the huts or even any Italian currency in circulation, though the Italians had decreed the lire the official legal tender.[17]

---

15 John Spencer quoting from his English translation of Haile Selassie's speech, *Ethiopia at Bay: A Personal Account of the Haile Sellassie Years* (Algonac, MI: Reference Publications, 1984), 74.

16 For a fuller account of the humiliation Haile Selassie received in Geneva see A. J. Barker, *The Civilizing Mission: A History of the Italo-Ethiopian War of 1935–1936* (New York: Dial Press, 1968), 294–9.

17 Edmond Stevens, "Italy Never Conquered Ethiopia," *Christian Science*

Italy invested heavily in roadbuilding, sometimes following well demarcated caravan tracks, other times surveying new routes that cut the distance between two points or, more often, wove the roads up steep gradients by following elevation contours and cutting hairpin turns into mountainsides for cars and trucks to pass. However, there were limitations. A road could track over one tabletop plateau, descend into a river gorge and up an escarpment to another tabletop and, apparently, the whole road could be protected by Italian troops and Eritrean *askaris*, yet one valley to the right or left could be terra incognito to those occupying forces. The prevailing narrative is that the infrastructure Italy left was of high quality. Angelo Del Boca lauds, "the Italians set about providing the empire with what it lacked, in other words, practically everything; roads, railways, factories, hospitals, schools, hotels, post offices, telephone exchanges, etc."[18] The reality is that many of the buildings, sewage systems, electric lines, and road grids were constructed with speed, inferior materials and little attention to durability.[19] City avenues often ended in refuse dumps. Richard Pankhurst assesses the labor practices, road building, urban infrastructure, industrialization (or lack thereof), and commerce, and concludes that the five years of occupation were "a time all in all of economic confusion and disequilibrium."[20] In the final analysis Italy's infrastructural contributions to Ethiopia were incontestable and irreversible but nonetheless rather "shoddy."[21] Once in place, however, there was no turning back. Years later roads were widened, mountain passes resurveyed by British, Swedish, or American civil engineers; water and sewage pipes replaced, and electric lines restrung.

Certainly, Italian expertise was an asset when it came to constructing infrastructure for it provided the platform for later enlargement or replacement, but the costs were prohibitively high, and the price tag was borne by Rome alone.[22] Ethiopia was a sinkhole for the Italian treas-

---

Monitor, reproduced in *New Times & Ethiopia News,* 271 (July 12, 1941).

18 Del Boca, *The Ethiopian War*, 232.

19 Shimelis Bonsa Gulema, "Urbanizing a Nation, Modernizing a City: Addis Ababa 1941–1974" (Ph.D. dissertation, University of California, Los Angeles, 2011).

20 Richard Pankhurst, "Economic Verdict on the Italian Occupation of Ethiopia 1936–1941," *Ethiopia Observer,* 14:1 (1971): 82.

21 Lord Francis James Rennell of Rodd writing the official record of the British liberation of Ethiopia, who was onsite during the occupation, said: "Italian Fascist architecture, rarely otherwise than shoddy and undistinguished even in Italy, had here run riot ... with the smallest element of craftsmanship, style or durability." See *British Military Administration of Occupied Territories in Africa During the Years of 1941–1947* (London: H.M. Stationery Office, 1948), 87.

22 Alberto Sbacchi, *Ethiopia Under Mussolini: Fascism and the Colonial Experience* (London: Zed Books: 1985), 111; Barker, *The Civilizing Mission*, 307.

ury. Moreover, Mussolini soon had commitments in Spain, Albania, and North Africa as the outset of World War II approached.

Spacio vitale or Italy's dream of empire depicted securing space for Italy's poor and landless peasants to settle and transform the country into an agrarian breadbasket for the benefit of the home nation. The late-nineteenth and early-twentieth centuris were characterized by migration of Italians to America and beyond. The rationale for establishing Italian East Africa stretching from Mogadishu to Asmara with the prize, Addis Ababa, at the center was to convince discontented Italians to stay in the Italian empire by promising them land, subsidies, and prospects for a good life in Africa. Marshall Badoglio prophesied that a million immigrants could be settled in Ethiopia.[23] That never happened. "On the eve of World War II ... only 3,550 families had been settled."[24] After liberation in 1941 the combined British and Ethiopian authorities spoke of the necessity to repatriate up to 50,000 Italians, likely the majority single men, with 5,000 of them deported to Kenya;[25] this was out of an estimate of 125,000 Italian soldiers, functionaries, and contractors in Ethiopia and another 45,000 in Eritrea in August 1941.[26]

Ethiopia never became a financially self-sustaining colony for it remained a garrison state. Costs skyrocketed because of the number of soldiers necessary to maintain security over rebellious Ethiopians. Originally, 68,000 troops were deemed sufficient to maintain control after conquest, but the Viceroy, General Graziani, insisted that 240,000 troops – the majority Eritrean *askaris* – were necessary to counter the Patriot resistance. Even the more "compassionate" Duke of Aosta, who replaced Graziani as viceroy in late 1937, determined it was necessary to maintain a standing army of equal size to that of his predecessor.[27]

Paranoia about the Patriots permeated all decisions and actions. The spiderweb of roads, bridges, and airports were strategic military objects built to rapidly deploy troops to the enclaves Italy had seized; they were

23 Robert Mallett traces the propaganda campaign of *spacio vitale* and how it became a cornerstone for the justification to invade Ethiopia from 1919 to 1935, *Mussolini in Ethiopia, 1919–1935: The Origins of Fascist Italy's African War* (Cambridge: Cambridge University Press, 2018).

24 Del Boca, *The Ethiopian War*, 235. Sbacchi claims only 3,200. For an in-depth analysis of the absurd level of burdensome government subsidies spent on Italian settlers – demographic colonialism – see *Ethiopia Under Mussolini*, 108–14.

25 "5000 Italians move from Ethiopia to Kenya," *New Times & Ethiopia News*, 281 (September 20, 1941): 2.

26 "Ethiopia Eritrea: Pro-Italian Talk in 'The Times', Sir Sidney Barton Defends Ethiopia," *New Times & Ethiopia News*, 275 (August 9, 1941).

27 Tekeste Negash, *Italian Colonialism in Eritrea, 1882–1941* (Uppsala: Uppsala University Press, 1986), 55–72.

not constructed to promote import/exports or enhance civilian transport. Resistance took many forms and repression was immediate. Upon entry into Addis Ababa executions commenced.

Crimes of occupation

General Pietro Badoglio entered Addis Ababa on 5 May 1936. In celebration, standing on the balcony of Rome's Piazza Venezia before an adoring crowd, Mussolini feted victory and shortly after promoted Badoglio to Viceroy over *Africa Orientale Italiana.* Badoglio envisioned ruling through a modified form of indirect rule by empowering traditional leaders. This did not sit well in Rome. Three days later the Minister of Colonies, Alessandro Lessona, articulated Mussolini's Fascist determination to expand suzerainty over Africa giving authority exclusively to Italians.[28] Badoglio resigned, and General Rodolfo Graziani was appointed Viceroy. Graziani wholeheartedly endorsed that what "Italy means by colonization [is] the system of implanting its race at the expense of the autochthon people, destined to systematic extermination."[29]

Marching through the countryside and into the city, Italian Blackshirts and conscripts defied the 1929 Geneva Convention on the Treatment of Prisoners of War: Ethiopians in remote areas who still bore arms, unaware of Haile Selassie's departure, were summarily executed; soldiers who surrendered were likewise shot, and those simply suspected of defying Italian occupation were bludgeoned, hung, decapitated. The Duce offered immunity to his firebrands. Few prisoners of war existed for they were killed. Upon entry into Addis Ababa, George Steer writes: "The Italians immediately instituted a death penalty for two crimes: the first was participation in looting of Addis Ababa, and the second was the possession of arms."[30] It did not matter that city dwellers were unaware of these edicts; a French official estimated "at least fifteen hundred were killed in this way."[31] Prison camps were filled with Ethiopian civilians awaiting their fate along with most of the Ethiopian aristocracy.[32] Upon liberation in 1941 a correspondent for the British East African Air Force visited the largest Italian prison camps in Addis and declared: "No words of mine can adequately describe the horror of life in these penitentiaries or probe the depths of the degradation of

28 Ian Campbell, *The Addis Ababa Massacre: Italy's National Shame* (London: Hurst, 2017), 26–7.

29 "Italy and the Colonies: Some Observations on Italy's Method of Colonization," *Ethiopian Herald*, 2:17 (October 21, 1944).

30 Steer, *Caesar in Abyssinia*, 402.

31 Steer, *Caesar in Abyssinia*, 402.

32 Campbell, *The Addis Ababa Massacre*, 38-41.

the human soul by the inhuman system which the Italians practice."[33] First and foremost the criteria for persecution and imprisonment was race: Greeks, Armenians, and Indian traders – all beneficiaries of Haile Selassie's hospitality and who had served and benefited from the Ethiopian state – were treated with kindness, Ethiopians were not.[34]

Resistance to colonial rule tracked Italian oppression. As their abuses increased, Ethiopians overtly and covertly challenged occupation. Haile Selassie's failed overture to the League of Nations became a veritable icon, the image of the lonesome, defeated figure standing up, with regal bearing, to world powers. This image galvanized Ethiopians of all walks of life. The Patriots played an ever-increasing role in resisting occupation.[35] Frustrated, Graziani decided to compete with his imperial nemesis and demonstrate affinity to Ethiopian traditions by holding an alms-giving ceremony on Friday February 19, 1937. The date was announced and hundreds of blind, destitute, lame, Orthodox priests and monks, plus merely curious city dwellers showed up to receive Italian charity in the only currency that was acceptable, thalers, an Austrian silver commodity currency.[36] Shortly after the speech and while money was being handed out two grenades were thrown onto the dais of the Gennete-Leul Palace (formerly Haile Selassie's palace and now the Institute for Ethiopian Studies at Addis Ababa University) where Graziani and other top officials stood. While no one was killed Graziani and others were wounded. In the ensuing mayhem the *carabinieri* along with soldiers and *askaris* fired into the unarmed crowd with rifles and machine guns. The palace grounds were littered with bodies, around 3,000 were slaughtered.[37] But that was only the beginning. Hearing that their Viceroy had fallen, soldiers quartering at the nearby Menilek II School were summoned and cordoned off the area, killing indiscriminately. Given *carta blanca*, violence and bloodletting climaxed late on February 19th. The Blackshirts roved through the city targeting "native quarters;" soldiers and *askaris* sought revenge in communities as far as fifty kilometers away; Italian citizens armed themselves with whatever weapons they possessed, forming vigilante groups moving

33 "Barbarous Italian Prisons in Addis Ababa." *New Times & Ethiopia News*, 269 (June 8 1941).
34 Interview with Avedis Terzian, Addis Ababa, November 19, 1986.
35 Semunguse Negese, "The Italian Occupation of Ankober and the Resistance Movement (1936-41)" (Addis Ababa University, Department of History, B.A. thesis, 1982).
36 In covert fashion Ethiopians erected ingenious barriers to the occupation, one of which was to insist on the use of thalers thereby rejecting the Italian lire, see Charles Schaefer, "Serendipitous Resistance in Fascist Occupied Ethiopia 1936–1941," *Northeast African Studies*, new series (n.s. hereafter), 3:1 (1996): 87–115.
37 Barker, *The Civilizing Mission*, 305–6.

from neighborhood to neighborhood.[38] "They began to play 'Hunt the Moor' on an unheard-of scale. They drenched *tukuls* with petrol, set them alight, and as the inhabitants rushed out, finished them off."[39] The insanity persisted into the night and for another three days. But the Graziani massacre did not stop.

Neurotic after his assassination attempt, Graziani went after Ethiopia's intelligentsia. Bahru Zewde calls their elimination "the missing generation," the results of which significantly impeded efforts to rebuild the nation after liberation.[40] More incriminating in the eyes of the population was his targeting of Orthodox monks and priests. At the prominent monastery of Debre Libanos, north of Addis Ababa, 425 monks and deacons were shot. Not content, Graziani ordered the execution of another 129 clerics from the monastery at Debre Berhan northeast of the capital on the suspicion that they were somehow complicit in the resistance.[41]

Violation of the rules of war was particularly alarming for Ethiopian Patriots resisting Italian occupation. Most Patriots were summarily executed. After Graziani's recall, due to a nervous breakdown, and replacement with the more cultured and humane Duke of Aosta, executions of Patriots continued, the only difference was that makeshift war trials were conducted. The sham of these "trials" was that Patriots were tried in the field by Italian officers and the verdicts were carried out on the spot. As one of his informants, Luigi Lino, told Angelo Del Boca: "At least the Patriots had the right to a valid trial even though they were almost invariably sentenced to be hanged."[42] Patriot leaders suffered, too. *Ras* Imru was fortunate, for upon surrender he was imprisoned and transported to Italy where he remained until the end of the war.[43] Others were less fortunate. *Ras* Desta Damteou, married to Princess Tanagne Worq, eldest daughter of Haile Selassie, "was the last Ras, to become the victim of the hatred of the Fascists ... who after having fought during seventeen months was taken prisoner, sick and exhausted." He was shot by firing squad four days after grenades were thrown onto the Palace stage. "It is thus obvious that it is through vandalism and cowardice, by a completely criminal act that Graziani ordered the

38 Ian Campbell meticulously deconstructs the events of February 19, 1937 and commemorates many of those who were killed on that day in subsequent purges, *The Addis Ababa Massacre*.

39 Del Boca, *The Ethiopian War*, 221.

40 Bahru Zewde, *Modern Ethiopia*, 170–1; and Bahru Zewde, *Pioneers of Change in Ethiopia: The Reformist Intellectuals of the Early Twentieth Century* (Oxford: James Currey, 2002).

41 Del Boca, *The Ethiopian War*, 224.

42 Del Boca, *The Ethiopian War*, 248.

43 "Addis Ababa was beflagged when the exiled patriot Ras Imru returned," *New Times & Ethiopia News*, 396 (December 4, 1943): 3.

killing of *Ras* Desta, prisoner and invalid."[44] To commemorate those who had fallen in the Graziani massacre, *The Ethiopian Herald* republished Haile Selassie's mid-March 1937 plea to the League of Nations where the emperor chastised: "All these crimes are in violation of the rules of public international law embodied in the fourth Hague Convention of 1907, concerning the Laws and Customs of Land Warfare."[45]

Imposed institutions

The wreck the Italians wrought extended beyond the crime of killing human beings: it dismantled many indigenous institutions and customs. *Spacio vitale* implied the creation of an ancillary Italy, a settler colony that replicated everything found in the homeland.[46] To repeat, this included constructing roads, hospitals, schools, post offices, municipal buildings, commercial and industrial properties, residential districts, even a football stadium. But Italy's transformation intentionally disrupted Ethiopian social structures and institutions. The three legs of the stool holding up the edifice of feudal Ethiopia – the emperor, the aristocracy, and the church – were cut off. Of course, Haile Selassie's evacuation simplified matters for it amputated the first leg.

Second, the Ethiopian aristocracy was severely curtailed.[47] Many were killed like *Ras* Desta Damtew and the three sons of *Ras* Kassa: Wonde Wossen, Aberra, and Asfa Wossen all with the rank of *Dejazmach* and all holding important governorships in northern Ethiopia. *Dejazmach* Wonde Wossen Kassa was invited to Addis Ababa to meet with Marshal Graziani in May 1936. This conformed with traditional protocol aligned with restorative justice, for new emperors often demanded regional governors come to the capital to submit. The intention, as seen in Chapter 1, was to show fealty to the ruler but depending on their relationship could involve a shaming ceremony or *wurdet*. Wonde Wossen Kassa was uncertain about Italian intentions and delayed going to Addis Ababa. Graziani interpreted this as treason, considering that his father, *Ras* Kassa, was one of the few aristocrats in England with Haile Selassie, for he thought Wonde Wossen was working with the resistance. After a long manhunt Wonde Wossen was found and executed in December 1936. Alarmed, his two brothers continued to evade Italian efforts to find them. In fact, earlier *Dejazmach*s Aberra Kassa and Asfa

44 "Honoring Ethiopia's Martyrs," *Ethiopian Herald,* 1:32 (February 5, 1944).

45 Whole issue on the Graziani massacre, *Ethiopian Herald,* 1:34 (February 19, 1944).

46 Fabienne Le Houerou, *L'Epopée des Soldats de Mussolini en Abyssinie 1936–1938: Les "Ensablés"* (Paris: L'Harmattan, 1994).

47 Sbacchi, *Ethiopia Under Mussolini,* 129–44; for a more pointed study see Sbacchi, "Italy and the Treatment of the Ethiopian Aristocracy, 1937–1940," *International Journal of African Historical Studies,* 10:2 (1977): 209–41.

Wossen Kassa led an unsuccessful attack on the outskirts of Addis Ababa that the Italians repulsed easily. Their situation was precarious. Using *Ras* Hailu Tekle Haymanot, who had earlier submitted, as go-between, guarantees were given Aberra and Asfa Wossen to spare their lives if they surrendered to *Ras* Hailu. They did and Hailu promptly handed them over to General Tracchia. The next day they were shot and beheaded, as stated in a telegram from Graziani: "In pursuance of my orders they were shot at dusk in the square in Fiche."[48] Stretching comprehension, Tracchia and Graziani publicly denied responsibility.[49]

Coercion worked, word spread, and lower ranking officials submitted to the Italians in large numbers, but even suspicion of supporting the resistance was sufficient for some to be executed. Italians were not interested in endorsing or even integrating Ethiopian political institutions; they were determined to stamp them out and plant their own. Many of the ruling class who survived were shipped off to Italian Somalia where they were imprisoned until liberation.[50] Connected to the aristocracy either through blood or political influence was the intelligentsia who were likewise assailed by the Italians. Haile Selassie claims that "75% of the educated young men [were] killed in cold blood."[51]

The third leg of traditional authority, the church, also was targeted. Even before the executions of the 554 monks and priests at Debre Libanos and Debre Berhan, Graziani decided to make a spectacle in Dessie's marketplace. Ordering a makeshift trial, *Abba* Petros, Bishop of Dessie, was accused of instigating the attack in Addis Ababa, carried out by Aberra and Asfa Wossen, and shot in front of the market-going public.[52] The crowd was traumatized. In the course of the five-year occupation *Abba* Petros and the three Kassa brothers were eulogized as martyrs of the resistance. To further neutralize the church, the Archbishop, appointed by the Patriarch of Alexandria, fled back to Egypt because of intense

48 *Documents on Italian war crimes; submitted to the United Nations War Crimes Commission by the Imperial Ethiopian Government*, Vol. 1 (Addis Ababa: Ministry of Justice, 1949), 10, document 13.

49 Sbacchi, *Ethiopia Under Mussolini*, 184–5.

50 Interview with Emmanuel Gabre Sillasse, Addis Ababa, 20 February 1987; Alberto Sbacchi, "Italy and the Treatment of the Ethiopian Aristocracy," *International Journal of African Historical Studies*, 10:2 (1977).

51 Haile Sellassie, *My Life and Ethiopia's Progress*, vol. 2, ed. Harold Marcus, trans. Ezekiel Gebissa (East Lansing: Michigan State University Press, 1994), 169; Bahru Zewde, *Pioneers of Change*, 35.

52 Anthony Mockler, *Haile Selassie's War: The Italian-Ethiopian Campaign, 1935–1941* (New York: Random House, 1984), 156–62. Market courts were common. Usually the *nagadras*, chief officer of the market, and a *dagna*, local judge, or two would dispense justice over commercial, land, and domestic disputes as the marketplace was the magnet drawing disputants together, Margery Perham, *The Government of Ethiopia* (Evanston: Northwestern University Press, 1969), 150.

pressure to validate the occupation. The Italians used this opportunity to appoint their own archbishop and declare the Ethiopian Orthodox Tewahido Church an autocephalous church where "the Abuna was made responsible to the Italian authorities."[53] The Coptic Church in Egypt promptly excommunicated the new *Abuna* Abraham, thus establishing two ecclesiastical centers. Within the Italians' efforts to mute church influence was a proclamation that stipulated that "the Abyssinian clergy were not allowed to undertake educational activities."[54]

This dictat undercut traditional education.[55] Again, referring back to Chapter 1, most educated Ethiopians attended their first school on the porch steps of their local church and, if exceptionally bright, devout, or high-class, continued their education by being assigned to or hiring priests or *debteras* – unordained church clerics – as tutors. National identity was as much a part of instruction as literacy, for the *Kibre Negest*, the national epic, grounded the religious and political ideology that formed the institutions of state and methods of governance. National identity was likewise molded by the *Fitha Negest* which articulated the law of the land that prized reconciliation. Forbidding religious education was designed to ensure that Ethiopian traditions were not passed on. The decimation of the clergy at Debre Libanos and Debre Berhan meant that two of the main centers of religious and legal learning were no longer shaping political discourse. Since identity was so connected to the polity, curtailing the aristocracy and the church effectively undercut the imperial government that had existed for millennia and had resisted Muslim, Portuguese, and nineteenth-century Italian attempts to unseat it. Having weakened traditional education, Italy invested little in any education for Ethiopians; in fact, the Tafari Makonnen School facilities were taken over and reserved for European children.[56] Begrudgingly scattered "native" schools were established, often "held in tents and huts"[57] with a decidedly fascist curriculum including marching and singing fascist military songs.[58]

---

53 "Italy and the Ethiopian Church," *New Times & Ethiopia News,* 259 (April 19, 1941): 3.

54 "Italy and the Ethiopian Church," 3.

55 Richard Pankhurst, "Education in Ethiopia During the Italian Fascist Occupation (1936–1941)" *The International Journal of African Historical Studies,* 3 (1972): 373.

56 Pankhurst, "Education in Ethiopia During the Italian Fascist Occupation," 371.

57 E. W. Polson Newman, *The New Abyssinia* (London: Rich and Cowan, 1938), 111.

58 Ladislav Sava, "Ethiopia under Mussolini's Rule, An Eye-Witness Account of What Happened When the Italians Marched In," *New Times & Ethiopia News* (September 27, 1940): 1.

The Italians were not without grounds for targeting the church. Seltene Seyoum in his article "The Role of the Ethiopian Orthodox Church in the Italo-Ethiopian War" states that many war proclamations and calls-to-arms issued by the palace were communicated to peasants through churches: "big and small churches became the most convenient and viable centers for public agitation and propaganda against Italy's colonial aspirations in Ethiopia."[59] Certainly, with all the *askaris* and collaborators in their employ, the Italians were well aware of the propagandistic role the church played, and as patriotic resistance increased it was one identifiable and powerful institution they could purge.

Italian demolition efforts extended into the legal realm as well. Imperial edicts disappeared. Moreover, the institutions of the *zufan chilot* (Imperial Court), the *afa negus* (Chief Justice or the 'Mouth of the emperor'), and *shaleqa* (provincial) courts, run by governors that adapted to local customs and religious practices, were abolished. Essentially all courts functioning under the precedent law of *atse serat*, which literally means 'the law of the sovereign,' that looked to the *Fitha Negest*, Ethiopian customary law, traditions of restorative justice and the updated 1930 Penal Code for antecedence to make law binding for either civil or criminal cases were jettisoned.[60] Below the decapitated high courts, the Italians allowed local *dagnas* (judges or magistrates) to decide village disputes, or Orthodox priests or Muslim *qadis* to deal with divorce and other socio-religious infractions, somewhat similar to British indirect rule.[61]

Dividing Ethiopia in half, the Italians applied laws developed in Eritrea over the previous fifty years for the predominantly Christian Orthodox north and somewhat modified laws enforced in Italian Somaliland for the Muslim populations in the eastern and southern half of the country. It was under these courts that the vast majority of Ethiopians were first exposed to European jurisprudence, for even though Haile Selassie's 1930 Penal Code had preceded Italian law, the Penal Code had little influence beyond Addis Ababa. While Italy's bifurcated system imposed variations of civil and criminal procedures in accordance with the Christian or Muslim beliefs of the regional populations, Italian laws were quite obviously fundamentally Italian with adaptations made to ensure colonial domination and impose a racist color bar. They were never intended to respect local customs.

---

59 Seltene Seyoum, "The Role of the Ethiopian Orthodox Church in the Italo-Ethiopian War: 1935–1936," unpublished paper, Unity University, no date.

60 Aberra Jembere, *Legal History of Ethiopia*, 126.

61 Esubalew Belay Fanta, "A History of the Ethiopian Imperial High Court and the Role of the British in the Juridical Development of Ethiopia (1942–1974)" Ph.D. dissertation, Addis Ababa University (2015), 40–2.

Special courts, of course, were set up for Italians and Italian commercial ventures.[62] To resolve interracial matters an alternate legal hierarchy was developed. At the top of the new legal system was the Criminal Court of Appeal presided over by the Viceroy. Just below was the Addis Ababa Criminal Court that adjudicated the vast majority of cases between Italians and Ethiopians in accordance with Italian laws.[63] As an addendum to its criminal and commercial duties, the Addis Ababa Criminal Court was the final court charged with enforcing Italian racial purity laws prohibiting the intermarriage or even sexual relations between Whites and Blacks. Children of mixed parentage were classified as native. While apartheid was still to be implemented, separation of races was codified into law in Ethiopia with severe penalties, at least theoretically.[64]

Combined, Italian colonialism, like the road-grid, affected only a small portion of the population – those mostly residing in urban centers – while the countryside was left relatively unscathed.[65] Its effects, however, were profound, less about what it constructed and more about what it destroyed. About the former, new institutions and infrastructure, though superficial and often shoddy, nevertheless furnished a six-year apprenticeship that embedded them into the national ethos and judicial architecture. About the latter, it undercut the feudal order. Not to be forgotten, memory-keepers were sidelined or eliminated and traditions forgotten or degraded. More detrimental, occupation halted autochthonous development in which innovators hybridized traditional customs with non-Ethiopian ideologies and jurisprudence. This was the trajectory to which Haile Selassie had committed himself, albeit slowly and with many false starts and ninety-degree turns.

Price of Liberation

Emperor Haile Selassie entered Addis Ababa on 5 May 1941, exactly five years after the Italians had entered. Perhaps to be anticipated, the price tag was high. True liberation was long in coming.

By 1941 the Blitzkrieg had made Europe a fascist continent with one democratic holdout, Great Britain and a few countries claiming

62 Perham, *The Government of Ethiopia*, 152.

63 Esubalew Belay Fanta, "A History of the Ethiopian Imperial High Court," 42.

64 Sbacchi assesses the problem of interracial conjugal rights in his section on "*madamismo*, the illegal cohabitation of an Italian man with an Ethiopian woman" in *Ethiopia Under Mussolini*, 170–3.

65 In conducting field research on the reach of the Penal Code of 1957, Paul Brietzke noted that Ethiopian efforts to codify law did not extend beyond the cities even by the late 1960s, see "Law and Rural Development in Ethiopia," *African Studies Review*, 18 (2007): 48.

neutrality. To inflict some pain and gain an elusive victory, Britain orchestrated a three-pronged attack on Italian East Africa: General Alan Cunningham attacking Somalia and southern Ethiopia from Kenya, General William Platt moving on Eritrea, and Major Orde Wingate leading a small brigade of British forces along with diasporic Ethiopians including Emperor Haile Selassie, known as the Gideon Force, pushing into Gojjam and central Ethiopia from Sudan. By rank and troop numbers British made their priorities quite clear. On the war chessboard the liberation of Ethiopia was a rook-move, only secondarily was it intended to liberate Ethiopia and restore Haile Selassie to the throne. Once liberated, Ethiopia was to remain under the Occupied Enemy Territory Administration (OETA) administered by the British military.

The wrench in the cogs was the Ethiopian Patriots.[66] While successful in wearing down Italian resolve and limiting *spacio vitale* to a garrison state, the Patriots were galvanized by the news that His Imperial Highness was in Khartoum making preparations to reenter Ethiopia. Patriots worked with Gideon Force yet oftentimes independently. What became apparent was that they were unaware of British OETA intentions. For the Patriots, ejecting the Italians and reestablishing Ethiopia as an independent nation with Haile Selassie as sovereign was their primary objective. Haile Selassie was caught in a double bind: placate the British or pursue his own ambitions which dovetailed nicely with the will of the Ethiopian people – at least that was his supposition.

The British radiated racial prejudice long refined in their colonies. In the lead-up to the liberation, Margery Perham, considered a respected Africa authority by Westminster as well as 10 Downing Street, wrote an op-ed to *The Times* expressing concern for the "massacre of [Italian] prisoners" by "wild tribesmen thirsting for revenge and loot."[67] The takeaway in 1941 was that Ethiopians could not be trusted to show restraint. General Cunningham certainly believed that.

After freeing Harar, General Cunningham commanded that Italian police retain authority and weapons to ensure Italians' lives and property were protected.[68] A Special Correspondent to the *New Times & Ethiopia News* reported: "Too many, especially of the [white] South and East Africans, are lacking in respect and consideration for the people they came to liberate; some consider the Ethiopian fair game for any sort of joke, not even excluding the robbery of his property or

66 Solome Gebre-Egziabeher, "The Patriotic Works of Dejazmatch Aberra Kassa and Ras Abebe Aragaye," *Proceedings of the Third International Conference of Ethiopian Studies*, vol. 1 (Addis Ababa: Institute of Ethiopian Studies, Haile Selassie I University, 1966), 293–314.

67 Margery Perham, "Abyssinia's Future," *The Times* (January 29, 1941): 5.

68 "Italian Surrender in Harar," *New Times & Ethiopia News,* 272 (July 19, 1941).

the mishandling of his wife."[69] After capturing Addis Ababa on April 4, 1941, Cunningham allowed Italian police and provincial authorities to continue to impose a color bar protecting Italian interests. Furthermore, preparations to evacuate five thousand Italians to Kenya were quickly arranged with many assurances that those who remained would receive British protection. Fear of retaliation, knowing the brutality that Italians had brought and the dehumanized prisons in which they incarcerated civilian Ethiopians, was the reason for keeping Haile Selassie and the Gideon Force from thrusting into Shewa and maybe beating Cunningham to Addis Ababa.

Within striking distance, Major Wingate was told to delay Haile Selassie and the Gideon Force at Debre Markos. To their mutual frustration, a month passed as Britain consolidated power, acting more like an occupation force as opposed to a liberation army. In the interim, White officers appropriated Italian hotels, villas, and commissaries; public spaces were restricted to whites – British, South African, and Italian – while Ethiopians were barred. The pretext for the holdup was to ensure Italians' safety. "We restrained [Haile Selassie] a bit because there are 100,000 Ethiopians there and 40,000 Italians and we don't want a massacre or incidents as the Ethiopians will all go mad at the triumphal entry."[70] Fundamentally, the British distrusted Africans. This despite repeated assurances by Emperor Haile Selassie and Empress Menen that Ethiopians would act with all the probity that they had shown Italians after the Battle of Adwa. In response to Margery-Perham-like accusations, Empress Menen vouched: "My Ethiopians are very kindly disposed towards any weak and helpless people, and the Italian women and children will not be ill-treated still less massacred by them."[71] The emperor packaged his response in terms of the language of the Bible and restorative justice. On first crossing the border between Sudan and Ethiopia, he reputedly said: "In the name of the gracious God whose mercy does so aid all of us, I now forgive those of you who have worked against the interests of your King and country, being, whether by force or choice, under Italian control."[72] Later during his May 5th Victory Speech he elaborated:

> What I would finally announce to you, my people, is that this day is a day of rejoicing for us all. Today is a day on which we defeated our

69 "Grave News from Ethiopia," *New Times & Ethiopia News,* 285 (October 18, 1941).

70 Douglas Newbold, Civil Secretary of the Sudan, quoted in Mockler, *Haile Selassie's War,* 372.

71 "Empress of Ethiopia Awaits Victory," *New Times & Ethiopia News,* 253 (March 8, 1941).

72 A quote from Haile Selassie recorded in an article by Emmanuel Abraham, "Abyssinia's Future," *New Times & Ethiopia News,* 257 (April 5, 1941): 2.

> enemy. Therefore, when we say let us all rejoice with all our hearts let not our rejoicing be in any other way but in the spirit of Christ. Do not return evil with evil. Do not indulge in the atrocities which the enemy has been practicing in his usual way, even up to the last moment. Take care not to soil the good name of Ethiopia by acts which are worthy of the enemy. We shall see that our enemies are disarmed and sent the same way they came. As St. George who killed the dragon is the Patron Saint of our army as well as of our Allies, let us unite with our Allies in everlasting friendship and amity in order to be able to stand against the godless and cruel dragon which has newly risen and which is oppressing mankind. I charge you to consider them as a brother and a friend and to show them kindness and consideration.[73]

In spite of his assurances the British continued to view Haile Selassie's government with skepticism, blocking Ethiopian sovereignty domestically and internationally. The Anglo-Ethiopian Agreements of 1942 and 1944, while loosening controls, nevertheless solidified the British grasp on political, military, and economic affairs. Haile Selassie, however, used every opening, every crack, every overture to assert his own prerogative as leader of a sovereign nation.[74] His approach towards the British exuded *seltaney* – polite, refined and restrained behavior.[75] Towards the conclusion of World War II, Haile Selassie perhaps ungraciously signaled a pivot to the United States by meeting President Roosevelt on the USS Quincy anchored in the Suez Canal after the Yalta Conference.[76] Sylvia Pankhurst's media barrage, war weariness, economic decline and a sustained independence campaign led by Mahatma Gandhi and Jamal Nehru in India but reaching into other colonies in Africa, undercut the resolve of the OETA to deny Haile Selassie's unwavering attempts to reassume authority over all of Ethiopia including the Ogaden and Eritrea. While dependence on Great Britain had been cut, Ethiopia continued to use British military and technical expertise to modernize bureaucracies and institutions for many years. The approach for achieving freedom was patience, a long-term view that incorporated using former adversaries as friends, and an inexorable determination to remain an independent nation.

73 "Emperor of Ethiopia to His People," *New Times & Ethiopia News*, 277 (August 23, 1941): 1–2.

74 Harold Marcus, *Ethiopia, Great Britain and the United States 1941–1974: The Politics of Empire* (Berkeley: University of California Press, 1983), 8–41.

75 Simon Messing, "Changing Ethiopia," *Middle East Journal*, 9:4 (Autumn 1955), 421–2.

76 Prior to meeting Roosevelt, Haile Selassie had dispatched Yelma Deressa to Washington D.C. to seek military and financial aid. The United States extended its Lend-Lease program to Ethiopia accompanied by American advisers. Later this was formalized as the Fellows Mission and still later became known as the Point Four Agreement of 1952, see Amanda Kay Mcvety, "Pursuing Progress: Point Four in Ethiopia," *Diplomatic History*, 32:3 (June 2008): 371–403.

Justice and Reconciliation

One of the first agenda items on Haile Selassie's list was to determine how to serve justice in order to bring reconciliation. Many parties required some form of justice as punishment for their actions and to expiate victims' animus by seeing perpetrators sentenced according to the law. Two immediate issues needed to be dealt with: Which parties? And what law? The first was relatively simple, the protagonists included the Italians, the *askaris* – Eritrean, Somali, and Libyan soldiers, and Ethiopian collaborators on one side, and Patriots and citizens on the other. The second issue was more muddled. Which set of laws was the sovereign state of Ethiopia to use? Customary law that local *dagnas* (judges or magistrates) used to decide village disputes, or Orthodox priests or Muslim *qadis* used to deal with divorce and other socio-religious infractions, time-honored traditions of restorative justice, the Penal Code of 1930, parts of Italian law that Ethiopians had been forced to endure, or inputs from British common law traditions that were newly introduce by the OETA? Esubalew Belay Fanta assesses these contending legal influences in his dissertation on the Ethiopian Imperial High Court.[77] While retroactively applying a term that would be coined decades later, Ethiopia in the early 1940s qualified as a country where "legal pluralism" reigned.[78] A contemporary, David Talbot, states: "This first half of the Twentieth Century has seen a tremendous amount of written precedents, from which the new civil code is being compiled."[79] Ethiopia was a country where African legal solutions carried legitimacy, but where imported European jurisprudence was viewed as a necessary step in the "law and development" movement to prove a nation was modernizing.[80]

The principals of restorative justice have been described at length. On the other hand, Ethiopia's early articulation of European codified law requires revisiting. The 1930 Penal Code's heavy reliance on

---

77 Esubalew Belay Fanta, "A History of the Ethiopian Imperial High Court," 40–2.

78 *Journal of Legal Pluralism and Unofficial Law* (1969 to present) demonstrates the breadth of legal pluralism and shades into legal anthropology whereby all social constructs that define human limitations are viewed as legal procedures. To understand the methods, see Norbert Rouland, *Legal Anthropology* (Stanford: Stanford University Press, 1994). With reference to the Horn of Africa, see Lyda Favali and Roy Pateman, *Blood, Land, and Sex: Legal and Political Pluralism in Eritrea* (Bloomington: Indiana University Press, 2003).

79 David Talbot, *Contemporary Ethiopia* (New York: Philosophical Library, 1952), 156.

80 Kaius Tuori, "Legal Pluralism and Modernization: American Law Professors in Ethiopia and the Downfall of the Restatements of African Customary Law," *Journal of Legal Pluralism and Unofficial Law*, 62 (2010): 43–70.

French codes devised for their distant colonies in Indochina, was not something haphazardly selected but was a choice based on decades of observation. While the Klubukowski Treaty in 1908 legitimated the existence of foreign Consular Courts in Ethiopia, they had actually been in existence for years. After the British and French got theirs, every other European power wanted their own courts to protect their citizens from the vagaries, in their minds, of Ethiopia's ill-defined commercial and criminal codes. As trade and politics became more entangled, Ethiopian merchants and politicians – often the same people – were dragged into those courts or barred from them. Either way the weight of foreign legal judgements was felt. Over time British common law and French codes were compared. The Napoleonic Code's clear divisions with branches for criminal, commercial, and civil law seemed more logical, more adaptable and easier to assimilate because the laws themselves were fixed, with none of the malleable reliance on precedent that typified British common law all based on the English precedent – not an easy task for Ethiopian legal scholars to comprehend and apply. Moreover, the Code de Indochine demonstrated how the fixity of French law paradoxically could be sufficiently flexible to accommodate Southeast Asian sensibilities.[81] This French example provided a roadmap. The incentive had everything to do with Haile Selassie's objective to modernize, for enhanced global connections and commerce required more legal wrangling. The 1930 Penal Code communicated to the world that Ethiopia was modernizing its legal system by starting at the beginning, constructing a system to punish criminals. Civil and commercial codes were in the works prior to the Italian invasion.

The reach of the 1930 Penal Code was essentially confined to urban centers, for out in the countryside criminals were dealt with according to local practices. Tension existed between the two systems for, while the new code attempted to construct a list of crimes together with corresponding penalties, it was generally considered softer. Mutilation was abolished, talion eliminated, criminal investigation was professionalized or at least made less arbitrary; certainly, the custom of *leba shay* was ended.[82] The Preamble attempted to reconcile tensions between old and new by claiming that the *Fitha Negest* was the inspiration for the Penal Code. The imperial aim was to apply criminal law uniformly and equitably. While governors were instructed to administer it throughout

---

81 Aberra Jembere, *Legal History of Ethiopia*, 11. Aberra also observes that the "completeness and economy of the French codes [provided] a better alternative for development," 198.

82 *Leba shay* involved elders from a community selecting a prepubescent boy ("the thief searcher"), administering a hallucinogen, following the boy around to where he collapsed and then arresting the individual in front of whose property the boy collapsed, Peter Garretson, "Leba šay" in *Encyclopaedia Aethiopica*.

their distant provinces, its application was spotty and large segments of the population were ignorant of its existence.

After 1936 Italian law superimposed itself. Where Italian interests butted against indigenous interests there was no prevarication, no compromise – Italian law won out every time. Ethiopians of all walks of life felt its finesse, fury, and finality. And yet, as described above, the Fascist regime was perfectly comfortable leaving local matters to *dagnas* to resolve disputes having to do with property rights, divorce, or petty crime. In this sense, Ethiopia's reform package was annulled, and local articulations of customary law given a boost at the village level. Talbot adjures that even the Italian penal code, despite its racialized application, was still used in the courts after liberation.[83] Restoring the 1930 Penal Code or formulating a new one would be a monumental task that required the government to seriously consider its shortfalls in light of new legal initiatives afoot in the country.

The main challenge was the OETA's enforcement of military law. To British eyes, Ethiopia was an occupied territory that fell under British law. Indeed decisions, disagreements, contracts, the whole gamut involved in ruling a country passed through the military hierarchy and at the top were generals Alan Cunningham and William Platt, with political issues left to Sir Philip Mitchell and Brigadier Lush. All were reluctant to cede any power to Ethiopians. Like the Italians before them, the British relied upon their own legal system which, for the first time, introduced British Common Law to Ethiopia. Some parts were improvements; other laws simply confused the picture.

As Haile Selassie's government considered how to bring justice to Italians, *askaris* and collaborators, juridical options seemed endless. As the following section demonstrates, procedures and verdicts were hodge-podge, some traditions taking precedent for certain enemies-of-state, other laws applying to other groups.

The Reckoning: Judging Italians, Askaris, and Collaborators.

Italians were of the first order not because the imperial regime viewed them as a priority but because British overseers insisted upon their speedy treatment. Being at war with Italy, Great Britain had skin in the game. Objectively the Axis countries dominated Europe and it looked like Rommel was on his way to securing North Africa. The manner in which Italians were treated could have repercussions on how Englishmen were treated if Egypt fell. The Battle of El Alamein that changed Allied fortunes in Africa was eighteen months away. Certainly, all the precautions the OETA employed, holding up Haile

83 Talbot, *Contemporary Ethiopia*, 156.

Selassie in Gojjam, authorizing Italian police to protect Italian interests after liberation, and quickly arranging for Italian evacuation, were deemed appropriate in the context of Britain's larger concerns.

Cocooned by the OETA, Italians continued to live in Ethiopia with as many as 30,000 residents in Addis Ababa in late 1941.[84] The British took their obligations seriously, they viewed themselves as "the occupying authority" until such time that an Anglo-Italian Peace treaty could be signed and issues of repatriation and property could be formally resolved according to their understanding of Laws of War. Conversely, Haile Selassie "regarded himself as the heir-at-law of the defeated Italian Government."[85]

For the British, repatriation of Italians was a top priority. If Italian civilians were allowed to stay on their farms or urban domiciles what would this communicate to Ethiopians about British commitment – paradoxical as it was – to restore Ethiopian sovereignty. If the British removed Italians from their land and dwellings but allowed them to stay in Ethiopia, they calculated that they would have to erect internment camps to protect the Italians which would cost manpower, equipment, and money, all in short supply during wartime. The solution was to evacuate them. Mussolini was offered free passage through the Suez Canal for ships destined for Mitsiwa and Assab to pick up the Italian soldiers and civilians. This never came to pass, and Italians clogged most Red Sea ports awaiting repatriation. In September 1941 the British resolved to relocate five thousand Italians to Kenya with some destined for Southern Rhodesia to be employed as skilled laborers for mining and roadbuilding.[86]

The Ethiopian government had a different view about the Italians and wanted some to stay, especially those who possessed needed technical skills. As previously asserted, Italian infrastructural contributions, while substandard, were groundbreaking for the time. Haile Selassie constantly admonished Ethiopians to treat Italians humanely. While Italian policemen were soon replaced with Ethiopians, Italians continued as truck drivers, electricians, mechanics, construction workers, and in a plethora of other activities the modern sector required. Retaliation was minimal. In fact, a significant percentage stayed in Ethiopia either as a distinct expat community, or marrying Ethiopian women and setting up shop even in the furthest corners of Ethiopia.[87]

---

84 Rennell of Rodd, *British Military Administration*, 67.

85 Rennell of Rodd, *British Military Administration*, 85.

86 "5000 Italians move from Ethiopia to Kenya," *New Times & Ethiopia News*, 281 (September 20, 1941), 2.

87 *New Times & Ethiopia News*, 262 (May 10, 1941): 3 confirms that: "Some of the Italian soldiers took unto themselves Abyssinian women and wanted to stay in the country against the wishes of their officers." Years later, the author's historical route tour to Gondar was saved by an Italian owned *gomist*

To an extent both groups were basing their actions on the Laws of War: the British emphasizing repatriation, Ethiopians stressing accommodation. The British feared reprisals and that the savage hoards would kill Italian men and ravage Italian women. The Ethiopians, instead, showed great kindness towards all Italians. In his autobiography Haile Selassie said, "in recognition of the benevolence of God to Us, We responded with kindness to the wicked acts of the enemy by declaring protection, instead of retribution and death, for the captured enemy troops."[88]

Despite all this *bonhomie* between Ethiopians and Italians who chose to stay, conflicts did emerge; however, they were relatively few.[89] By contrast, as noted by Leonard Mosley, a contemporary journalist, homicides were mostly carried out by "Greeks and Armenians seeking revenge upon their former occupiers, who had ruined them"[90] by dismantling their commercial enterprises.[91] Young Italian women were not accosted by Ethiopian men, rather they "found themselves the objects of sexual attentions" by white Allied troops.[92]

Friction between the OETA and the Ethiopian government grated on many surfaces since the British viewed Haile Selassie as an ingrate. Powerful British officials viewed Ethiopia as another colony by insisting upon control over domestic policy and foreign affairs, this included staffing of the civil service and judiciary, and by controlling telegraph, telephone, and railroads. They had the temerity to take over banking and require the use of the East African shilling, and even had the audacity to insist on driving on the left-hand side of the road.[93] To thwart Ethiopian development, the British stripped the country of everything

---

(tire repair shop) somewhere between Debre Markos and Bahir Dar on a late night in 1986 during the tumultuous days of the Derg. In 1992 an elderly Italian emerged from the back of a garage in Gambela to supervise a welding job for our election observer team's Toyota Landcruiser. In conversation both old men claimed they had married local women, had lived in their communities since the 1940s, raised families and had never entertained the idea of returning to Italy.

88 Haile Sellassie, *My Life and Ethiopia's Progress*, vol. 2, 167–8.

89 Rennell of Rodd, *British Military Administration*, 68.

90 Leonard Mosley was a British journalist attached to Gideon Force who remained in Ethiopia after liberation, reporting on the situation. He was highly critical of the leadership of the OETA while appearing sympathetic to Ethiopians, *Haile Selassie*, 279.

91 Richard Pankhurst, "Economic Verdict on the Italian Occupation of Ethiopia 1936–1941," *Ethiopia Observer*, 14:1 (1971).

92 Mosley, *Haile Selassie*, 279. Also depicting instances of the "robbery of his [Ethiopian's] property or the mishandling of his wife" see "Grave News from Ethiopia, by A Special Correspondent," *New Times & Ethiopia News*, 285 (October 18, 1941): 1.

93 Rennell of Rodd, *British Military Administration*, 69–71, 81–4.

modern or of value. Sylvia Pankhurst, in her booklet, *Why Are We Destroying the Ethiopian Ports?* condemned the British removal and relocation of all Italian communications technology and naval installations from Mitsiwa and Assab to Sudan, Egypt, Yemen, and India. She makes the point that the OETA decreed that none of these items were to remain in Ethiopia.[94] Leonard Mosley, roving around Ethiopia in 1941, lamented the fact that all Italian war materials – troop transports, bulldozers, artillery, and small arms – often well-used or old-fashioned but nevertheless in abundance, were to be removed from Ethiopia for the war effort. He states: "So the whole of the material was taken out of the country, and much of it was left to rot on the roads south into Kenya and across the deserts of the Sudan."[95]

After the Battle of Adwa in 1896, Italians were used as pawns to broker Ethiopian sovereignty. Emperor Menilek could fashion the terms of transitional justice to meet Ethiopian interests thereby forcing Italy and all other colonial powers to acknowledge Ethiopian independence. Circumstances were radically different in 1941, for the British monopolized the realm of transitional justice with respect to Italians rendering Haile Selassie powerless.[96] A week after arriving in Addis Ababa, the emperor appointed a seven-member cabinet.[97] Brigadier Lush informed Haile Selassie that he did not have such authority, saying "His Majesty Haile Selassie cannot fully reassume his status and powers until a peace treaty with Eritrea has been signed by Italy. Until that happens, the King of Italy must remain the legal ruler of Ethiopia."[98] Haile Selassie did not back down and the rift only grew.

Without resorting to the formalized restorative justice modalities previously discussed, Ethiopians, nevertheless, employed portions of the process that allowed atrocities to be forgiven but never forgotten. Again, in the best interests of the Ethiopian state, shards of the old justice system were imposed, when they were not overruled by the British. One such example was when Colonel Maraventano surrendered

94 Sylvia Pankhurst, *Why Are We Destroying the Ethiopian Ports*? (London: New Times & Ethiopia News Books, Woodford Green, 1952).

95 Mosley, *Haile Selassie*, 281. By contrast, Rennell of Rodd maintained that, although there was great demand for war material in North Africa and the Middle East, "little material was taken out of Ethiopia," *British Military Administration*, 94.

96 Alberto Sbacchi, "Haile Selassie and the Italians 1941–1943," *African Studies Review*, 12:1 (April 1979): 32, 35–7.

97 Haile Sellassie, *My Life and Ethiopia's Progress*, vol. 2, 167.

98 Christine Sandford, *The Lion of Judah Hath Prevailed, Being the Biography of His Imperial Majesty Haile Selassie I*, reprint (Chicago: Lushena Books, 1999), 109. Rennell of Rodd in writing the official history of the British liberation of Ethiopia paints a different picture attributing the fracas to a "misunderstanding regarding appointments," *British Military Administration*, 72.

his brigade of 8,000 to *Ras* Kassa's troops and a portion of the Gideon Force. Major Wilfred Thesiger, the same person who had observed the *wurdet* ceremony in Addis Ababa after the Battle of Segale as a young boy in 1916, was dispatched to inform Maraventano that Haile Selassie intended to hold a parade of surrendering Italian prisoners at Fiche, *Ras* Kassa's ancestral home to show their submission. After complaints about how denigrating it would be for white prisoners to be paraded before a black army, Maraventano was reprimanded by Thesiger about the atrocities Italians committed over five years and how restrained and magnanimous the Ethiopians were to merely insist on this symbolic act. In Thesiger's words,

> the Emperor sat in an open-sided tent with his son Asfa Wossen, Chapman-Andrews and a few retainers. The presence of this small, indomitable man endowed the proceedings with a strange dignity and significance. For him, as ruler of a warrior race, the parade may well have been a necessary manifestation of victory, but no hint of triumph showed on his face; he watched in silence, his expression sombre and rather sad. Ras Kassa, old and heavy, sat his mule between Johnson and myself, and watched with an impassive face the parade of the men who had murdered his sons. Nor did the assembled crowds, women as well as men, give vent to their feelings, though the relatives of many had died at Italian hands.[99]

Other sources indicate that *Ras* Kassa wanted to execute all 198 Italian officers to avenge the killing of his two sons, yet the emperor reasoned magnanimity.[100] While Ethiopians upheld the honoring, evidence insinuated that Italians disregarded the performative shaming that connotes contrition. It should be noted that there was never an "honest voice of contrition for the hideous crimes they committed" by the Italian government.[101] Justice, however, was years and successive Italian governments away.[102]

Insulated by the British and the whole Allied war strategy, the Ethiopian government was constrained by Western rule of law conceived during and applied after World War II to redress mass violence. The Nuremburg Trials were criticized as victors' justice; nevertheless, they brought Axis leaders to trial, originally convicted 21 to death, imprisoned others from fixed terms to life imprisonment and acquitted a few.

---

99 Thesiger, *The Life of My Choice*, 351.

100 David Shirreff, *Bare Feet and Bandoliers: Wingate, Sandford, the Patriots and the Part they Played in the Liberation of Ethiopia* (London: Radcliffe Press, 1995), 211.

101 Sylvia Pankhurst, "Address of Miss Sylvia Pankhurst Over Radio Addis Ababa," *Ethiopian Herald*, 32:2 (January 27, 1945): 2.

102 Providing an Italian interpretation on the impasse see Giampaolo Calchi Novati, "Re-establishing Italo-Ethiopian Relations after the War: Old Prejudices and New Policies," *Northeast African Studies*, n.s. 3:1 (1996).

The wheels of justice were slow, and Ethiopia was destined to wait. As early as 1943 the Allies initiated the United Nations War Crimes Commission to identify, classify and try war criminals from the European and East Asian theaters – but not Africa. The Commission assisted in over 30,000 cases and brought over 2,000 to trial. Seventeen Allied countries were members of the Commission – but not Ethiopia. Controversy exploded even in Whitehall with Labour parliamentarian, Creech Jones, demanding to know why Ethiopia was excluded. This caused mass circulation of memoranda within the Foreign Office arguing for and against Ethiopia's exclusion. The British government remained adamant that Ethiopia was to be excluded for three reasons. First, that the War Crimes Commission was limited to the investigation of only "the present war" meaning from 1939 to 1945. This compelled Richard Law, a spokesman for the Foreign Office to argue that the majority of war crimes were committed in 1935 through 1937 and "[t]hat was another war."[103] This contention did not hold up as China, one of the seventeen members, insisted that Japan be prosecuted for crimes dating back to 1928. Second, that the politics of allowing others besides the seventeen original members would cause future political problems as still other countries would insist on inclusion. Third, that the British government believed it was "unlikely that the Ethiopian representative would be in a position to contribute much to the Commission's proceedings."[104] Blatant racism was on display in the third yet, indirectly, may have compelled the Ethiopian government to undertake heroic efforts to overcome prejudices by developing a Ministry of Justice capable of drawing up charges against fifty Italian officials and military leaders, conforming to United Nations directives and then to mount legal proceedings against Marshals Badoglio and Graziani within severe time constraints.

A blow-by-blow account of Ethio-British machinations is provided by Richard Pankhurst in his article "Italian Fascist War Crimes in Ethiopia."[105] Suffice to say Ethiopia won yet lost. Public opinion forged by the *New York Times* article, "Ethiopia Awaits War Crime Action" persuaded Commission members, led by the United States, to allow Ethiopia in.[106] Accommodations were written into the Italian Peace Treaty of 1947, ratified in Paris, acknowledging that World War II started in October 1935 for Ethiopia, and that it retained *postlimitrium*, the understand-

---

[103] Richard Pankhurst, "Italian Fascist War Crimes in Ethiopia: A History of Their Discussion, from the League of Nations to the United Nations (1936–1949)," *Northeast African Studies*, n.s. 6:2 (1999): 96.

[104] Pankhurst, "Italian Fascist War Crimes," 100.

[105] Pankhurst, "Italian Fascist War Crimes," 83–140.

[106] Sydney Gruson, "Ethiopia Awaits War Crime Action," *New York Times* (January 31, 1945). The article documents how the British ignored a list of Italian war criminals submitted by Ethiopian diplomats.

ing that Haile Selassie's government-in-exile exercised jurisdiction after the 1935 invasion. This was crucial, since it enabled Ethiopia to argue that abuses during the whole occupation were not the internal affairs of *Africa Orientale Italiana* but were aggressions waged against another sovereign state. The treaty also included provisions for Ethiopia to try Italian war criminals through the agency of the War Crimes Commission. Here is where things were stymied, for Great Britain was still reluctant to allow Ethiopia to prosecute Badoglio for during his Prime Ministership he had sent secret communications to Britain indicating his willingness to abandon Germany and negotiate peace with the Allies. For the British, how could a key player in bringing about the cessation of hostilities face a war crimes tribunal?

Perhaps because of Ethiopia's lowly place within the Commission, perhaps because of the weight of other cases and the power of their plaintiffs, or perhaps because of British stalling tactics Ethiopia was consigned to the last five days to plead their case before the Commission was officially disbanded. All this was communicated to Ethiopia five months before its termination. In that constricted time period Haile Selassie directed the Ministry of Justice to assemble material documenting war crimes. It involved sifting through evidence to prepare charges and then bringing them before the Commission. With a decimated staff – recall Italy eliminated much of Ethiopia's intelligentsia – and reliance on some Swedish, American and, in fact, British legal advisers, Ethiopia managed to comply with the legal morass of international law. In addition, comprehending the importance of propaganda Ethiopia published *La Civilisation de l'Italie Fasciste en Ethiopie* (1948), a two-volume compendium of telegrams between Rome and fascist generals in Ethiopia ordering the use of gas and other human rights abuses, that would sway public opinion their way.[107]

In the end Ethiopia prepared two cases for the War Crimes Commission, but were preempted from ever trying them. Graziani was tried for his crimes in Europe and sentenced to nineteen years yet only served one. Ethiopia's case against Badoglio was never tried. Ethiopia's legal efforts were unsuccessful.[108] Possibly to enhance its legal stance in international circles, Ethiopia published its evidence in *Documents on Italian War Crimes; Submitted to the United Nations War Crimes Commission by the Imperial Ethiopian Government* (1949), a two-volume, airtight litigation that would be shelved in United Nations archives as a historical record of gross human rights abuses orchestrated by

---

107 *La Civilisation de l'Italie Fasciste en Ethiopie* (Addis Ababa: Ministry of the Press and Information, 1948).

108 Pankhurst, "Italian Fascist War Crimes," 135.

Ethiopia's two most reviled war criminals Marshal Rodolfo Graziani and Marshal Pietro Badoglio.[109]

The lesson of its failed attempt was to push Ethiopia to adopt international law even more. Ethiopia had to commit wholeheartedly to Westernizing its legal codes and judiciary; "legal pluralism" would no longer suffice. This becomes evident in the following chapter.

Askaris Again

Askaris again come out on the short end, but not nearly as badly as after the Battle of Adwa. That the *askaris* shouldered the brunt of the fighting and later security detail is indisputable.[110] According to British military records, the majority of the Italian fighting forces were Eritreans, Libyans, and Somalis. Each defeated Italian Colonial Battalion was comprised of mostly *askaris* who were then under the protection of British forces. *Askaris* as well as Italian soldiers were classified as enemy combatants. A tactic first employed by Orde Wingate and then later copied by other British commanders was to send a message to an Italian officer claiming that they were about to disengage and leave the battlefield to the Ethiopian Patriots to finish them off. This often convinced the Italians to surrender precisely for the protection the British afforded for both white and African troops.[111]

Well before the thorny issues of the Anglo-Ethiopian Agreements of 1942 were ratified, the War Cabinet took a more belligerent approach, dispatching Sir Philip Mitchell in June 1941 to dictate terms between the OETA and Haile Selassie. The first two points essentially put the Ethiopian government under British advisement – something like what the Italian version of the Treaty of Wechale of 1889 inferred. The third point was that jurisdiction over foreigners was "to be reserved to British courts."[112] The last two ceded Ethiopia to British military operations if required. Most galling was that Haile Selassie was not permitted to mobilize Ethiopian forces to put down internal insurrections. All of the points were hotly disputed and eventually resolved in Ethiopia's favor except point three. *Askaris*, including those from Eritrea, were subject to British law and therefore decommissioned, repatriated, or induced to serve new white officers. No severing of right hand and left foot was

109 *Documents on Italian War Crimes; Submitted to the United Nations War Crimes Commission by the Imperial Ethiopian Government*, two volumes (Addis Ababa: Ministry of Justice, 1949 & 1950).

110 Araya Habtai, "The Role of Eritrean Askaris in the Italo-Ethiopian War & under the Occupation (1935–1941)" (Addis Ababa University, Department of History, B.A. thesis, 1970).

111 Shirreff, *Bare Feet and Bandoliers*, 265.

112 Rennell of Rodd, *British Military Administration*, 75.

undertaken, no executions were ordered, in fact, imprisonment fell under prisoner of war protocols for *askaris*. In some distant regions retribution took place against identified *askaris* who had brutalized or killed local inhabitants, but all of those instances were outside the law. Conducting interviews for his B.A. thesis at Addis Ababa University, Girma Kassaye found a trace community of Eritrean *askaris* who had settled in Shashemane suggesting that some had been allowed to settle and not return to Eritrea.[113] Yet no formal edict was issued about them by the Ethiopian government.

Collaborators and the indifferent

Furnishing justice to Ethiopian citizens was the duty of the Ethiopian government and judiciary. The citizenry can be broken down into collaborators and the indifferent. Addressing them in reverse order, the indifferent comprised the bulk of the population yet their actions do not infer that they were indifferent to the loss of Ethiopian sovereignty or to becoming colonial subjects, nor does it mean that they did not take micro-actions to thwart Italian occupation. Rather, it supposes that many lived beyond the reach of the Italian garrison state and had almost no contact with the occupational forces. For them life's challenges were rudimentary: planting, reaping, and storing sufficient grain for themselves and their livestock, meeting their social responsibilities and complying with the religious obligations of whatever religion they adhered to. Other Ethiopians who lived under direct colonial occupation in cities or along transportation corridors chose to remain inactive, neither enhancing nor impeding the Italians. In Haile Selassie's autobiography it is apparent that he was aware of the material and psychological trauma indifferent Ethiopians endured for five years and recognized that the burdens of war were imposed by both the Italians and the Patriots. In many ways Haile Selassie comprehended the complexities and contradictions in lives lived and with his knowledge of the human condition he was open to reconciliation.

> It was the resident of the rural areas who bore the brunt of the wartime difficulties. It was he who was taxed by two authorities: helping patriots by providing them with provisions and protection, while also suffering from the enemy's ... weapons which burned and killed him ... The work of rehabilitating a people who had experienced moral breakdown, and whose culture had been undermined, requires going back and revisiting what had happened.[114]

---

113 Girma Kassaye. "A History of Eritrean Askaris with Special Emphasis on the Askaris who settled in the Sima Tir Hamassen Safar in Shashemane after 1947" (Addis Ababa University, Department of History, B.A. thesis, 1995).

114 Haile Sellassie, *My Life and Ethiopia's Progress*, vol. 2, 169.

Perhaps recognizing Ethiopia's reliance on agrarian output, as did the members of the *zufan chilot* or Imperial Court of preceding centuries, the first order from Haile Selassie's government was to create stable conditions for peasants to cultivate their land, or in his words: "Aware that peacetime requires one to work with as much energy and strength as in wartime, We worked tirelessly ... to alleviate all these problems."[115] Beyond the economic and infrastructural hurdles encountered to revive commerce and trade, the emperor also had to address the "moral breakdown" that divided Ethiopian society right down the middle. How does the state administer justice to sufficiently punish collaborators to placate those who thought themselves Patriots, be they actual fighters or the indifferent?

History indicates that it was exceedingly difficult to identify and prosecute collaborators. For *Dejazmach* Belay Zeleke, a Patriot leader with an unsurpassed record and a mass following, Haile Selassie's promotion of collaborators was one of the main reasons he fell out with the emperor. Identifying collaborators may have been the easier task, deciding who to bring to trial was another matter. A criterion was that the state desperately needed educated and technically savvy Ethiopians to operate the country. Italy had eliminated or caused the evacuation of a high percentage of Ethiopia's intelligentsia and even those who were refugees were delayed returning. Conversely, some Ethiopians under Italian rule had been taught how to run generators, repair electric transformers, maintain water and sewage pipes and pump stations, employ modern architectural techniques, and perform as bureaucratic functionaries. Haile Selassie judged that the state needed all these people. There was no mass amnesty, no Truth and Reconciliation Commission like in South Africa, where the accused could publicly confess, receive forgiveness and resume their careers; rather, there was just an inclination to forgive and forget, an individualized, haphazard process that reintegrated a sizeable proportion of the collaborator population. As Angelo Del Boca states, "the reader might just as easily be appalled at the unscrupulous manner with which Hayla-Sellase recycled the mediocre servants of Mussolini."[116]

There was precedent for centuries, after feudal wars soldiers and low-ranking officers were generally forgiven for their support for a wayward *Ras*. In Chapter 1, attention was given to the socio-economic nature of feudal Ethiopia and the necessity for peasants to return to their land before the rainy season to plant next year's crop. Fighting was an off-season extravagance; tilling the soil was an annual necessity. Peasants did both but societal survival was dependent on the latter. Similarly, the state was dependent on workers returning to work

---

[115] Haile Sellassie, *My Life and Ethiopia's Progress*, vol. 2, 169.

[116] Del Boca, *The Negus*, 219.

after May 1941. Another rationale surfaced: there was risk in negating all the local preferments the Italians had made especially in the countryside as their lustration or purging could have led to aggrieved *balabbats* (local elites) becoming *shifta* (brigands) using readily available Italian weapons.[117] Some collaborators, less mediocre ones, were employed in Haile Selassie's cabinet and given noteworthy portfolios. In short, those individuals' integration without reprisal was the order-of-the-day.

While the list of collaborators is lengthy, the intention here is to assess the form of justice administered by the government or sought by the offender. For this reason only a select few of the noted traitors' cases will be assessed. Essentially, these cases can be broken down into three categories. First, where conditional forgiveness was awarded and the collaborator abided by the conditions. Second, where whose who received conditional forgiveness but abused the lenient conditions were resentenced to harsher conditions. Third, where collaborators appealed to British law, thus muddying legal protocols within Ethiopia by introducing foreign procedures.

The most celebrated case in the first category was *Ras* Hailu Tekle Haymanot of Gojjam, the same man who assisted *Lij* Iyasu's escape in 1932 and for whom restorative justice had already been conditionally applied before the Italian occupation. The 1932 escape involved Italian complicity to overthrow Emperor Haile Selassie for which *Ras* Hailu was confined, yet through his agents he was still able to manage his enormous wealth which theoretically had been confiscated. After the invasion, the Italians remembered his duplicity and restored his titles and properties; in addition, they paid him 40,000 lire per month (equivalent to US $53,500 in 2024).[118] *Ras* Hailu served them well and had a role, implicitly or perhaps naively, in the executions of *Dejazmach*s Aberra and Asfa Wossen. Moreover, his own forces, comprising of up to 30,000 men, participated in counter-guerilla operations against the Patriots. *Ras* Hailu's stance was not altogether welcoming when the Gideon Force marched into Gojjam in 1941. Ultimately after holding out for two days he surrendered, after which Haile Selassie sent him back to Addis Ababa for future sentencing. Incomprehensibly, Haile Selassie merely put *Ras* Hailu under house-arrest.[119] Haile Selassie showed similar leniency towards other top-tier collaborators like *Ras* Kebede Mengesha Atikam, *Ras* Getachew Abata, and *Dejazmach* Mengesha Wube. Even *Ras* Seyoum Mengesha, the eleventh-hour Patriot who assisted British forces in liberating Tigray, was pardoned for treason as

117 Richard Greenfield, *Ethiopia: A New Political History* (New York: Frederick A. Praeger, 1965), 277.
118 Bahru Zewde, *Modern Ethiopia*, 167.
119 Greenfield, *Ethiopia: A New Political History*, 278.

a pawn in Italy's subjugation of Ethiopia.[120] His sympathies were hard to decipher; *Ras* Seyoum performed a masterful balancing act between supporting Italy and supporting Ethiopia. In the end he was appointed *Negus* over Tigray in 1941 by the Italians to hinder its liberation. Not only did Haile Selassie forgive him but appointed him titularly governor of Tigray while keeping him under his nose in official residence in Addis Ababa. To occupy him, *Ras* Seyoum was appointed sporadically to the Crown Council (the updated *zufan chilot* or Imperial Court).

While seeming to replicate the restorative justice modalities of old, two key differences were present. First, after liberation Haile Selassie relied upon his own judgement more, partly because the senior tier of aristocrats had been depleted or had shown disloyalty, thus, advice from the *mekwanint* did not have the gravitas of the *zufan chilot* where in former times a council of nobles voiced their opinions and declared how a certain action would affect their province or the nation as a whole by either granting amnesty or advocating punishment. Second, Haile Selassie had been determined to replace the nobility with professional bureaucrats. The Italian occupation simply gave Haile Selassie the opportunity to do so at an accelerated rate. Moreover, *shum shir* (appoint-demote) had forever been an imperial strategy, but after liberation when the landed aristocracy was at its weakest, Haile Selassie elevated it to become a governing principle. *Shum shir* allowed him to keep remnants of the old aristocratic class and ambitious, young aspirants from gaining solid regional power bases from which they could challenge him.[121] Emperor Haile Selassie's decreeing who was to be granted conditional forgiveness in many ways fit within the paradigms of *shum shir* for it kept some of disgraced collaborators in the mix and counterbalanced the emergent Patriots who believed they were owed governorships and patronage.

Illustrating the erosion of restorative justice was the case of Belay Zeleke, arguably Ethiopia's most effective Patriot and an immensely popular national hero.[122] He had fought tirelessly throughout the occupation, gaining wide recognition amongst rank-and-file soldiers, yet his ego made it difficult for other Patriot leaders to work with him.[123] Kept hanging around in Addis Ababa for nine months, Belay Zeleke observed less noted Patriots and even collaborators receiving promotion. This infuriated him and increased his animosity towards Haile Selassie especially when the position of Governor General of Gojjam was passed

120 Del Boca, *The Negus*, 216.
121 Donald Levine, *Interpreting Ethiopia* (Los Angeles: Teshai, 2014), ch. 23 "Šum Šir".
122 Asfa-Wossen Asserate, *King of Kings*, 177.
123 Zelalem Assefa, "Dajazmach Baläy Zallaqa (1912–1945)" B.A. thesis, Department of History, Addis Ababa University (1983), 49–50.

to Hailu Balaw. Finally, Haile Selassie elevated him to a *dejazmach* and made him sub-governor of Bechana, a small district of Gojjam. Belay Zeleke felt slighted and set about governing his district as if a sovereign. He bestowed titles such as *fitawrari*, *dejazmach*, and even *ras* on his relatives and followers, conferred *gult* rights to land in his area and neighboring districts, kept tax revenue, and defied directives from the Governor of Gojjam and the emperor to rescind those decrees.[124] In addition, Belay Zeleke began accusing the emperor of having fled the country, having betrayed those who fought in the resistance and having promoted collaborators. Relations continued to deteriorate, even after Crown Prince Asfa Wossen tried to mediate. They ended in open insurrection in early 1943. Fighting lasted three months and on the brink of defeat Belay Zeleke surrendered in what is known as the Battle of Somma. Despite the promise of amnesty given on the battlefield, Belay Zeleke was put on trial soon after he arrived in Addis Ababa and sentenced to death. The most spirited advocates for his execution were two of the other most respected Patriot leaders, Abebe Aregay and Mesfin Sileshi. The execution was to take place back in Gojjam but because of the rainy season, Belay Zeleke and his jailers returned to Addis where the emperor commuted his sentence to life imprisonment. This was a rather stiff penalty. Restitution was not out of the question. In the case of Worku Itateku, the telegraphist who had passed secret messages to Marshal Graziani, the court decreed death for high treason, yet Haile Selassie commuted the sentence to twenty years and when Worku Itateku had served his time, the emperor restored all his property.[125]

Belay Zeleke, however, abused the terms of his punishment. In Waliso prison, Belay Zeleke conspired with three other disgruntled Patriots, plotted an escape and with their supporters from outside wounded and killed a number of guards in the breakout.[126] Recaptured on the outskirts of the city, the offenders stood trial for murder, not insurrection, and were hanged on January 12, 1945 in accordance with Ethiopia's Penal Code. One of the conspirators, Mammo Hailu, was the son of the arch-collaborator *Ras* Hailu Tekle Haymanot, who had been treated leniently. Here, the father was forced to sit as one of the judges at his son's capital punishment trial.[127]

Two issues can be decoded from Belay Zeleke's case about the erosion of restorative justice. First, honor and shaming had little place after liberation. No shaming ceremony or *wurdet* was choreographed, nor were the terms of conditional forgiveness noted by official memory-

---

124 Zelalem Assefa, "Dajazmach Baläy Zallaqa," 63–6.

125 Del Boca, *The Ethiopian War*, 263.

126 Zelalem Assefa, "Dajazmach Baläy Zallaqa," 72–3; Asfa-Wossen Asserate, *King of Kings*, 177.

127 Greenfield, *Ethiopia: A New Political History*, 279.

keepers. The trial, if it can be called such, was concealed from the public, although their hangings were in public squares. Second, as already alluded to, the judges at this trial were not the *mekwanint* of old, although *Ras* Hailu would have qualified as one. The trial platform adjudicated the case based on codified law, not on what would be best for societal reconciliation. The only similarity to traditional restorative justice was that when conditional forgiveness was abused the offender could be resentenced to harsher conditions including death.

The third category of cases introduced legal confusion which reached its height following liberation. In this case "Italian-made *Ras*" Haile Selassie Gugsa appealed to British law to shelter himself from Haile Selassie's wrath.

Son of a prominent line of Tigrean nobles, Haile Selassie Gugsa was a young, volatile man who felt slighted after his father died in 1933 when most of Tigray was put under the authority of *Ras* Seyoum Mengesha. To assuage his anger, Haile Selassie gave him the title *dejazmach*, governorship of Mekele region and integrated him into the royal family by arranging the marriage of the emperor's youngest daughter Zenebe Work, age fifteen, who died a year later from influenza.[128] Well before the invasion, Haile Selassie Gugsa was feted by Italian officials in Asmara who promised him nearly anything. In response he said, "I am ready to obey whatever Italy orders; ready to join with Italian troops."[129] Indeed he did: at the beginning of hostilities he defected with 10,000 men to the Italian side, doing irreparable damage to Ethiopia's northern offensive. During the occupation Haile Selassie Gugsa served as a faithful Italian lackey.[130]

Tigray was one of the last places where Italian troops resisted British forces. Understanding the end was near, Haile Selassie Gugsa surrendered to the British.[131] Surprisingly, the OETA rewarded Haile Selassie Gugsa with the governorship of half of liberated Tigray. Showing no remorse or sense of gratitude, he continued to correspond with Fascist Italy.[132] Infuriated, though still turning down Ethiopia's extradition request, the British secreted Haile Selassie Gugsa to the Seychelles where they kept him in confinement until 1946.[133] Contending interpretations of the laws of war appear to be at the heart of the impasse between the OETA and the Ethiopian government. To finally attain his extradition Ethiopia had to promise that Haile Selassie Gugsa would be

128 Marcus, *Haile Sellassie I*, 140–2. Mosley claims Princess Zenebe-Work was married at age thirteen and died two years later "beaten, bullied and humiliated by her drunken husband," *Haile Selassie*, 198.

129 Marcus, *Haile Sellassie I*, 141.

130 Mosley, *Haile Selassie*, 197–200.

131 Gruson, "Ethiopia Awaits War Crime Action."

132 Haile Sellassie, *My Life and Ethiopia's Progress*, vol. 2, 174.

133 Haile Sellassie, *My Life and Ethiopia's Progress*, vol. 2, 174, ft. 289.

tried in the High Court in which foreign judges sat and with a promise that there would be no execution. The trial record published in *The Ethiopian Herold* was a far cry from traditional forms of restorative justice.

Arguments for the defense were made by Ato Gila Mikael Bahta who basically argued that Haile Selassie Gugsa was a very young man under psychological duress because his wife and expected child had died, and later his father. In an unsound state of mind, the Italians wined and dined him in Asmara and showed him the awesome power of their military, and "because of his youth and the lack of counselors" he did not betray the emperor but "surrendered" to Italy.[134]

The guilty judgement was read on July 30, 1947 in an opinion of 8 to 1. According to the Ethiopian Penal Code, Haile Selassie Gugsa was found guilty for High Treason, guilty for Aiding the Enemy, guilty for Rebellion Against Government, guilty for Collaborating with the Enemy, but not guilty for Insubordination.[135] Each one of these verdicts listed multiple Articles that had been broken.

The whole trial was conducted on European terms. The verdict of the "The Dedjasmatch Gugsa Trial" as recorded in *The Ethiopian Herald* on August 4, 1947 could have been a part of the court record in any European country. Seven of the eight judges in the Majority Opinion were Ethiopians, Sigard Lund was a Swede. The Minority Opinion was written by Leonard Robert Mullen, an Englishman. In the end, Haile Selassie Gugsa spent thirty-eight years in prison where he died in 1985.[136]

Leniency Still a Hallmark of Ethiopian Justice

Back in 1943 when Ethiopia was denied admittance to the United Nations War Crimes Commission, the pretext was that the Italian invasion took place before World War II, therefore, it was another war. The rejoinder was to ask, why wasn't China excluded when it insisted that Japanese war crimes went back to 1928? Upon that logic, Ethiopia eventually was admitted. As China and Ethiopia were early victims of Axis aggression, it is relevant to compare how they treated collaborators. In short, the manner in which Ethiopia administered justice was far more lenient than the way China dealt with collaborators who worked with Japanese occupiers. As Yun Xia records in *Down with Traitors: Justice and Nationalism in Wartime China*, collaborators were called *hanjian* (literally, traitors of the Han Chinese). The effort was to root them out and prosecute them. The trials were little more than showpieces but very popular and widely covered in the media. Verdicts were impris-

134 "The Dedjasmatch Gugsa Trial," *The Ethiopian Herald*, 5:6 (August 4, 1947): 2.
135 "The Dedjasmatch Gugsa Trial," *The Ethiopian Herald*, 5:6 (August 4, 1947): 3.
136 Haile Sellassie, *My Life and Ethiopia's Progress*, vol. 2, 174, ft. 289.

onment or execution. Cleansing China of *hanjian* was a policy shared by the Nationalists and Communists alike even during the civil war leading to Mao Zedung's victory in 1949 and for years afterwards in both China and Taiwan. Both parties looked upon them as enemies of the state such that the term *hanjian* became an epithet. "Any unpatriotic opinion or action can be branded as *hanjian*."[137] No attempt was made to restore the *hanjian* into society much less the administration. Ethiopia was far more humane, more forgiving.

[137] Yun Xia, *Down with Traitors: Justice and Nationalism in Wartime China* (Seattle and London: University of Washington Press, 2018).

7

The 1960 Coup d'État: Restorative Justice Ignored

The 1960 Coup d'État, led by brothers Germame and Mengistu Neway, marks the abrupt right turn in Emperor Haile Selassie's reign, ending his struggle to consolidate power against foreign and domestic challengers and inaugurating his determination to hang on to power while deaf to the counsel of trusted advisers and blind to societal signposts. As Bahru Zewde states: "In the three decades between Liberation and Revolution, no event shook the imperial regime or attracted as much public attention as the abortive coup d'état of December 1960."[1] The plotters tested the regime to its core and their suppression challenged the monarchy to implement a just solution.

Serving justice, or not, is the focus of this chapter. The first section probes a wide-ranging analysis of the intellectual currents coursing through Ethiopia at the time. It concentrates on the Qachane Club, for many of the drivers of the coup and countercoup were members of this social and intellectual club. The second section outlines the adoption of European legal practices in Ethiopia by focusing on procedural developments in the courts and the reorganization of the Ministry of Justice. This is followed by an account of the coup d'état as background for the trial of the plotters, the most noted of whom was Mengistu Neway. Comprehending how hanging from a rope in the middle of a square in Addis Ababa would ensure his place in history as a revolutionary martyred for his cause, Mengistu Neway did not appeal his death sentence or seek other means of redress. The trial was an outright rejection of restorative justice and, if probed further in cases of less prominent supporters of the coup d'état, the tricky reconciliation process showed elements of traditional restorative justice long practiced by the state, yet with omissions that reduced its ability to bring about reconciliation.

Qachane Club and Intellectual Fermentation

Quantum changes affected Addis Ababa between 1941 and 1960, not so much in terms of infrastructure and outward appearance, although the

1 Bahru Zewde, *The Quest for Socialist Ethiopia: The Ethiopian Student Movement c. 1960–1974* (Woodbridge: James Currey, 2014), 55.

city saw improvements and growth, but in terms of the psychology of the population. The intelligentsia and aristocracy had been decimated by the Italians and yet within less than twenty years a new generation of Western-educated intellectuals had returned to assume ever more important positions in government. Government expanded at an astounding rate: ministries came into being, civil institutions formed, and bilateral development projects multiplied. Employment in salaried, bureaucratic positions offered easy access to bank loans for houses and cars. The screening criterion was education. Schools feeding University College improved their curricula dramatically to meet the expectations of Ethiopia's preeminent institution of higher education whose faculty was largely comprised of foreign academics. Bright Ethiopians were recruited from all provinces, their university enrollment attesting to formalized tracks for meritorious advancement and elite family connections. At the apex were those who studied in foreign countries under government scholarships.

The private sector rebooted quickly with the Mercato (Ethiopia's largest market) drawing merchants who established supply chains stretching to the borders and beyond.[2] Foreign firms were apportioned import/export licenses so as to politically accommodate European, American, and Asian interests, yet all were staffed with Ethiopians in the mid and lower tiers. The sprouts of a capitalist middle class were emerging. *Berhanena Selam*, the government's newspaper, gave the literati license to express alternate viewpoints – within reason. Art and theater became professionalized. In the economic sector a sense of optimism prevailed. The adage that Ethiopia could become the "breadbasket of Africa" pointed to a belief in the transformation of agriculture that animated strategists who gauged Ethiopia's potential and believed that, if only some cultural impediments were removed, Ethiopia's future was assured.[3] Walt Rostow's "take off theory," was the ideology that buttressed this optimism for it outlined how certain socio-cultural conditions had to be overcome to enable a society to jump from primitive production to extractive industries and finally towards mass consumption.[4] The problem for many educated Ethiopians was that tackling the entrenched feudal order was not happening quickly enough.

---

2 The government provided a comprehensive assessment of Ethiopia's economy that demonstrated how far it had come, see *Economic Handbook: December 1958* (Addis Ababa: Ministry of Commerce and Industry, 1958).

3 For a patronizing and pejorative inditement of traditional Ethiopia and an unabashed celebration of modernity see Edith Lord, "The Impact of Education on Non-Scientific Beliefs in Ethiopia," *Journal of Social Psychology*, 47 (1958): 339–53.

4 W. W. Rostow, *The Stages of Economic Growth: A Non-Communist Manifesto* (Cambridge: Cambridge University Press, 1960).

The Qachane Club was located on the grounds of *Ras* Imru's Addis Ababa compound, a short walk from Haile Selassie's palace – now Addis Ababa University, Sidist Kilo campus. Its history is rather opaque; nevertheless, it appears *Ras* Imru gave his only son, Mikael Imru, permission to invite his friends over to fraternize and discuss global issues. By 1954 property was given or lent to the club to erect a library into which many members deposited their personal book collections. All was not serious as there appeared to have been ample time for casual conversation, games, alcohol, and recreation.[5]

Ras Imru – cousin and confidant to His Majesty, Patriot leader, prisoner-of-war in Italy and progressive thinking aristocrat – was appointed Ambassador to the United States in 1947. *Ras* Imru's own political leanings spanned the spectrum and certainly were not limited to American capitalist dogma; if anything, *Ras* Imru was receptive to aspects of socialist and communist ideology as demonstrated in his land reform initiatives to empower peasants on his properties back in Ethiopia. Beyond his diplomatic portfolio, *Ras* Imru cared for and cultivated the intellectual growth of the first post-war generation of Ethiopian scholarship students to study in America. Parenthetically, there were few other Ethiopians residing in or traveling to America so consular duties were minimal. While his own son, Mikael, pursued a degree in England, many of the scions of Ethiopia's elite did study in America. *Ras* Imru took personal interest in the Ethiopian students, corresponding with those who were distant, and engaging with those who studied near Washington D.C., one being Germame Neway – generally considered the brains behind the eventual coup – who received his B.A. from the University of Wisconsin and his M.A. from Columbia University. *Ras* Imru's mentoring went as far as to encourage this rather small cadre of elite students to organize to better prepare themselves to assume leadership positions once they returned to Ethiopia. The Qachane Club was one manifestation of this sentiment.

It is important to note that Germame Neway's radicalization likely took place after he returned to Ethiopia, especially after he began to gain administrative experience as governor of Wollamo and Jigjiga successively.[6] Germame's M.A. thesis at Columbia was on white set-

5 Tekeste Melake, "The 1960 Coup d'État in Ethiopia," M.A. thesis in History, Addis Ababa University (1990), 50.

6 Donald Levine, "On the December 1960 Coup Attempt," *Africa Today,* 8:5 (May 1961), republished in the anthology *Interpreting Ethiopia: Observations of Five Decades* (Los Angeles: Tsehai, 2014), ch. 24. This was the piece that made Levine persona non-grata for the Haile Selassie regime, a state ultimately to be rescinded through the intervention of University College, Vice President Harold Bentley on the grounds of academic freedom. In a carbon-copy of a private letter Levine wrote to Haile Selassie thanking him for withdrawing the order and appointing him to the new Haile Selassie I University, he wrote, "I

tlement policy in Kenya. It only concludes with reference to the Mau Mau insurrection in the last pages of the typed manuscript even though Mau Mau dominated Kenyan media at the time.[7] What is noteworthy about his thesis is its staid bibliography – its lack of radical thinkers or Marxian theorists. The thesis is bland, yet a few passages illuminate his deep-seated desire for revolutionary change. Reflecting Hegelian dialectics, he states:

> Social institutions display organic characteristics in their evolvement. Left to their normal course of development, they undergo a metamorphose change usually from a lower stage to a higher and more complex structure. Because of the time the normal course would take ... it might essentially be found necessary to introduce into society ... a higher form of political institutions [*sic.*]. Under such a transplanting process of properly selected and adaptable new institutions into an old social climate, planning and carrying out of certain preparatory activities become absolutely necessary. For instance, the indigenous institutions which are genial to the new ones must be systematically cultivated, and the ones which are actively anachronous in their qualities must be either neutralized or rendered impotent by the proper measures.[8]

It is difficult to conclusively describe Germame Neway's personality. In a highly accusatory and antagonistic correspondence about the attempted coup two years afterwards, Willard Park, an American anthropologist who undertook 200 interviews with credible sources after the coup d'état states that a classmate of Germame's viewed him as "a 'Little Hitler", even in the school days, he was not at any time interested in human welfare or Ethiopian development, his only interest was in getting himself in a position of power."[9] Responding with equal conviction, Donald Levine counters, "True, he was authoritarian to a degree; all political leaders are. But I saw him at work in Jigjiga, a performance far superior to any of the dozens of other provincial governors whose work I observed firsthand." Levine admits that Germame was not the man to have led the coup; however, he "talked with [Germame] at length about the Somali problem, and heard

---

have been deeply moved by the letter from Your Imperial Majesty dated July 31 [1961]. The message it brings is an eloquent expression of Your Majesty's magnanimity ... If I have written somewhat rashly in the article ... it is because for the moment I loved Ethiopia 'not wisely, but too well.'" Correspondence Donald Levine to Emperor Haile Selassie, August 18, 1961.

7 Surprisingly Jomo Kenyatta's own work *Kenya, the Land of Conflict* (1945) is not referenced.

8 Germame Neway, "The Impact of the White Settlement Policy in Kenya," M.A. thesis in Political Science, Columbia University (1954), 95–6.

9 Willard Park, letter to Donald Levine, Addis Ababa, May 2, 1962.

generous and enlightened thoughts on the matter unparalleled by anything else I heard in the country."[10]

The Qachane Club appeared popular and inviting at the beginning as a place where those privileged sons could meet, talk, play games, include wives or girlfriends, and party, but soon talk turned to serious discussions over the direction Ethiopia should take. Its membership was like a roster of offspring with ancestral lineages to the highest families. Discussions ranged broadly. Praise for the Pan Africanist ideas of George Padmore and other Marxist-leaning authorities radicalized Germame and other Qachane members.[11] Examples from Russia, China, and India offered pathways towards liberation. For Ethiopians, the issue was less about obtaining liberation from the colonialism that consumed the rest of Africa and more about release from the strictures of a stifling feudal order. The Free Officers Movement which led to the Egyptian Revolution and the downfall of King Farouk illustrated how a monarchy could be overthrown. Mohamed Naguib and Gamal Abdel Nasser were not bashful in denouncing the corruption, nepotism, and injustice of Egypt's monarchy.[12] Ethiopia's literati saw parallels to their own country. Flaming discord among Qachane members was the issue of how to bring substantive change while accommodating Ethiopia's three-legged stool: the monarchy, the aristocracy, and the church. Realizing "the abyss between Addis Ababa and the rest of the country [was] deeper than the Blue Nile gorge,"[13] Qachane members assessed the importance of the triumvirate to determine what could be changed and what the population could tolerate – which "anachronous [institutions] must be either neutralized or rendered impotent."[14] Eliminating the aristocracy was nearly impossible because ethnic relations were bound up in longstanding communal ties that coursed up and down the social economic ladder. Changing the church was a no-go from the start for religious beliefs defined the hegemonic Christian population. It was agreed that the monarchy unified the nation, but history had shown the form and embodiment of the monarchy had been subject to change.[15] Once identified, questions about what shape the monarchy should take produced divisions among Qachane members.

10 Donald Levine, letter to Willard Park, Detroit, Michigan, May 8, 1962.

11 Richard Greenfield, *Ethiopia: A New Political History* (New York: Frederick Praeger, 1965), 343–6.

12 Gamal Abdel Nasser, *Egypt's Liberation: The Philosophy of Revolution* (Washington D.C.: Public Affairs Press, 1955); Anwar el Sadat, *Revolt on the Nile* (New York: John Day, 1957); and Joel Gordon, *Nasser's Blessed Movement: Egypt's Free Officers and the July Revolution* (Oxford: Oxford University Press, 1992).

13 Jeanne Contini, "The Winds of Change and the Lion of Judah," *The Reporter,* 24:2 (May 25, 1961): 34.

14 Germame Neway, "The Impact of the White Settlement Policy in Kenya," 96.

15 Donald Levine, "Legitimacy in Ethiopia" (1964) in *Interpreting Ethiopia*, ch. 4.

Over time the Qachane Club divided into three groups led by Germame Neway, Mikael Imru, and Amha Abera the grandson of *Ras* Kassa. Differences between the first two were both semantic and pragmatic yet sufficient to create barriers in their push to change the socio-economic positioning of Ethiopia. Germame Neway sought radical change; Mikael Imru took a more incrementalist stance pushing the progressive ideas of his father steps further. Amha Abera's more moderate group, which included Zewde Gabre-Selassie and Endalkachew Makonnen, both future prominent officials within Haile Selassie's government, "did not have much of a quarrel with the existing regime."[16] Fast forward, the list of Qachane Club members who were implicated in the 1960 Coup d'État included Germame Neway, Lemma Frehiwot, and Germame Wondafrash; those involved in its resolution included Zewde Gabre-Selassie as Minister of Justice, with Endalkachew Makonnen and Mikael Imru trying to mediate once they returned to Ethiopia from their ambassadorial assignments.[17]

While there is no record of the issues discussed or minutes depicting who said what at Qachane, the evolution of progressive thought can be traced by perusing published student journals. The first student publication was *The Lion Cub* published by the Ethiopian Student Society (ESS). Started in 1949 in Britain, it had as its objective to bring together Ethiopian students studying in Europe and to assist in their acculturation into Western society. Mary Tadesse's list of society officers almost replicates Qachane Club membership with Zewde Gabre-Selassie, Mikael Imru, Endalkachew Makonnen, Mengistu Lemma, plus herself all being officers of ESS and most of them serving as its presidents.[18]

On the other side of the Atlantic, Ethiopian students in the United States and Canada formed the Ethiopian Students Union of North America (ESUNA) in 1948. In 1950 ESUNA organized a retreat at Lake Esquagama in Minnesota which fifty-five of the sixty-five Ethiopian students attended. To open the retreat an address was read, reputedly written by Emperor Haile Selassie, encouraging them to study hard as the nation was relying on them. Overseeing the retreat was Ambassador *Ras* Imru.[19] Both student unions were subsidized by the emperor and, as such, much praise was lavished on him while criticisms were veiled – "wax-and-gold" yet again. ESUNA appeared somewhat directionless until its second president, Germame Neway, took control. He started a newsletter called *Ethiopian Student News* (later

16 Tekeste Melake, "The 1960 Coup d'État in Ethiopia," 52. Greenfield also refers to them, *Ethiopia: A New Political History*, 355.

17 Tekeste Melake provides a longer list of members, "The 1960 Coup d'État in Ethiopia," 51.

18 Mary Tadesse, *My Life, My Ethiopia: A Diary of History and Love* (Trenton: Red Sea Press, 2021), 122.

19 Bahru Zewde, *The Quest for Socialist Ethiopia*, 98–9.

to become *Challenge: Journal of the Ethiopian Students Association of North America*), and under his leadership changed the tone of ESUNA to address the serious responsibilities his cohort of educated elites owed to their native land, ironically on the same wavelength as the emperor. Some of the provocative articles lamented the level of illiteracy in Ethiopia. Students always prefaced criticism of the educational system by acknowledging the massacre of Ethiopia's prewar intelligentsia by the Italians and the extraordinary measures Haile Selassie had taken to rebuild and staff schools that raised enrollment from approximately 30,000 in 1946 to nearly 135,000 in 1958.[20] Yet, despite the Ministry of Education's avowal to raise literacy through community schools, Ethiopia lagged miles behind other African countries. For Mulugetta Wodajo and many others, the aim of education was social change – "a reflection of the nation's deliberate efforts to undergo gradual social and political changes."[21] The question was how to implement change. The easy solution was education, but the timeframe appeared inestimable and patience was running out.

While considered tame in comparison to the vitriol of the 1960s and 1970s, cumulatively the criticisms added up to such an extent that Mary Tadesse states in her autobiography that before the coup d'état there were "rumblings here and there of dissatisfaction" in the 1950s.[22] On the whole, the writings up to the 1960 Coup were satirical, poking fun at the culture and state, while largely remaining apolitical although pointing to issues that needed remedy, like education and land tenure. Noteworthy is that few of these issues were original, in fact, most of these issues were being raised with the emperor, his inner circle or by the newly elected parliamentarians who took their seats in 1957.[23]

The three pillars characterizing the assault on the old order as seen in the student journals *Challenge* and *Struggle*, published after the coup, were class struggle, the nationalities question, and land tenure. Each had some influence on Germame Neway and other putschists. Marx's writings on class struggle were certainly well known by Qachane members through their own readings and through the influence of professors, for some American and European social scientists were sympathetic to Marxism.[24] Marxist-Leninist books were hot items on library shelves across America both among left-leaning Americans

20 Mulugeta Wodajo, "Ethiopian Education: A Medium for Social Change," *Phi Delta Kappan: A Journal for the Promotion of Research, Service, and Leadership in Education*, XLI:4 (January 1960): 159.

21 Mulugeta Wodajo, "Postwar Reform in Ethiopian Education," *Comparative Education Review*, 2:3 (February 1959): 29.

22 Mary Tadesse, *My Life, My Ethiopia*, 142.

23 Reidulf Molvaer, *Black Loins: The Creative Lives of Modern Ethiopia's Literary Giants and Pioneers* (Lawrenceville: Red Sea Press, 1997), 117–18.

24 Elleni Centime Zeleke, *Ethiopia in Theory: Revolution and Knowledge Production, 1964–2016* (Chicago: Haymarket Books, 2020), 99–102.

and foreign students. Germame Neway was presumed to be a Marxist yet, looking ahead, there was no active intervention from Moscow and there was no overly Marxist tone to the coup d'état, discounting its Leninist violence.[25] Moreover, the Soviet Union was among the first countries to congratulate Haile Selassie on stamping out the insurrection.[26] Class struggle was the fuse that ignited the Red Terror after 1974 because it was so clearly impossible to easily and universally apply to Ethiopia. Fighting between the Ethiopia Peoples' Revolutionary Party (EPRP) and Meison (the All-Ethiopian Socialist Movement, an alternate student-led party), and later the military Derg was largely over each party's interpretation of Marxism.[27] This was nowhere to be seen in 1960. The nationalities question was bandied around before the coup but with less fervor for in reality Qachane Club members were largely Amhara[28] or Tigrean. While Haile Selassie began to diversify his scholarship students to reflect Ethiopia's ethnic diversity, these graduates were the new returnees still going to the Central Personnel Agency every day to wait to be placed in government positions. They did not have the panache to place ethnicity into the center of the political debate at that time.

Land tenure, however, was an age-old problem. "Land to the Tiller" was a popular refrain. Power and income disparities based on access to land and labor underpinned the political economy of Ethiopia. Everyone recognized that something should be done about it, even the emperor. In a speech delivered a year after the abortive coup, Haile Selassie, perhaps to quell lingering revolutionary zeal aroused by the Neway brothers, perhaps because he believed in it, stated:

> The fundamental obstacle to the realization of the full measure of Ethiopia's agricultural potential has been, simply stated, lack of security in the land. The fruits of the farmer's labor must be enjoyed by

25 A long debate surfaces in the literature as to whether Germame Neway was a communist. A foreign contemporary who knew him well maintains he was not, Greenfield, *Ethiopia: A New Political History*, 346, 352.

26 Czeslaw Jesman, *The Ethiopian Paradox* (New York: Oxford University Press, 1963), 71.

27 Standard works on the Ethiopian Revolution expose the deep cleavages between combatting parties claiming their authentic Marxist interpretation, see for example, Fred Halliday and Marine Molyneux, *The Ethiopian Revolution* (London: Verso, 1981); René Lefort, *Ethiopia: An Heretical Revolution?* (London: Zed Press, 1981); Christopher Clapham, *Transformation and Continuity in Revolutionary Ethiopia* (Cambridge: Cambridge University Press, 1988); and Edmond Keller, *Revolutionary Ethiopia: From Empire to People's Republic* (Bloomington: Indiana University Press, 1991).

28 Reidulf Molvaer notes that Germame Neway's grandfather, who shares his name, "was one of Menilek's loyal followers and the one who proposed and engineered the removal of non-Shewan nobles from the centre of political power by posting them in remote areas, thus ensuring the rise of Shewan nobility," *Black Loins*, 130, n. 109.

> him whose toil has produced the crop. The essence of land reform is, while fully respecting the principle of private ownership, that landless people must have the opportunity to possess their own land ... It is Our aim that every Ethiopian own his own land.[29]

The difficulty was how and when to implement land reform. The "how and when" befuddled the regime and its critics.

The pressure to reform intensified throughout 1960, for in that year nearly all of the French colonies became independent and Nigeria, Africa's most populous country, won independence from Great Britain. The Belgians abruptly and calamitously pulled out of Congo. Closer to home Somalia received independence in July of 1960. Optimism, voiced by a younger generation of African leaders, was in the air.

The Courts and the Ministry of Justice

Turning from the intellectual milieu that planted the seeds for the coup d'état to the judiciary that prosecuted the coup-makers, the following pages will be given over to developments in the legal realm that drew the Ethiopian regime away from restorative justice mechanisms previously used to bring societal healing. The 1950s introduced numerous initiatives from the first Five-Year Plan to installing the first parliament. Judicial reform was equally impressive, in 1957 the revised penal code was proclaimed,[30] followed by the civil code, commercial code, and amended maritime laws all with the imprint of French jurists that was in keeping with Haile Selassie's consequential decision to favor French codified law that shaped the Ethiopian Penal Code of 1930. Remember, strict delineation in law was anathema to restorative justice. The place to begin to determine how the judiciary assumed the veneer of modern, Western legal procedure is to look at the transformation of the courts.

A lasting effect of the Occupied Enemy Territory Administration (OETA) was to plant British jurists in the Imperial High Court where their commitment to procedural reform renovated how law was carried out in Ethiopia. While there were courts above and below the Imperial High Court (see Chart 1), the Imperial High Court was where the majority of civil, criminal and commercial cases were tried, and its verdicts set precedents for other Ethiopian courts to follow. "The High Court ... visited all parts of the empire" setting standards on how

---

29 Quote found in Hagos Gabre Yesus, "Land Reform: Plus ça change ... .?" *Challenge: Journal of the Ethiopian Students Association of North America,* vol. 5 (March 1965): 7.

30 Penal Code of the Empire of Ethiopia, *Negarit Gazeta* – Extraordinary issue, No. 1, 1957.

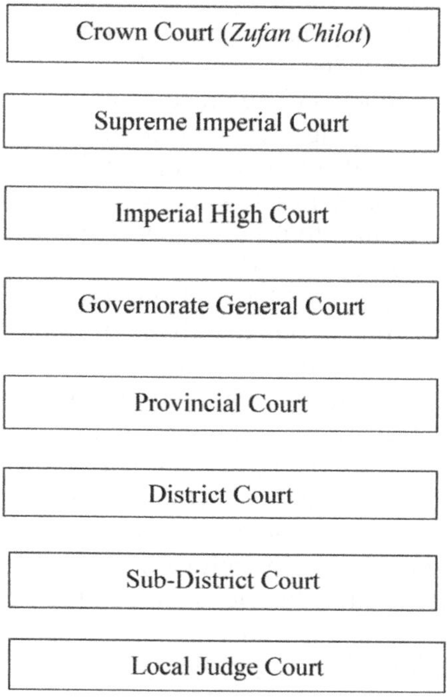

Chart 1 Imperial Ethiopian Court Structure between 1947 and 1961. Source: Originally promulgated in Administration of Justice Proclamations of 1942. The court structure was later added to by Aberra Jembere, *Legal History of Ethiopia*, 221.

to conduct trials.[31] British judges were a minority within the court, but their influence belied their numbers as the President was always British until 1967 and the British judges, such as Nathan Marein, often taught fellow Ethiopian judges how to operate a modern court including insistence on appropriate police procedures for the accused beforehand, use of statutory evidence during the trial, appropriate sentencing, and humane prison conditions for the imprisoned afterwards. In his own words, Marein's book, *The Ethiopian Empire: Federation and Laws*, was to "make this a practical book for lawyers and judges in the Empire of Ethiopia and foregone theoretical divisions for the sake of practicality."[32] Given the theoretical underpinning of British legal procedure

31 "Ethiopia Today: A Review of the Progress Made in the Last Three Years," *The Ethiopian Herald*, 11:2 (September 9, 1944): 2.

32 Nathan Marein, *The Ethiopian Empire: Federation and Laws* (Rotterdam: Royal Netherlands Printing and Lithographing Company, 1955), 16.

by their British colleagues and witnessing its practical application in the courts, the Ethiopian judges began "developing professional confidence to the extent that they began to stand in dissent against their foreign colleagues while deciding on court cases."[33] Because they had the numbers, Ethiopian judges were often in the majority. Essentially, their dissent was a result of developing confidence in the hybridization of Ethiopian jurisprudence, the amalgam of divergent legal strains previously discussed that, to briefly repeat, included the *Fitha Negest*, French codified law brought to Ethiopia via Indochina and written into the Ethiopian Penal Code of 1930 and carrying on into the Penal and Civil Codes of 1957 and 1960 respectively, Italian inputs forced upon the Ethiopian population and, after 1941, traces of English common law but mostly British legal procedures. That Ethiopian judges had a better handle on this admixture likely stems from the fact that they were immersed in it. They were forced by their nationality to make a workable legal tradition that represented Ethiopian interests.

As an aside, Haile Selassie appeared blind to this eclectic mixture; to his mind he was rationally reforming law to serve Ethiopians. "Justice," His Majesty said, "is the prime life for freedom and government and it is because of this that We have dedicated Our life since the age of 18 to codify laws for Our peoples concerning all aspects of their activities in life."[34]

All did not go smoothly in the Imperial High Court. To dilute British influence, Emperor Haile Selassie invited Sweden to recruit jurists to serve on the court. Stemming from Lutheran missionary efforts in the nineteenth century, Sweden had a long history in Ethiopia, always trying to ply a semi-neutral stance between European imperial interests and Ethiopian independence.[35] In 1946 Baron Eric Leihondfound and Sigard Lund were appointed as Solicitor-General and Assistant Solicitor-General to take charge of public prosecution.[36] Soon Baron Leihondfound was chosen to lead the Ethiopian War Crime Commission (see chapter 6), to the dismay of the British. A "long, drawn-out tug of war" between the British and Swedish judicial staff ensued. The British viewed the Swedes as "stooges" and "yes men" of the Ethiopian government and particularly the Ministry of Justice, which, they maintained, dictated to the Swedish judges whom to prosecute.[37]

---

33 Esubalew Belay Fanta, "A History of the Ethiopian Imperial High Court," 111.
34 "His Majesty Receives Judges," *Ethiopian Herald,* 3:200 (August 26, 1961).
35 Gustav Aren, *Evangelical Pioneers in Ethiopia* (Stockholm: Forlaget, 1978); and Fekadu Gurmessa, *Evangelical Faith Movement in Ethiopia: Origins and Establishment of the Ethiopian Evangelical Church Mekane Yesus* (Minneapolis: Lutheran University Press, 2009).
36 Esubalew Belay Fanta, "A History of the Ethiopian Imperial High Court," 106.
37 Esubalew Belay Fanta, "A History of the Ethiopian Imperial High Court," 107.

The break between the British and the Ethiopians was over the independence of the judiciary. The British wanted guarantees of non-interference; the Swedes were less insistent. The Ethiopian government sought to influence court proceedings, such that the Ministry of Justice, arguably the arm of government most concerned with security-of-person and justice, wanted to guide the selection of cases that the Imperial High Court tried and even influence its verdicts. Often the Swedish and Ethiopian judges deferred to the ministry. Two British Presidents of the Imperial High Court resigned over the issue of judicial independence and by the mid-1950s the British Consulate and the Foreign Office basically washed their hands of facilitating court reform.[38]

The Ministry of Justice, 1943 to 1960, was an institution rife with dysfunction and contradictions. It was popularly referred to as *Yefidda Minstere* or Ministry of Injustice.[39] Theoretically the advent of the ministerial system in 1943 was to modernize government agencies along European lines. One problem was there were very few Western-educated Ethiopian lawyers or staff. The Ministry of Justice was led by an appointee from the upper crust of Ethiopian feudal society who spent all his time at the palace. Real decision-making power was held by the Vice Minister, usually someone from the lower aristocracy who knew French and/or English, acquired at a French Catholic school or a modern government school. The staff was made up of "scores of *debteras*" according to Bereket Habte Selassie. "These were the products of traditional Ethiopian Church education and formed the backbone of the administration at the time."[40] They were the same smart, unordained clerics so highly versed in *qiné*, as extolled in Chapter 1, who were able to perceive unintended consequences of actions, who excelled at capturing deep meanings and who could articulate subtle criticism of prevailing socio-political norms. They were the intellectuals of traditional society. *Debteras* were adept at cross-examination techniques, framing issues and side-arguments, and interpreting the law. In many ways employing *debteras* was a rational stop-gap strategy to staff the Ministry of Justice because their traditional education emphasized justice and social reconciliation. The problem was in entrenching them in a ministry dedicated, in name at least, to modern, efficient jurispurdence and the application of tort law. Bereket Habte Selassie saw them as

---

38 Esubalew Belay Fanta, "A History of the Ethiopian Imperial High Court," 106–13, 129–35.

39 Bereket Habte Selassie noted that in the 1950s when he started his career at the Ministry of Justice the license plates for ministerial vehicles carried the Amharic initials F.M. for *Fird Minstere*; people quickly renamed it *Yefidda Minstere* or Ministry of Injustice.

40 Bereket Habte Selassie, *The Crown and the Pen*, 131.

"masters of obscurantist thought and obfuscation"[41] with a penchant to delay action and sabotage reform efforts.

Bereket Habte Selassie was the second Western-trained lawyer appointed to the ministry. Within three months he had written a lengthy report that was brought to the emperor's attention on how the ministry and courts could coordinate workload and be more efficient while the latter still retained its independence.[42] The dysfunction between Western-educated lawyers and the *debtera* staff circled around interpretations of justice, legal systems, court procedure, and views on society – whether to allow society to return to its feudal equilibrium or agitate for social and political change through legal measures.

The contradictions fixated on the role of an independent judiciary. The Imperial High Court's British judges insisted upon it. But the Imperial High Court had two courts above it that were directly controlled by the emperor (see Chart 1 above). The Ministry of Justice was answerable to all the courts, not just the British-dominated one, and whenever cases were deemed political or dealt with the sovereignty of the state, the ministry was tasked to reassign the cases to the Supreme Court or Crown Court. Executive privilege was inscribed in the function of the Ethiopian monarchy and certainly remained evident in the Revised Constitution of 1955 in which Article 35 gave Haile Selassie supervision over the courts, including the ability to grant pardons.[43] In some instances, the Ministry of Justice backed Western legal verdicts in the Imperial High Court to set precedents. Other times, when it appeared a judgement might go against the emperor's will or the interests of other high officials, Ethiopian judges in the Imperial High Court were "bullied and bulldozed" into reconsidering "making their decisions on the cases in question."[44] While a long way from being capricious, justice did favor the monarchy and its elite allies.

Ethiopia's legal structure from the Revised Constitution, to the ministry, and on down to the courts reflected the tension between the movement towards representational government and the "prerogatives of the Crown."[45] Through the screening of the Minister of the Pen, later successive Prime Ministers, and as a last resort the Crown Council, few efforts at proportional representation made it to the emperor for him to veto; thus, Haile Selassie could maintain the fiction of supporting reform. This illusion, however, was proved after the coup d'état both in the political and judicial spheres as his distrust increased and his willingness to delegate decreased.

41 Bereket Habte Selassie, *The Crown and the Pen*, 131.
42 Bereket Habte Selassie, *The Crown and the Pen*, 132.
43 Aberra Jembere, *Legal History of Ethiopia*, 174–5.
44 Esubalew Belay Fanta, "A History of the Ethiopian Imperial High Court," 132–4.
45 Spencer, *Ethiopia at Bay*, 257.

Figures 5a and 6b Brigadier-General Mengistu Neway and his brother Germame Neway, leaders of the abortive coup d'état of 1960.

The Coup d'État of 1960

Although only five days in duration, the 1960 Coup d'État profoundly redefined the politics, the intellectual milieu and the perception of justice for the remainder of Haile Selassie's reign. During the evening of December 13, 1960 Brigadier-General and Commander of the Imperial Bodyguard, Mengistu Neway and his brother Germame Neway, Governor of Jigjiga, capitalized on the emperor's absence to deceive top cabinet officials and noted aristocrats that the empress was dying and that they had to come to the palace immediately. Deception went further to insinuate that the Army was plotting to overthrow Haile Selassie and that the Bodyguard had been mobilized to save the regime. Rank-and-file Guardsmen believed this lie. Confusion reigned on the night of the 13th. So spontaneous and so secretive were the brothers in initiating the coup that their two main conspirators, General Tsige Dibu, Chief of Police and Lieutenant-colonel Warqenah Gebeyahu, Chief of Security Service for the Private Cabinet, arguably Haile Selassie's most trusted intelligence agency, did not know that the coup was underway until summoned.[46] Some accounts suggest that Tsige Dibu was reluc-

[46] While the execution of the coup was hurriedly decided by the two brothers to capitalize on Haile Selassie's trip to West Africa and Brazil, the planning had been a long time in the making. Meetings had been held at the home of Brigadier General Mengistu Neway where Germame Neway recruited General Tsige Dibu and Lieutenant Colonel Warqenah Gebeyahu as well as other high officials and officers. All were reputedly devoted patriots interested in advancing Ethiopia and who believed the place to start was to topple the authoritarian monarchy and replace it with a constitutional monarchy answerable to the people, Marcus, *Ethiopia, Great Britain and the United States*, 120–1. Girma

tant and took hours before deciding to cast his lot with Mengistu and Germame.[47] Other sympathizers, men later accused of conspiracy leading to the trials like Gaitachew Bekele and Lemma Frehiwot, were kept at arm's length even though they tried to insert themselves.[48]

Two narratives emerge, one following the putschists' efforts, the other tracking the loyalists' determination to put down the coup d'état. Richard Greenfield, a sympathizer, devotes three chapters to the coup d'état, the first on Germame Neway, the intellectual streams of political disaffection and Germame's radicalization. The second about the coup, and the third about Mengistu Neway's capture, trial and martyrdom. In detail Greenfield traces events, personalities and successes, but mostly the blunders. By the morning of December 14th the Bodyguard had secured the State Bank, Ministry of Finance, state radio station, and two telecommunication stations. With Tsige Dibu agreeing to join, policemen were deployed around the city to ensure stability. Guardsmen were stationed at strategic places sometimes on rooftops around Addis Ababa.[49] From start to finish the rebellion was an urban affair hardly branching beyond the commercial/political hub of the city.

Not all telecommunications were cut – a blunder for, late at night, Crown Princess Medferiyash-Work Abbebe was able to call *Ras* Asserate Kassa to inform him that her husband, Crown Prince Asfa Wossen, had not returned from Empress Menen's palace where he had gone for dinner and to watch a film and that her calls to inquire about his whereabouts had gone unanswered. Sensing something amiss, *Ras* Asserate drove over to the Crown Prince's palace and called a number of trusted dignitaries including *Balambaras* Metheme-Sillase Welde-Mesqel, who recorded the loyalist experiences to quell the insurrection. Quickly they learned that the Crown Prince, *Ras* Imru, *Ras* Abebe Aregay of Patriot fame, Major-General Mulugetta Bulli and other high officials had been driven under guard and detained at the Imperial Bodyguard headquarters which was a short distance from the two palaces. Working through the night *Ras* Asserate contacted Major-General Merid Mengesha to inform him of developments and ascertain which side the army was on. General Merid assured fealty to the crown and the First Army Division headquarters became the center of resistance. Quick thinking Metheme-Sillase also suggested that a telegram be sent to Haile Selassie in Brazil informing him of the coup d'état. Taking a circuitous route to the British Embassy, *Ras* Asserate, Metheme-Sillase and *Fitawrari*

Tsehay also makes much of the pre-planning, "The Abortive Coup d'État of December 1960" B.A. thesis in History, Addis Ababa University (1979), 34.

47 Greenfield, *Ethiopia: A New Political History*, 391.

48 Gaitachew Bekele, *The Emperor's Clothes: A Personal Viewpoint on Politics and Administration in the Imperial Ethiopian Government, 1941–1974* (East Lansing: Michigan State University, 1993), 101.

49 Greenfield, *Ethiopia: A New Political History*, 391–2.

Warqenah Welde-Amaneul implored the British Ambassador to send a telegram alleging Mengistu Neway and Tsige Dibu's sedition and signed it with the names of the core loyalists, the most important of which were generals Merid Mengesha of the army and Kebbede Gebre of the air force.[50] All this took place before 6:30 AM December 14th.

For most city-dwellers it was a normal Wednesday morning, except for the fact that there were more police and troops positioned at some intersections. Most government offices and stores opened. By this time many of Haile Selassie's cabinet members as well as prominent nobles had been detained and details were scarce. The first full day of the putsch rebels devoted to propaganda while the loyalists consolidated their ranks and strategized a countercoup. In addition, the loyalists sent an emissary to the Bodyguards HQ to probe the brothers' receptivity to some form of reconciliation. It went nowhere. More strategically they brought in the Patriarch and a number of Bishops to ensure ecclesiastical authority was on their side which they used effectively the next day.[51]

For the rebels, the signature piece was a revolutionary proclamation written by Germame and Warqenah which the Crown Prince read – allegedly under duress – and which was broadcast over the radio. It declared the ills of the ancien regime, social stagnation, economic underdevelopment, and political corruption plus the promise that under the new government the new monarch, Asfa Wossen, would serve as a salaried official devoted to the constitution. Neither Haile Selassie nor God were mentioned, the language was Western nomenclature devoid of Ethiopian allegory. The proclamation made clear that Ethiopia was to be a constitutional monarchy and that it had the support of "the armed forces, the police, the younger educated Ethiopians and by the whole Ethiopian People ... from this moment on!"[52] Mimeographs of the proclamation were distributed throughout the city, but neither the radio message nor the leaflets clarified the nature of the rebellion to a surprised population. An eleven-point plan gave more details about the new government;[53] it declared that *Ras* Imru was appointed Prime

---

50 Metheme-Sillase Welde-Mesqel, "About the Abortive Coup Attempt in Addis Abeba from 5 Tahsas to 8 Tahsas 1953" (December 14–17, 1960), compiled, trans. Reidulf Molvaer, *Northeast African Studies,* n.s. 3:2 (1996), 97–101.

51 Metheme-Sillase Welde-Mesqel, "About the Abortive Coup," 102–4.

52 Translation found in Greenfield, *Ethiopia: A New Political History,* 398–9. There is much debate as to whether Crown Prince Asfa Wossen was coerced to read the proclamation.

53 Christopher Clapham assessed the plan against directives from Haile Selassie's government and concludes that the difference was "largely one of tone." The revolutionary element of the putschists, he maintains, was their commitment to restructure government as opposed to the tradition of simply replacing the emperor but keeping the socio-political structure intact, "The

Minister and the popular Mulugetta Bulli was made Chief of Staff of the Ethiopian armed forces. An enticement to bring over soldiers to their cause was the promise of higher salaries and defined privileges.[54] Internal disputes within the Revolutionary council arose with Warqenah and Tsige Dibu urging that *Ras* Asserate and General Merid be seized to thwart a loyalist backlash. Mengistu Neway vetoed the idea for he believed the next step was to solidify the popular uprising instead of neutralizing the two counter-revolutionary kingpins – another blunder.[55]

Believing in the need to raise popular support, Mengistu Neway went to the university and addressed the students who were already abuzz after reading the Crown Prince's proclamation. Appealing to their patriotism, their ambitions and their victimization at the hands of the elite, Mengistu Neway asked students to march in the streets as the vanguard of a popular uprising. It took a day of consensus-making and preparation, but after a long night constructing posters and composing slogans and songs students took to the streets on Thursday the 15th. "The students carried placards which endorsed 'Peaceful Change' and 'Prosperity for Ethiopia.'"[56]

The same day the loyalists made their own appeal to the populace. More effective than a demonstration, they had the Patriarch Basilios inform the people that "a few IBG officers have broken their oath to protect the Imp. Family but that the Army, Air Force and Police are loyal."[57] The force behind coaxing the Patriarch to make a statement was Major-General Merid Mengesha who sought two outcomes: pacify the population and justify the use of armed force. To drive home these objectives General Merid, using army radio and dropping pamphlets from helicopters, issued four more messages on December 15th and 16th calling the rebels "criminals," telling the rank-and-file guardsmen that they "will be made responsible for the shooting and bloodshed; therefore go home," furthermore, exhorting the people to "hand over I.B.G. officers in your neighbourhood," and finally that "H.I.M. [Emperor Haile

---

Ethiopian Coup d'Etat of December 1960," *Journal of Modern African Studies,* 6:4 (1968): 503.

54 Greenfield, *Ethiopia: A New Political History*, 402–3.

55 Greenfield, *Ethiopia: A New Political History*, 401.

56 *News and Views,* IV:10 (December 16, 1960), Mengistu Neway trial file, Manuscript Room, Institute for Ethiopian Studies, Addis Ababa University. Greenfield writes that this issue of *News and Views* was pulled and destroyed before publication but that five copies were saved by Jesuit staff members. This must be one of the five, *Ethiopia: A New Political History*, 491, fn 14.

57 Address from Abuna Basilios (December 15, 1 pm), Mengistu Neway trial file, Manuscript Room, Institute for Ethiopian Studies, Addis Ababa University.

Selassie] is amongst you."[58] Invoking religious legitimacy as well as the emperor's suzerainty, the loyalists won the propaganda war.[59]

Fighting broke out Thursday afternoon and continued all of Friday. Finally, events catalyzed citizens. Every memoir of age-appropriate Ethiopians devotes space to where they were at that time, their actions or reasons for their inaction, and finally retrospective rebranding – years later – of their political affinity, usually to side with the Neway brothers as clairvoyants of the revolutionary direction Ethiopia was to follow in the decades ahead. Fighting erupted on the streets potentially mixing combatants with student demonstrators. To prevent casualties, university faculty coaxed students back to the safety of the University College campus.[60] Kasa Inches, a centrally located neighborhood, was where some of the first pitch battles took place. A citywide curfew was declared. Small arms fire dominated with machine guns, mortars and tanks adding to it. The barrage, according to Emmanuel Abraham, spread throughout the city as "whoever possessed a firearm let it off [for] many people desired to warn off those who had a mind to loot."[61] The Bodyguard were outnumbered and outmaneuvered. Strafing by F-86 Sabre fighter jets targeted the Imperial Bodyguard headquarters then other Bodyguard strongholds. General Merid Mengesha is reported to have said that "seventy-five per cent of the battle against the abortive coup d'état was won by the air force."[62] Combat spread towards Piassa and the Merkato, and on Friday edged up towards the palace and Imperial Bodyguard headquarters. Many of the Guardsmen had by this time lost heart as they understood that they were fighting against the emperor, the church, and the will of the people. The death toll was 174 Bodyguards, 29 soldiers, and 120 civilians. In addition, 300 Bodyguards, 43 soldiers, and 442 civilians had been wounded.[63]

The last-ditch effort by Mengistu and Germame to ensure their revolution was remembered took place at the Genete-Leul Palace, where all the hostages had been taken sometime earlier and which now functioned as the rebel headquarters. Complicating the battleplan was the fact that the American Ambassador, Arthur Richards, was in the building trying

58 Notices and army radio addresses from Major General Merid Mengesha (December 15 & 16, 1960), Mengistu Neway trial file, Manuscript Room, Institute for Ethiopian Studies, Addis Ababa University.

59 Girma Tsehay, "The Abortive Coup d'État of December 1960," 34.

60 Greenfield, *Ethiopia: A New Political History*, 416.

61 Emmanuel Abraham, *Reminiscences of My Life* (Oslo: Lunde forlag, 1995), 180.

62 Greenfield, *Ethiopia: A New Political History*, 422.

63 "Life In Capital Back To Normal," *Ethiopian Herald*, 2:301 (December 21, 1960) corroborated by Robert Hess, *Ethiopia: The Modernization of Autocracy* (Ithaca: Cornell University Press, 1970), 141.

to broker the release of the hostages.[64] This did not stop army tanks from breaking down the palace gates and rolling right up to the portico. Ambassador Richards along with his aides were quickly shown to a window in the back of the building by Lieutenant-colonel Warqenah and told to jump and flee. After jumping they took a car and returned via backroads to the American embassy.[65] At the palace entrance, Captain Dereje Haile Mariam, married to one of Haile Selassie's granddaughters, descended from one of the tanks and shouted, "In the name of the Emperor, I call you to surrender!"[66] Germame Neway leveled his pistol and shot him. Soldiers reacted killing some and sending round after round into the palace walls, windows and doorways. General Tsige Dibu fought on, taking out a number of soldiers but in the end finally succumbed, body riddled with bullets.[67]

As the battle raged, Mengistu Neway went upstairs to check in on Crown Prince Asfa Wossen and *Ras* Imru, who were kept in a separate room on the top floor, informing them of the situation. Next the brothers, comprehending that all was lost, entered the Green Room carrying submachine guns and strafed the palace reception room where all the other hostages were held. Leaving and then coming back a second time, after hearing moans, Mengistu and Germame shot and killed those who showed signs of life. A few lived by feigning to be dead. In all fifteen prominent dignitaries were killed including *Ras* Seyoum Mengesha, Governor of Tigray; *Ras* Abebe Aregay, Prime Minister and famed leader of the Patriot resistance; Mekonnen Habte-Wold, Minister of Commerce and brother of the future Prime Minister; and Major-General Mulugetta Bulli, Minister of National Community Development who the putschists had elevated to their Chief of Staff two days before. In all eleven ministers or vice-ministers, two senators, a governor and the *qes atse* (Imperial Chaplain) were slaughtered.[68] Months later at the trial of Mengistu Neway one of the survivors,

> Haji Farah testified that he had heard someone outside the room shouting 'exterminate' as fighting had approached the Palace. Almost immediately the first round of shots poured into the room from the door side where he had seen about eight men in battle dress. He himself was wounded in the third round and had seen Brig. Gen. Mengistu once between rounds of firing.[69]

---

64 American involvement and mediation in the abortive coup are meticulously detailed in Harold Marcus's *Ethiopia, Great Britain and the United States*, 116–69.

65 Gontran de Juniac, *Le Dernier Roi des Rois* (Paris: Plon, 1979), 266.

66 Asfa-Wossen Asserate, *King of Kings*, 231.

67 Greenfield, *Ethiopia: A New Political History*, 429.

68 "Life In Capital Back To Normal," *Ethiopian Herald*, 2:301 (December 21, 1960)

69 "Brig. Gen. Mengistu Newaye's Trial," *Ethiopian Herald*, 3:59 (March 10, 1961).

The massacre indelibly inked the abortive coup d'état into history.

Mengistu, Germame, and Warqenah along with other putschists escaped through back doors and faded into the city. Lieutenant-colonel Warqenah was found the next day near Piassa and after a gun battle put a pistol in his mouth and pulled the trigger, but not before invoking the name of Emperor Tewodros who also killed himself instead of submitting. Mengistu and Germame Neway escaped to Entoto and then onto Mount Zuqwala located between Debre Zeit and Mojo. Revealed by peasants, police confronted them about a week later. In the skirmish, after losing some of their comrades, Germame shot his brother and then himself.[70] Mengistu, however, survived his deep facial wound and after three months in hospital was tried for treason.[71] In capital letters, Germame Neway wrote at the end of his Columbia University master's thesis: "FOR ONE PHASE OF A PEOPLE'S STRUGGLE ENDS WHERE THE VICTORY OF THEIR CAUSE BEGINS."[72] Similar sentiments about the enduring nature of a "cause" were expressed to Donald Levine, who claims he was one of the last people to see Germame alive: "Don, please tell our story to the world. Even if we are defeated and killed, at least a word of truth will have been spoken in this land of deception."[73]

On Saturday, December 17, 1960, Haile Selassie returned to Addis Ababa from Asmara to joyful ululation. His trip home from Brazil in a DC-6 B turbo-prop was long and eventful including flying the last segment on only three engines successfully piloted by Captain Green, an American and one of the original cohort of Ethiopian Airlines pilots seconded from TWA.[74] Haile Selassie was welcomed in Asmara by his son-in-law Brigadier-General Abiye Abebe and *Ras* Makonnen Endalkatchew, President of the Senate. They pledged their loyalty to the emperor and helped disseminate His Imperial message to bewildered and confused Ethiopians throughout the rest of the country that he was returning. Stepping off the plane Emperor Haile Selassie was met at the airport by Crown Prince Asfa Wossen, Patriarch Basilios, Generals Merid Mengesha and Kebbede Gebre – heroes of the resistance, *Ras* Asserate Kassa and core loyalists, other aristocrats, government officials, and townsfolk. His heavily armed caravan then made its way to the Jubilee Palace which was to become his residence until deposed and escorted from it in an unmarked Volkswagen Beetle in 1974. On Sunday,

70 "Mengistu Captured, Ghermame Killed," *Ethiopian Herald,* 2:305 (December 26, 1960).

71 Greenfield, *Ethiopia: A New Political History,* 434–5.

72 Germame Neway, "The Impact of the White Settlement Policy in Kenya," 112.

73 Donald Levine, "*Kwillo amekkiru we-ze-senay atsni'u*" (remarks on the occasion of receiving the award of Honorary Doctorate from Addis Ababa University, July 24, 2004) in *Interpreting Ethiopia*, 160.

74 Arefaynie Fantahun, "The attempted coup d'état of 1960 as reported by Paris Match," *Ethiopia Observer* (April 26, 2023).

Haile Selassie spoke over the radio calming the people and stating that the rebellion was the result of a few disaffected criminals. Reports in *Berhanena Selam* and the English newspaper, *The Ethiopian Herald*, paid tribute to the heroism of the army, air force, police and, not to be overlooked, the Ethiopian people who remained steadfast. Condemning "a very small group of Body Guard officers and minor civil servants," Haile Selassie made a plea for peace: "Peace is justice, justice peace; the two are complementary."[75]

Measured Justice

Like all threats to the nation, this one required delicate calibration for not all the participants were involved equally. The Neway brothers, of course, were the ringleaders and final executioners, whereas most of the Bodyguards were following orders that they believed were in keeping with their primary responsibility to ensure the safety of the royal family. Involvement of other putschists ranged from vital to tangentially aligned. Aroused students floated banners, sang revolutionary songs, and started marching on the streets only to hear rifle fire and be quickly shepherded back to their dorms. Immediately afterwards, the question surfaced, did Crown Prince Asfa Wossen willingly participate in the coup d'état by reading the prepared pronouncement or was he forced to do so? Depending on the person or the group, the emperor and his severely reduced cabinet had to determine how to administer justice, whether perpetrators were to stand trial in a court or be forgiven according to time-tested modes of restorative justice. Reversing the order, the following analysis will start with the blanket amnesty given to soldiers and university students, alternate solutions arrived at for the Crown Prince, address more complicated and somewhat harsher punishments associated with those linked to the Neway brothers, and finally culminate in the Imperial High Court trial of Mengistu Neway and two accused co-conspirators, Kifle Woldemariam and Degafe Tedle. What is apparent is that the form of restorative justice, in those cases where it was applied, jettisoned many of the lessons associated with conditional forgiveness and reverted to a facile understanding of forgive and forget by fiat. This was something that the next fourteen years, until the Ethiopian Revolution of 1974, would call into question.

Soldier/combats of the Imperial Bodyguard

Imperial Bodyguard privates and non-commissioned officers were essentially given amnesty like soldiers hundreds of years earlier. As

[75] "Imperial Majesty Pays Tribute to the Heroic Ground and Air Forces, Police and People," *Ethiopian Herald*, 2:301 (December 21, 1960).

Arnauld d'Abbadie noted in the early nineteenth century such forgiveness was mandated and clemency was to be shown to the vanquished.[76] In this sense, Emperor Haile Selassie's pardon of the privates and non-commissioned officers was time honored. In his decree he acknowledged society's dependence on the soldiers saying, "taking into consideration the hardships of the wives and children and other dependents, We have given mercy to those who were misled."[77] In short, the act of pardoning was more to restore the social order, as of old.

The emperor ultimately pardoned the "misled" on January 9, 1961.[78] Why the delay of three weeks? In keeping with improvements in restorative justice modalities, "conditional forgiveness" augured for delay in granting amnesty. Already on December 22, 1960, there were indications that the emperor was going to amnesty rank-and-file soldiers and policemen, yet the delay likely had to do with devising a forum for the public spectacle. In the end no honor and shaming ceremony occurred, instead forgiveness was decreed by the emperor through the media. This was hardly symbolic, and it hardly brought about a sense of reconciliation, for the perpetrators and the public were kept apart.

For those of higher rank, an investigating commission classified defendants into two groups.[79] The first consisted of the top thirteen defendants of whom only three would be tried before the Imperial High Court, see below. The second group consisted of one hundred eighty Bodyguard officers who were tried at a special court martial. Approximately seventy-eight were sentenced to three years imprisonment and deprived of their rank; forty-nine were sentenced to two years again and deprived of rank; fifty-three officers were sentenced to two years while retaining their rank.[80] Most were paroled early.

University College students

Student demonstrators were forgiven almost immediately.

> Like good prodigal sons they marched to the Palace to tell HIM, the father of Ethiopian education and the Monarch of enlightenment and refinement, how they were compelled by the leaders of the rebellion to demonstrate against their will. HIM forgiveful [*sic.*] as ever, judging the situation in its correct perspective dismissed the whole thing as a sad item of the past which should not cast a dark shadow on the present and called upon them to pursue their studies diligently.[81]

---

76 d'Abbadie, *Douze ans*, 455.

77 "His Majesty's Christmas Message to The Nation," *Ethiopian Herald*, 3:9 (January 9, 1961).

78 "His Majesty's Christmas Message to The Nation," *Ethiopian Herald*.

79 Editorial, "Justice Must Prevail," *Ethiopian Herald*, 2:309 (December 30, 1960).

80 Tekeste Melake, "The 1960 Coup d'État in Ethiopia," 186.

81 "Editorial: Students Loyal to HIM," *Ethiopian Herald*, 3:4 (January 3, 1961).

Emperor Haile Selassie always had a soft, paternalist attitude towards students and invested heavily, both in time and treasure, in developing education in Ethiopia. At the top the nation's pride and joy was University College. Haile Selassie routinely visited the university, checking on curriculum and services and offered something between encouragement and admonishment in explaining the duty to country that each student bore.[82] That these coddled students defied their benefactor and supported an overthrow was an affront, an indelible insult to His Imperial Majesty. Yet Haile Selassie swallowed his pride and quickly pardoned the students. *The Ethiopian Herald* headline on January 2, 1961, read "Emperor Receives College Students Forgives, Forgets." Further down in the article the emperor is quoted as saying: "We are regarding what has taken place as if it never happened. May God help you that you too will be guided by the same spirit to continue your studies with diligence."[83] As with the Bodyguards, Haile Selassie was bypassing all the lessons learned in the later nineteenth century and reverting to forgive-and-forget. Absent was pageantry – the *wurdet* – instead some student leaders marched to the palace to plea to the emperor himself. Absent was an obligation on the part of the students to physically show contrition by wrapping a *shemma* around the waist, known as *metat'eq*, as a symbol demonstrating shame or carrying a milling stone on their shoulders in public to show submission. Absent was a public acknowledgement on the part of the students to live according to the terms specified in the forgiveness proclamation. And, like defeated contenders for the throne of bygone years, students were left free to harbor resentment and dream revolutionary thoughts. During the *Zemene Mesafint*, war resolved little simply because restorative justice returned everything to the status quo. Likewise, forgive-and-forget returned things to the way they stood before the coup – pampered.

Tamru Fayessa, "President of Cultural Activities for academic year October 1960 to July 1961" and one of "the 'Big Five' of the Cabinet of the Student Council of the University College," marched to the palace with many other students to ask for forgiveness, which was given, as previously stated, "on receipt of their somewhat insincere apology."[84] Proof, if it can be called such, was written into an article written by Haile Fida titled "Dull Christmas Vacation at U.C." where he complains that in the roiled city of Addis Ababa, shortly after fighting destroyed infrastructure and left dead people in the streets, "[t]here were no shows, no films, no real picnics for all; nothing at all that one could call special." Further, "it was evident that many [students] did not even

82 "H.I. Majesty Visits University College," *Ethiopian Herald,* 3:72 (March 25, 1961).

83 "Emperor Receives College Students Forgives, Forgets," *Ethiopian Herald,* 3:1 (January 2, 1961).

84 Richard Greenfield, letter to Donald Levine, Addis Ababa, February 5, 1962.

possess the little sum of money [government stipends] that was necessary to take them around the night-clubs in town."[85] How audacious, how lacking contrition!

Crown Prince Asfa Wossen

One of the more vexing cases revolved around the Crown Prince Asfa Wossen Haile Selassie. Did he knowingly condone the coup d'état or was he coerced to read the revolutionary statement over the radio? That he was front and center kneeling on the tarmac to welcome his father back at the airport indicates that many, if not all, notables thought he had been coerced.[86] Yet at the airport Haile Selassie was reputed to have said, as related by *Ras* Asserate Kassa standing nearby: "We would have been very proud of you if We were coming to attend your funeral. Get up!"[87] Was he that insensitive or had Haile Selassie thought his son should have bravely faced death as he had at Maychew where: "He was always in the zone of artillery fire and continually exposed himself to danger."[88] Whatever Haile Selassie's personal opinion was, the official stance was coercion, no better certified than in the Ethiopian government accusing *Time* and *Newsweek* magazines of libel, stating the papers "started from the wrong assumptions and drew preposterous conclusions on the unfortunate happening of the previous week." And that the putschists' attempt "to implicate the Crown Prince in the conspiracy was well understood by all Ethiopians from the very start of the abortive Coup d'État and to suggest anything else is preposterous."[89] Unpacking "well understood," it likely refers to the fact that the populace comprehended the Neway brothers' effort to legitimize the overthrow by placing Asfa Wossen and *Ras* Imru and a few other prominent figures as the leaders of the new government without their consent.[90] What was surprising, though, was the brothers' disregard for the power of the church and the aristocracy in general.

---

85 Haile Fida, "Dull Christmas Vacation at U.C.," *Ethiopian Herald*, 3:21 (January 24, 1961).

86 A secondary sources claims that Asfa Wossen approached his father shouldering a large rock in the time-honored gesture of penitence, Hans Wilhelm Lochot, *The Mission: The Life, Reign and Character of Haile Selassie I* (London: Palgrave Macmillan, 1989), 83.

87 Asfa-Wossen Asserate, *King of Kings*, 233.

88 Steer, *Caesar in Abyssinia*, 316.

89 "Editorial: Libellous Magazines Banned," *Ethiopian Herald*, 2:305 (December 26, 1960).

90 This certainly was the case with Mulugeta Bulli, Minister of National Community Development, who was one of the dignitaries imprisoned by the Neway brothers and who only heard that he had been elevated to their Chief of Staff of the Armed Forces a day after the public announcement when Gaitachew Bekele came to visit him, *The Emperor's Clothes*, 108.

Yet the discord between father and son persisted. Five years later Richard Greenfield wrote, "The rift between the Crown Prince and the Emperor has grown no narrower nor had the former been encouraged to play a more prominent role in public affairs."[91] Forgiveness, if there was any, takes many forms. An oft repeated trope was that Asfa Wossen was consigned to follow his father everywhere, to every ribbon-cutting for each new hospital or school, to Timket (Epiphany) ceremonies, to attend funerals.[92] But this contradicts the record. Tabulating reports on Haile Selassie's whereabouts on the front page of *The Ethiopian Herald* for eighteen months before and eighteen months after the coup, it is evident that the emperor surrounded himself with family members – specifically his sons Asfa Wossen and Prince Sahle Selassie, and his cousin *Ras* Imru – more prior to the abortive coup d'état than after. Before the rebellion it almost appeared that the imperial family relished each other's presence and could not stand being separated. After the coup Haile Selassie appears more solitary, yet even more fixated on dominating the news cycle with coverage of his greeting heads of state, receiving ambassadors, signing trade agreements, or launching development projects. Father and son were together at the opening of Africa Hall in February 1961. Certainly, Asfa Wossen accompanied his father on many domestic trips always showing diffidence by appearing two steps in back and to the side. They did travel in the same vehicle on many occasions and it is only logical that they spoke often, but the differences in personality and political persuasion never endeared one to the other neither before nor after December 1960.

Forgiveness and reconciliation may have been elusive, but part of "conditional forgiveness" was to demonstrate contriteness, to atone for whatever was held against you. Crown Prince Asfa Wossen lived atonement. Penitent, he forever deferred to his father, the emperor. As his wife, Crown Princess Medferiyash-Work Abbebe, relates in a revealing article in the German *Stern* magazine published after the 1974 revolution, "so far my husband has never had the chance to do something for the country. His father, ex-Emperor Haile Selassie, isolated him for years. He treated him like a puppet."[93] In the same article the Crown Prince appears to clarify his participation in the abortive coup. "I was always for a transition in Ethiopia. As you know, I was involved in the coup d'état against Haile Selassie's regime, and voluntarily and not, as

91 Greenfield, *Ethiopia: A New Political History*, 454 (tense disagreement in original).

92 Peter Schwab, *Haile Selassie I: Ethiopia's Lion of Judah* (Chicago: Nelson-Hall, 1979), 119.

93 "*Dern König, der nur nichen darf* [The King who is only allowed to nod in agreement]," *Stern* (October 3, 1974), 152. Translation was provided by my colleague Timothy Malchow, Professor of German Studies, Valparaiso University.

was claimed, forced. And I always believed that only the military could one day bring about a transition in Ethiopia."[94] Is this the last word? Perhaps, but princes like paupers often reconstruct the past to better suit their present.

The putschists

Pardoning soldiers, policemen, and students was a far cry from serving justice for the ringleaders. Calibrations had to be made over just how involved each individual was in the plot to overthrow the regime. Figures differ but the original reports were that 4,000 men had been apprehended with the majority of them being privates and non-commissioned officers who were quickly amnestied. Hundreds of officers and civilian accomplices were imprisoned for an indeterminant period while their cases were investigated. Compounding the problem was that reorganizing a decimated cabinet took some time. The Ministry of Justice was not spared as Tadesse Negash, Minister of State in the Ministry of Justice, was one of those killed.[95] A reform commission was created to advise the emperor on cabinet appointments and other issues pertaining to the abortive coup which took additional time. In early 1961 *Dejazmach* Zewde Gabre-Selassie was appointed Minister of Justice precisely to deal with Mengistu Neway and others who had engineered the coup. Recall Zewde Gabre-Selassie was a member of the Qachane Club along with Germame Neway and others who would ascend the political ladder in the coming years. Zewde Gabre-Selassie, of exceptionally prominent birth, had been educated at the University of Exeter and Oxford University. His grasp of British politics and jurisprudence meshed nicely with that of the British judges serving on the Imperial High Court. One of the first decisions the cabinet had to make was where and how to dispense justice. Either the Crown Court or the Imperial Supreme Court would have been the logical forum to try the rebels since those courts dealt specifically with affairs of state and challenges to sovereignty. However, those courts, which were controlled by the ministry and thus the emperor, operated in a rather opaque manner, totally incomprehensible to the non-Ethiopian. Since the abortive coup d'état had been covered by *Time*, *Newsweek*, *Paris Match* and a host of other foreign papers and the inference was, at least in the first two, that the Haile Selassie regime was corrupt and repressive, there was

---

94 "Dern König, der nur nichen darf," *Stern* (October 3, 1974), 154. Asfa-Wossen Asserate provides a slightly different translation, *King of Kings*, 234.

95 According to Bereket Habte Selassie, who worked with him, Tadesse Negash was "related to the Neway brothers on his mother's side." He further states, "Germame was an equal opportunity revolutionary; he did not spare his blood relatives," *The Crown and the Pen*, 143.

enormous pressure to hold the trial in the Imperial High Court where, as described above, British magistrates had fashioned legal procedures codifying the use of statutory evidence and sentencing, giving the impression of an independent judiciary to rival those of Europe. This was important since the coup-makers had denounced the backwardness of the country and Haile Selassie had to prove the falsehood of their allegations.

Gathering evidence for hundreds of putschists was a huge task. Some spent time in prison, others received demotions, still others were exonerated. A question posed at the trial of Mengistu Neway was, why were only three people tried when so many others could have been brought to justice? A short answer is the slow grinding maw of the justice system precluded trying any more.

On December 2, 1960 *The Ethiopian Herald* published a list of the fifteen dead dignitaries as well as ten ringleaders of the plot of whom five would perish, three would be captured and two turned themselves in.[96] Of these, two alleged ringleaders were never taken to court; rather, their cases were dealt with using traditional methods of restorative justice that (a) expedited the process, (b) insisted on conditions, (c) allowed ambiguities to remain, and (d) brought reintegration into society. These two men were Gaitachew Bekele, Assistant Minister to Department of Marine, and Lemma Frehiwot, Secretary General of the National Coffee Board. It is worth assessing both cases to comprehend which features of restorative justice were applied, which were missing, and how the partial application of restorative justice was less effective than in the past.

Gaitachew Bekele provided a detailed account of his activities during the coup and his travails afterwards in his autobiography, *The Emperor's Clothes: A Personal Viewpoint on Politics and Administration in the Imperial Ethiopian Government, 1941–1974*. He confesses that if he had known about the overthrow beforehand, he would have supported it for, like many progressives of that era, he found the regime too indebted to tradition and backward looking. Like most Ethiopians, the coup d'état caught him by surprise and to find out why there were Bodyguards at road junctions on that fateful Wednesday morning stopping vehicles and forcing drivers to get out and walk home, he prevailed on his brother, Melaku, a major in the Bodyguard, to drive him to the headquarters. Gaitachew Bekele's account of the next three days where he went in and out of the headquarters, talked with the top four conspirators, visited prisoners and basically offered advice – soundly ignored – as to how to successfully topple the regime, points to the chaos, the obstinacy of Germame and the strategic incompetence of the brothers.

96 "Life In Capital Back To Normal," *Ethiopian Herald*, 2:301 (December 21, 1960).

> I found Germame to be a stubborn and headstrong man, unable to listen to reason. On the other hand, his elder brother, the commander of the Imperial Bodyguard, was docile and easily manipulated. That is the main reason why a golden opportunity for change was lost – a stubborn man at the helm with no proper plan and a pliant stooge following his every whim.[97]

The one time where Gaitachew Bekele could be accused of complicity was when, somehow, he was invited to accompany Germame Neway to the Ministry of Information to broadcast the Crown Prince's message. While being afforded free access in and out of the Imperial Bodyguard headquarters, Gaitachew Bekele, according to his account, spent considerable time with Colonel Warqenah Gebeyahu. Countervailing his support, Gaitachew Bekele was also in contact with some of the prisoners assaying ways to resolve their plight and negotiate a settlement without bloodshed.

On Thursday, as fighting started, Gaitachew Bekele "decided to give myself up and dissociate myself from the embarrassing affair."[98] Sneaking out of the city in disguise, he wrote a confession days later and had it delivered to *Dejazmach* Kebede Tessema who had been appointed by the emperor to be the face of the state for those civilian accomplices who wanted to give themselves up. Acting as his guarantor, Kebede Tessema went to the Palace and arranged a meeting for Gaitachew Bekele. Haile Selassie, never one to commit himself, listened to Gaitachew Bekele's confession while having the written one in his hand.

His case went before Judge Nathan Marein, a Dutch-born Israeli lawyer trained in England. As Attorney General, he ordered a police investigation and then dismissed the case as without merit and even recommended Gaitachew Bekele's reinstatement to his government position. The emperor was furious and called in the Minister of Justice, *Dejazmach* Zewde Gabre-Selassie, and ordered him to fire Marein. Pointing to the intense international scrutiny the regime was already under, Zewde Gabre-Selassie advised differently arguing that Marein's contract be allowed to expire and Gaitachew Bekele's case be removed from the docket and resolved discreetly per time-honored juridical traditions.[99] All we have on this matter is Gaitachew's account; nevertheless, some mechanisms of Ethiopia's traditions of restorative justice stand out.

While there never was a formal public forum, Gaitachew Bekele was taken to the Palace and forced to wait on the lawn before meeting with the emperor. In his account many dignitaries and bureaucrats

97 Gaitachew Bekele, *The Emperor's Clothes*, 104.
98 Gaitachew Bekele, *The Emperor's Clothes*, 110.
99 Gaitachew Bekele, *The Emperor's Clothes*, 113–14.

were there casting malevolent eyes on him.[100] It hardly qualified as a shaming ceremony, but it did communicate who was victorious and who had lost, or who was in and who was out.

Gaitachew Bekele spent time in prison while his case was discussed, perhaps even in the Crown Court, for it appears many of the highest officials had input on his case. He does not provide dates, but it appears his punishment was decided quickly. The conditions associated with the terms of restorative justice were classic. Gaitachew Bekele was to be banished, *gizot*, to a remote city and removed from his position until such time that his reintegration could be considered. Conditions in the 1960s were far different from the nineteenth century when *gizot* effectively removed a wayward *ras* from his patrimony. Gaitachew Bekele was removed from his government position, salary, and certainly from his network of friends and associates, but there was no inherent connection to peasants, other producers or the population at large. In short, Gaitachew Bekele had to atone for his participation by willingly agreeing to live within the stipulations issued by the state. What is not spelled out is how widely members of the regime came together and agreed to those terms, nor who were the memory-keepers or enforcers. Gaitachew Bekele's *gizot* was problematic for in Gondar, his first place of banishment, it was determined that he would be at risk of retaliation. In Wollisso, his second place of banishment, it was found he had too many family connections and after only ten days he was reassigned. A parade of friends came to visit him in Wollisso including Mikael Imru. The third try in Jimma appeared suitable yet, according to his autobiography, Gaitachew Bekele ingratiated himself with the governor to the extent that he was appointed head of the Jimma Town Council.[101] He even had time to write a little book titled *Mirror for a Public Servant* that explored "the relationship between the public and public servants," for which he had to obtain the emperor's approval to publish. Surprisingly, he did receive approval and Haile Selassie even paid for its publication.[102]

The whole affair allowed the Haile Selassie regime to overlook details and be satisfied with Gaitachew Bekele's ambiguous support of the attempted coup. A court trial would require scrutiny of every action and each word of his confession in cross examination; restorative justice allowed Gaitachew Bekele's revolutionary intent to be forgiven because of his abiding love for his country. Ambiguity encapsulated in the ideology of *sem inna werq* allowed the state to see beyond past indiscretions to the promise of full political restoration. Reconciliation came in November 1961 when Gaitachew Bekele was appointed Governor of Bahr-Dar. As he says: "To be called from banishment to Addis

[100] Gaitachew Bekele, *The Emperor's Clothes*, 110.
[101] Gaitachew Bekele, *The Emperor's Clothes*, 114–21.
[102] Gaitachew Bekele, *The Emperor's Clothes*, 123–4.

Ababa and to be appointed as governor the same day was the work of an emperor and all the credit must go to him."[103]

The case of Lemma Frehiwot is less documented although it should be otherwise.[104] Lemma Frehiwot having pursued a master's degree in Social Science in America, was a member of the Qachane Club and distantly related to the Neway brothers.[105] Details of his involvement in the coup are sketchy, although he told me in passing that he conversed directly with Mengistu and Germame Neway during the coup and had access to the Imperial Bodyguard headquarters – perhaps similar to Gaitachew Bekele's passing in and out of the headquarters. According to Willard Park: "Apparently Lemma was the bag man of the revolt" with no explanation about what that entailed.[106] Lemma Frehiwot disavowed that he had anything to do with the planning or fighting and certainly not the massacre in the Green Room of the Genete-Leul

103 Gaitachew Bekele, *The Emperor's Clothes*, 143.

104 Lemma Frehiwot was a good friend of my adviser, Donald Levine. Their friendship began at the University of Chicago where Lemma pursued a master's degree in Social Science specializing in Planning between 1953 and 1955, according to the university's Registrar. Concurrently, Levine was finishing his master's and starting his Ph.D. there. Levine said Lemma was his first Amharic instructor while still in Chicago. After completing his Ph.D. on social theory Levine went out to Ethiopia to conduct field research, influenced by the ethnographic work of Robert Redfield, ultimately leading to his book *Wax and Gold*. From 1957 through the abortive coup, the two were constant companions in Addis Ababa when Levine returned there from his fieldwork in Manz. Lemma was the one to advise Levine to go to Manz for he claimed the purest form of Amharic was spoken there. Levine was in Addis Ababa during the coup, which he recounted to me during an evening sitting at the bar of the Ras Amba Hotel and from which I later made notes when I returned to my hotel room. Levine gave me Lemma Frehiwot's contact information before I went to Ethiopia for dissertation research in the mid-1980s. I immediately looked him up and through that connection had a standing invitation to visit Ato Lemma's home. I formally interviewed him seven times. Unfortunately, my dissertation was about Ethiopia's integration into the world economy hence my questions were more about trade, commodity extraction, labor practices, land tenure, currency issues, and his experiences as Director of the National Coffee Board – which was ideal since coffee was Ethiopia's largest export. I knew of his involvement in the 1960 Coup d'état and in passing he referred to it, but I never pressed him for details. This brief account is pasted together from my notes of Levine's account at Ras Amba, reference to a series of highly accusatory letters between Levine and another American anthropologist Willard Park that Levine gave me along with much of his collection from this time period, published accounts, a conversation with Richard Pankhurst, and one account in one of my interviews with Lemma Frehiwot.

105 Tekeste Melake, "The 1960 Coup d'État in Ethiopia," 242; Gaitachew Bekele, *The Emperor's Clothes*, 116–17.

106 Willard Park, letter to Donald Levine, Addis Ababa, May 2, 1962.

Palace.[107] Levine adjures: "I am very fond of Lemma, but remain fairly certain that he had no part at all in the planning of the coup."[108] Lemma Frehiwot's name, however, did appear in the first listing of ringleaders and the authorities did consider him an accomplice.[109] Whether he was captured or turned himself in is unknown; however, Richard Pankhurst claimed that he saw Lemma Frehiwot shortly after the coup sitting on the lawn in front of the Jubilee Palace in handcuffs,[110] likely waiting to be brought before the emperor to explain his involvement, with *Dejazmach* Kebede Tessema again acting as his interlocutor.

It is reported that Lemma Frehiwot was removed as Secretary General of the National Coffee Board and banished to Asmara.[111] It is noteworthy that *Ras* Asserate Kassa, loyalist of the first order, was appointed governor over Eritrea during Lemma Frehiwot's *gizot*[112] which may explain why he was "quietly reinstated in his former position after a suitable period of 'exile.'"[113]

How does Lemma Frehiwot's story reflect restorative justice? Handcuffed and sitting on the lawn in front of the palace, Lemma Frehiwot received the critical eyes of the establishment as they passed in and out of the palace. Again, it was not analogous to an honor and shaming ceremony for the public was absent, but he was in a position of submission before his bureaucratic peers. Second, judgement about his activities appears to have been swift, not only for his crimes but also for his atonement. Third, there were conditions placed upon him and who better to judge whether he was penitent than *Ras* Asserate Kassa. He acted as the memory-keeper and judge. Fourth, his case was shrouded in the ambiguity over where to draw the line between passive and active participation in the insurrection. Fifth, reconciliation with the Haile Selassie regime was speedy; Lemma Frehiwot was reinstated as – new title – the Director of the National Coffee Board in 1962.[114] Restorative justice always has an eye out for discerning what is best for society. Perhaps because of Lemma's knowledge of world markets, his connections to

107 Interview with Lemma Frehiwot, Addis Ababa, December 5, 1986.

108 Donald Levine, letter to Willard Park, Detroit, Michigan, May 8, 1962.

109 "Life In Capital Back To Normal," *Ethiopian Herald,* 2:301 (December 21, 1960).

110 Conversation with Richard Pankhurst, Addis Ababa, July 3, 2016. Also see Richard and Rita Pankhurst, *Ethiopian Reminiscences: Early Days* (Los Angeles: Tsehai, 2013), 269.

111 In a conversation with Donald Levine at the Ras Amba Hotel in Addis Ababa about his account of the coup, he related that Lemma Frehiwot "was tortured with electricity learned from the Israelis" while in prison in Addis Ababa before banishment to Asmara (January 28, 2010).

112 Asfa-Wossen Asserate, *King of Kings*, 241.

113 Robert Hess, *Ethiopia*, 143.

114 Interview with Lemma Frehiwot, Addis Ababa, December 5, 1986.

coffee exporters and, first and foremost, his relations with coffee producers throughout Ethiopia, he may have been the best person in Ethiopia to handle the country's coffee collection and export. As postscript, Lemma Frehiwot only stayed with the Coffee Board a few more years then became a commercial farmer free to travel the country buying and leasing land, employing peasants and producing cash crops.[115]

The trial

The trial of Brigadier-General Mengistu Neway, Captain Kifle Wolde Mariam, and Lieutenant Degafe Tedla of the Imperial Bodyguard proceeded rather quickly from inditement, to prosecution, to verdict. It ignored restorative justice. After a forty-day period of mourning decreed by the emperor to honor the ministers lost, the trial started on February 28 and ended one month later, on March 28, 1961, the sentence read:

> Mengistu was then sentenced to death by public hanging and an order made confiscating his property and depriving him of this rank and decorations. The Court found mitigating circumstances which did not justify the imposition of the death penalty on the second accused. The second accused was sentenced to 15 years imprisonment and deprivation of rank and decorations. The third accused was sentenced to 10 years imprisonment and deprivation of rank and decorations.[116]

The more lenient sentence for the latter two was partially due to the fact that they had no prior knowledge of the coup.[117]

Two days later, on March 30th at 7 AM in the Mercato, Mengistu Neway, deprived of his rank as Brigadier General and Commander of the Imperial Bodyguard, stood with pride and indifference, and reputedly put the noose around his own neck.[118] Before jumping off the stand, he announced the adversaries of the regime were emboldened by what had been done.

The trial was not without complications. Immediately after the failed coup, a power struggle developed between relatives of the victims and some of the elderly aristocracy who sought harsh measures versus Aklilu Habte-Wold, soon to be appointed Prime Minister, and Zewde Gabre-Selassie, the new Minister of Justice, who recommended an open trial with each defendant represented by defense counsel with an added feature to prove impartiality which was to encourage foreign observers to attend. Their leniency is remarkable because one had lost

---

[115] Interview with Lemma Frehiwot, Addis Ababa, December 5, 1986.

[116] "Mengistu and Two Others Convicted On All Charges," *Ethiopian Herald*, 3:75 (March 29, 1961).

[117] It is noteworthy that Kifle Wolde Mariam appealed his sentence to the Supreme Court months later where he was found guilty a second time and sentenced to death by hanging.

[118] de Juniac, *Le Dernier Roi des Rois*, 274.

his brother and the other had lost his grandfather in the massacre. As Seyoum Haregot noted, "Aklilu and Zewde won the day, as the Emperor had the wisdom to heed the voices of counselling magnanimity rather than vengeance."[119]

Resolved to try the accused in court, the defendants were charged on three counts according to the revised Ethiopian Penal Code of 1957. They included Article 250, outrages against constitutional authorities, Article 252, armed uprising against the government, and Article 522, aggravated homicide.[120] The court was presided over by three Ethiopian judges of notable experience,[121] and the proceedings were conducted in Amharic. The courtroom was largely full of relatives of victims, but space was left for foreign correspondents to monitor the case. Some procedural issues slowed the trial but on March 10th the prosecution wound up its case after receiving testimony from twenty-six witnesses. Participants as well as victims testified, with a couple of the former declining to testify for fear of self-incrimination at their own trials.[122] The two most damning statements were from survivors of the Green Room massacre. Haji Farah, Vice Minister of Interior, testified in the days leading up to the shooting they were denied food and shortly before shots were fired, he heard "someone outside the room shouting 'exterminate.'" Haji Farah's testimony vacillated between gravity and humor.[123] By contrast Brigadier-General Mekonnen Deneke, another survivor, could not hold back his emotions as he gave his deposition from a hospital where a special courtroom was erected. "Makonnen Deneke burst into tears while describing the scene of massacre in the Gennete Leul Palace. He wept and even screamed during the one-hour description of the murder scene. He identified the defendants who had taken part in the Palace massacre."[124] From outset to closure, Mengistu Neway admitted to everything including the killings of the fifteen dignitaries and claimed full responsibility for the planning and execution of the coup d'état, never even implicating his deceased brother.

Towards the beginning of the trial Mengistu Neway appealed to the Supreme Court on four counts, the most consequential was the right to secure a foreign advocate. He argued that an Ethiopian lawyer would be subject to future harassment if he were to have defended him too

119 Seyoum Haregot, *The Bureaucratic Empire: Serving Emperor Haile Selassie* (Trenton: Red Sea Press, 2013), 31.

120 Edvard Hambro, "The Rebellion Trials in Ethiopia: Comments of an Observer," *Bulletin of the International Commission of Jurists,* 12 (1961): 31, 33–5.

121 de Juniac, *Le Dernier Roi des Rois*, 272–3.

122 "Prosecution Wound Up Case," *Ethiopian Herald,* 3:59 (March 10, 1961).

123 "Prosecution Wound Up Case," *Ethiopian Herald,* 3:59 (March 10, 1961).

124 "Brigadier General Makonnen Give Evidence at Hospital," *Ethiopian Herald,* 3:57 (March 8, 1961).

energetically because Ethiopia did not possess "a strong and well-organized Bar" to insulate him against societal backlash.[125] Mengistu appears prescient for, after his appeal was rejected, he was appointed Ato Getahun Munagnaw. Getahun Munagnaw put up a weak defense, one time feigning illness and admitting himself into a hospital to avoid going to court.[126]

In all, defense counsel called eight witnesses to the stand, including the main defendant. Prosecuting attorney, Colonel Teffera Gebre Mariam, therefore, had the opportunity to question Mengistu Neway's actions touching closest to the three charges brought against him. Greenfield gives a translation of the cross examination, emphasizing Mengistu's altruistic intent to "improve the standard of living, not just of the soldiers but of the whole population," knowledge that he was violating the constitution, and his assumption of power in order to change government – "I did this on my own authority."[127] But there was no denying his culpability.

Foreign pressures manifested themselves. The International Commission of Jurists insisted on sending a representative to monitor the trial.[128] Edvard Hambro from Norway was selected as foreign observer. He traveled to Ethiopia and observed the trial for one week. A skilled translator interpreted the proceedings to Hambro in English; moreover, full access was given to him to interview officials and defendants, and even inspect their prisons. With cautionary things to say about the independence of the judiciary and the autocratic nature of government, Hambro, nevertheless, concluded that "a real effort has been made to conduct the trial as fairly as possible."[129]

As stated above, sentence was rendered at the end of March 1961 and Mengistu Neway was hanged two days later in a public square. His body was left hanging for some days for people to see. Mengistu Neway indicated that he did not wish to appeal saying, as recounted by Donald Levine:

> I will not appeal your decision. You have already denied me justice by not letting me have proper defense in this trial. I have done what you say, but I am not guilty. Ethiopia has been standing still, while our African brothers are moving ahead in the struggles to overcome poverty. What I did was in the best interest of my country.[130]

---

125 The foreign observer, Edvard Hambro, remarks about the lack of a strong Bar which he believed was necessary for impartial trials, "The Rebellion Trials in Ethiopia," 30, 32.

126 "Prosecution Wound Up Case," *Ethiopian Herald,* 3:59 (March 10, 1961).

127 Greenfield, *Ethiopia: A New Political History,* 442–3.

128 "Third Day Trial of Brig. Gen. Mengistu Newai," *Ethiopian Herald,* 3:54 (March 4, 1961).

129 Edvard Hambro, "The Rebellion Trials in Ethiopia," 32.

130 Levine, "On the December 1960 Coup Attempt" in *Interpreting Ethiopia,* 230.

New Direction

The die was cast. The trial had satisfied the international community; America and other donor nations granted financial support and investments poured in.[131] Emperor Haile Selassie's position was secure. The verdict left no room for equivocation, for the codified articles of law proved him guilty. Sentencing was also immutable for French law decreed capital punishment. To an extent the results were too irreversible, too finite. Restorative justice always held the option of reversing course along the continuum between magnanimity and punishment depending on the penitence of the perpetrator and/or the will of the people. Codified justice did not allow that.

Shortly after the abortive coup, Haile Selassie had said, "Peace is justice, justice peace; the two are complementary."[132] They were not. While amnesties had been granted to the majority of Bodyguards, police, students, and collaborators, the protocol involved was less than satisfactory to bring about societal reconciliation. Part of this was that the honor shaming ceremony that certified victor and vanquished and recognized a return to the status quo was gone. Forgiveness was more like the forgive-and-forget type that typified the *Zemene Mesafint* of the nineteenth century where the vanquished could harbor sentiments for revenge. In fact, after the December coup d'état these sentiments were not long in coming.

Salacious pamphlets began to appear around Addis Ababa decrying the imperial regime and praising the revolutionary martyrs. They were unsigned. What is remarkable about this barrage of leaflets is their vehemence, the forcefulness with which they denounced the regime and the emperor. One distributed on Haile Selassie's birthday read, "You the Lion of Judah, known for not being satisfied by eating human flesh and crunching bones are a despicable, miniscule creature." Beyond more *ad hominen* accusations of corruption and embezzlement, the pamphleteer warned, "Now that Ethiopia understands that you are careless of her and has begun to retaliate against your wrongdoings Ethiopia will avoid the confusion that has been set in the Decembrist [the eulogized, new name for the coup-makers] Movement. She has fully recognized now that her enemies are you and your lackeys."[133]

There are many other versions of what Mengistu Neway said in rejecting an appeal, for example see Greenfield, *Ethiopia: A New Political History*, 451.

131 Marcus, *Ethiopia, Great Britain and the United States*, 161.

132 "Imperial Majesty Pays Tribute to the Heroic Ground and Air Forces, Police and People," *Ethiopian Herald*, 2:301 (December 21, 1960).

133 Unsigned pamphlet in Amharic titled "The Birthday of a Tyrant" (July 23, 1961) from Donald Levine's collection of clippings that he gave to me in the mid-1980s when he was Dean of the College at University of Chicago and assumed the Derg's days would never end. Translation was provided by Gebru Wolde, my neighbor and friend.

The use of double meanings, found in *sem inna werq*, to criticize the emperor was also employed to articulate growing resentment. Tamru Feyessa, student leader and budding poet, read his Amharic poem called the "poor man speaks" over a loudspeaker on College Day a few months after the failed coup. According to Richard Greenfield, it "was innocuous only on the surface. There was great clamour in the country for copies of this verse."[134]

Mengistu Neway understood the evolutionary path Ethiopia was on – that the country was headed towards univocality in law and other spheres of governance and commerce. This was an explicit rejection of the ambiguity associated with restorative justice, for restorative justice reasserted tradition, the old antiquated way of doing things. Yet the cultural ideology that held Ethiopia together for centuries was unraveling. Various pressures, both foreign and domestic, not least of which was Emperor Haile Selassie's campaign to minimize the power of the nobility and assert the power of the throne, led to its undoing. Mengistu Neway knew that forgiveness in 1960 would not bring his sincere atonement; rather, for him it would only postpone insurrection. He also had learned that sacrifice was necessary to become a cultural icon for future revolutionaries. Ironically, Mengistu Neway had been Belay Zeleke's executioner, the man who had placed the noose around the neck of the Patriot hero beloved by the peasants of Ethiopia.[135] He had also witnessed how, rather than descend into infamy, Belay Zeleke had risen to martyrdom, a beacon of a more equitable Ethiopia. Whether in protest for what he believed was an unfair trial or for entry to hero status, Mengistu Neway chose to forgo all effort at legal redress and instead opted to die for his cause.

The trial brought justice, swift and fixed, and satisfied the victims' families' desire for vengeance. It also pleased the emperor and the cabinet for it proved to the world Ethiopia's adoption of modern jurisprudence. It unequivocally demonstrated that overthrowing the monarch, killing to thwart Ethiopia's functioning government, and taking the law into one's own hands was punishable by death. Retributive justice ruled. No longer were circumstances considered, conditional forgiveness granted, and atonement expected, for Ethiopia's codified laws spelled out what punishment served what crime.

134 Richard Greenfield, letter to Donald Levine, Addis Ababa, February 5, 1962.
135 Asfa-Wossen Asserate, *King of Kings*, 178.

Epilogue

Peace Not War: Traditions of Restorative Justice in Imperial Ethiopia, 1769–1960 traces the use and improvements made to restorative justice practices that characterized Ethiopian history into the early twentieth century. Overlapping, the book also assesses the pull of modernity that both forced and lured Ethiopia to cast aside its endogenously evolved legal remedies and adopt European jurisprudence that aligned more with retributive justice. This Epilogue demonstrates how thorough and encompassing was this transition to retributive justice, for when the Ethiopian People's Revolutionary Democratic Front (EPRDF) overthrew the Marxist dictatorship in 1991 and felt the necessity to apply transitional justice to try Derg members (Amharic for Committee and the term popularly used to refer to the military junta) in a court trial for their crimes against humanity and genocide, the EPRDF leadership did not even entertain the use of Ethiopia's traditions of restorative justice.

Peace Not War's agenda is twofold. First, it contributes to the literature on restorative justice by showing how Ethiopia, through trial and error, corrected the "forgive and forget" ideation of restorative justice as one-and-done, blanket amnesties that, as was shown (Chapter 2), did not bring about reconciliation, but rather encouraged enmity and war. It also demonstrated that historical analysis can uplift significant improvements that were made to restorative justice modalities through the development of "conditional forgiveness" that evinced ingenuity, flexibility, and adaptability to, in fact, reconcile warring parties and bring about lasting peace. Second, the historical method possesses a perhaps unintended consequence, for, by focusing on the way national threats to the sovereignty of the state were resolved, it outlined how one legal remedy was supplanted by another – restorative for retributive justice. Ethiopian history shows how restorative justice was shelved out of preference for European-inspired, codified law to the degree that Ethiopia's robust tradition of restorative justice was forgotten. However, since the election of Prime Minister Abiy Ahmed, Ethiopia is experimenting with differing ways to bring about peace, equity, and justice. Perhaps lessons from its past would help Ethiopia achieve national reconciliation.

The Derg Trials, End of Restorative Justice

The years between the coup d'état of 1960 and the 1974 revolution were similar to the interwar years of the twentieth century, for some they were the best of times, for others the looming clouds only grew darker. Finally, the city of Addis Ababa took on a different appearance. Open spaces, fields and pasturelands were subdivided, water pipes and electric lines were laid. The downtown was burnished, commercial activities expanded, and construction was ongoing. A new airport was built and leading out to it an upscale neighborhood, Bole, was platted. While never large, an entrepreneurial class began to gain sway signaled by ownership of larger villas. Salaried government functionaries had more disposable income and with it purchased cars adding to traffic congestion which necessitated widening streets and paving them. As Addis had become the center for the Organization of African Unity, the number of diplomats multiplied increasing opportunities for clerical workers by an even larger factor. Destination tourism took Ethiopians and resident foreigners to Debre Zeit, Ambo, and Lake Langano. Private schools appeared, often associated with different expatriate communities, but all welcomed Ethiopian students who could pay. Peace Corps workers were dispatched to remote locations to, if nothing else, introduce an alternate pedagogy, one that questioned authority structures. Abebe Bikila won back-to-back Olympic marathons in 1960 and 1964 followed by Mamo Wolde in 1968 vaulting Ethiopia into the pantheon of world-class runners and they became an inspiration for countless Ethiopian youth in the years to follow. Possibilities seemed infinite for those on top; life remained stultifying for those at the bottom.

The unsigned, salacious pamphlets distributed after the 1960 Coup d'État grew into open protests and organized parties in the ensuing years. Haile Selassie I University was the hub of the ideological ferment.[1] The Ethiopia People's Revolutionary Party (EPRP) was the hotbed of revolutionary activity before differing interpretations of Marxism/Leninism separated one group of students from another. From their written denunciations came the passage of revolutionary party constitutions which pitted them against the monarchy but also against one another. To appeal to those at the bottom, land reform was demanded and a classless society advocated. The years 1960 through

1 University College of Addis Ababa was renamed Haile Selassie I University in December 1961 and relocated to the Genete-Leul Palace after the emperor moved to the Jubilee Palace and gave the Sidist Kilo compound to the university to become the main campus and serve as the university's administrative facility, see *Inaugural Address of His Imperial Majesty Haile Sellassie I on the Occasion of the Founding Ceremony of the Haile Sellassie I University*, Addis Ababa (December 18, 1961).

1974 were not without political turmoil. Other coups were squelched, and assassination attempts prevented through an ever more invasive security system, yet rumblings became demonstrations became riots.

Starting in the Afar region, Ethiopia suffered widespread famine in 1973 with millions affected and tens of thousands dying of starvation in northern Shewa, Wollo, and Tigray. While likely aware of the magnitude of the famine, Haile Selassie, in the public's judgement, appeared oblivious and unmoved. Reinforcing this opinion was the fact that while government resources should have been diverted to famine relief, instead the regime spent lavishly on celebrating the emperor's eightieth birthday and other commemorative occasions.[2] The hypocrisy was broadcast on October 18, 1973 in Jonathan Dimbleby's *Ethiopia: The Unknown Famine* documentary, becoming an embarrassment for educated Ethiopians and a catalyst for the overthrow of an indefensible monarchy. The Ethiopian Revolution of 1974 had many instigators: soldiers mutinying for better pay, teachers calling a general strike against an educational reform bill that obstructed comprehensive education, taxi drivers striking to demand a 50 percent increase in fares to offset the rise in fuel prices and frustrated, impatient students. It had a populist feel to it, "the soldiers and junior ranks against the high officers, the poor against the rich, employee against employer and labour against management."[3]

The uproar climaxed in February 1974 causing Haile Selassie's long-governing cabinet to resign. There ensued two cobbled-together administrations led by Endalkachew Makonnen and Mikael Imru respectively. Note that these men were members of the Qachane Club years before (see Chapter 7) and therefore were viewed as politically progressive, yet both governments swore loyalty to the emperor which hindered their effectiveness to bring about necessary reforms. Like many revolutions the pendulum for change gained momentum. Law and order broke down between February and September as the weak cabinets' security apparatus was unable to quell growing unrest. Gradually the vacuum was filled by the Derg made up of communist-leaning military officers who adopted more radical positions and assumed additional powers. Jockeying within the Derg led to firefights amongst the leadership with Mengistu Haile Mariam, a major from the Third Division of the Army, ultimately seizing control through sheer brutality. Upon his orders Emperor Haile Selassie was deposed, driven away from the Jubilee Palace in a proletarian Volkswagen Beetle to be jailed, and murdered a year later. Then sixty generals, ministers, and high-ranking officials were summarily executed with Mengistu Haile Mariam reputedly pulling the trigger to ensure an irrevocable break with the past,

2 "Haile Selassie is 80," *New York Times* (July 24, 1972): 17.

3 Bahru Zewde, *Modern Ethiopia*, 231.

just like his revolutionary predecessors Mengistu and Germame Neway. Next the Derg turned on the EPRP, essentially the student-led leftist wing that taught Mengistu and the rest of the Derg the fundamentals of Marxism. The EPRP was not passive and turned against the Derg as well as Meison (All-Ethiopian Socialist Movement) who quickly sidled up to the Derg for protection but also for the misbegotten idea that they would become the cardinals of Marxist orthodoxy. This lasted for less than a year after which the Derg devoured Meison as well. Many *kebele* (neighborhood administration) officials and militiamen were illiterate or common criminals, yet Mengistu's Derg empowered them with the right to determine who was a monarchist or counter-revolutionary and then authorized them to take justice into their own hands and imprison, torture, disappear, or kill whomever, whenever with impunity. Bodies were left out on the streets to putrefy the air and pacify the population. To add to their suffering, families who identified the bodies of loved ones were often required to pay for the bullets that were used to kill them before they were allowed to retrieve the corpses for religious burials.[4]

Estimates range from 10,000 to 150,000 persons killed, almost all of them from Ethiopia's cities.[5] Far more were imprisoned without charge for indefinite periods of time. The Red Terror or the "ferreting-out" campaign endured for two years and rendered the population traumatized and quiescent. The Marxist-Leninist dictatorship lasted until the summer of 1991 when the collapse of the Soviet Union, the ascendancy of ethno-nationalist parties fighting to overthrow the regime with Western support, and decay from within the totalitarian one-party state contributed to its collapse.

Competition to become the successor regime was intense; however, after weighty political maneuvering and a disputed election in 1992 the EPRDF emerged as the dominant party controlling Ethiopia for the next twenty-six years. With economic stasis, political insecurity, a consti-

---

4 The literature on the Ethiopian Revolution is vast, see Andargachew Tiruneh, *The Ethiopian Revolution 1974–1987: A Transformation from an Aristocratic to Totalitarian Autocracy* (Cambridge: Cambridge University Press, 1993); Fred Halliday and Maxine Molyneux, *The Ethiopian Revolution*; René Lefort, *Ethiopia: An Heretical Revolution?* For the perspective of a contrite former member of the Derg, see Dawit Wolde Giorgis, *Red Tears: War, Famine and Revolution in Ethiopia* (Trenton: Red Sea Press, 1989).

5 The scale of violence makes estimates imprecise. Babile Tola provides both low and high estimates, see *To Kill a Generation: The Red Terror in Ethiopia* (Washington D.C.: Free Ethiopia Press, 1997), 160, 163. Other figures can be found in Kiflu Tadesse, *The Generation Part II: Ethiopia Transformation and Conflict – The History of the Ethiopian People's Revolutionary Party* (New York: University Press of America, 1998), 269; and Barbara Harff and Ted Robert Gurr, "Toward an Empirical Theory of Genocides and Politicides," *International Studies Quarterly*, 32:3 (1988): 364.

tutional crisis, and juridical confusion, the situation the EPRDF inherited was chaotic. Prime Minister Meles Zenawi, its undisputed leader and a brilliant tactician, turned Ethiopia around in a remarkably short time. Meles Zenawi's accomplishments were internationally heralded, and along with Isaias Afeworki of Eritrea and Yoweri Museveni of Uganda, they were branded Africa's "new generation of leaders" partly for their commitment to transparency and accountability. However, some years after the euphoria of the "political spring" of the early 1990s had subsided *The Washington Post* noted, "each attained power through the barrel of a gun, and none have been able to put his weapon down."[6] Notwithstanding, in the 1990s Western imports began to arrive and stores began to restock their shelves; EPRDF soldiers – initially – were the paragons of discipline ensuring security of person in a war-torn land; broadly recruited committees, in terms of educational attainment, ethnicity and gender, were charged with drafting a constitution which was ratified in 1995 inaugurating a federalist government; finally, a transitional justice system was put in place to account for the atrocities of the Derg.

The Transitional Government of Ethiopia, with the EPRDF the dominant party, assumed the responsibility to bring Derg officials to trial.[7] To this end the Special Prosecutor's Office (SPO) was established in 1992 with a dual mandate: to try the accused and "to record for prosperity the brutal offenses ... in order to prevent the recurrence of such a system of government."[8] The latter hamstrung the SPO for, remarkably, *kebele*s and other government offices kept detailed records of the atrocities which overwhelmed the SPO staff. Foreign computer experts were requisitioned from the Carter Center to create a database of this vast trove of abuses.[9] By mid-1994, 301,000 pages of Derg documents had been collected in the capital, and additionally three-hundred Ethiopian, SPO contractors were dispatched to *kebele*s throughout the country to begin compiling the records of imprisonment, torture, and murders perpetuated by the "unleashed *kebele* officials" in 1977/8. Finally, with the assistance of the Argentinian Forensic Anthropology Team, the SPO exhumed graves creating a map of mass graves throughout Ethiopia. As the trial got underway the influence of foreign investigators and legal experts decreased, although they kept criticizing trial procedures to

6 Karl Vick, "New African Leaders Turn on One Another." *The Washington Post* (September 2, 1999).

7 Kjetil Tronvoll, Charles Schaefer, and Girmachew Alemu Aneme. eds., *The Ethiopian Red Terror Trials* (Rochester: James Currey, 2009).

8 "Transitional Government of Ethiopia," Preamble of Proclamation 22/1992.

9 The foreign contribution, particularly the role of the Carter Center, is assessed by Todd Howland, "Learning to Make Proactive Human Rights Interventions Effective: The Carter Center and Ethiopia's Office of the Special Prosecutor," *Wisconsin International Law Journal*, 407 (Spring 2000).

the very end. Over time the flagship trials in Addis Ababa languished. The public initially clamored to testify about their mistreatment and throngs crowded into courtrooms to hear testimony, but delays led to apathy. Even the Prime Minister Meles Zenawi, in a 2002 interview, was candid enough to venture that because of the protracted nature of the trial "the exercise became more and more irrelevant."[10] Problems abounded: for example, judges rotated on and off the three-panel bench, breaking basic legal procedure. Other questions surfaced about the rights of the accused and impediments to documentary evidence for the defense. Political support to prosecute past atrocities waned as the EPRDF was increasingly accused of abuses itself. Disputes over Ethiopia's own definition of the genocide that included political groups – students and party members – ground the trials to a virtual halt. In the end, verdicts for the top fifty-five officials were given in December 2006, fourteen years after the start of the trial; moreover, the appeals process further protracted it for another two years.[11]

If nothing else, "the contribution of the Red Terror trials to transitional justice [was] predicated precisely on their autochthonous nature,"[12] where the law, prosecutors, defense lawyers, and judges were all Ethiopian. Moreover, it added a new element to adjudicating genocidal acts. The victims of the Red Terror came from every ethnic, religious, and social group in Ethiopia, but what they shared were political opinions – from ultra-leftist ideologies to conservative yearnings for a constitutional monarchy. Politics and politics alone was Mengistu's rationale for the killings. It just so happened that Article 281(a) of the 1957 Ethiopian Penal Code, conveniently and perhaps sagaciously on the part of Haile Selassie's legal advisers, defined acts of genocide to include political groups, where, in fact, the 1948 U.N. Convention on Genocide confined the definition to include only national, ethnical, racial, and religious groups.[13]

---

10 Kjetil Tronvoll interview with Prime Minister Meles Zenawi, Addis Ababa, January 16, 2002. Transcript of interview referenced in *Ethiopian Red Terror Trials*, 6, 69.

11 For contending views on the efficacy of the SPO see Sarah Vaughan, "The Role of the Special Prosecutor's Office" in *Ethiopian Red Terror Trials*, ch. 4; and Teshome Gabre-Mariam Bokan, "A Plea for the Trial of Dergue and/or WPE Members," unpublished paper (August 25, 1994).

12 Kjetil Tronvoll, Charles Schaefer, and Girmachew Alemu Aneme, "Concluding the Main Red Terror Trial: Special Prosecutor v. Colonel Mengistu Hailemariam et al." in *Ethiopian Red Terror Trials*, 136.

13 Article 281 of the 1957 Penal Code in its English version reads: "Whosoever, with intent to destroy, in whole or in part, a national, ethnic, racial, religious or political group, organizes, orders or engages in, be it in time of war or in time of peace..." (underlining mine).

But the trials hardly brought reconciliation. The public was inured; a national identity barely existed; forgiveness was forgotten; and atonement was not even part of the equation. When finally the verdict was read, news reporters interviewing Ethiopians on the street found that there had been a dramatic shift away from viewing the Red Terror trials as a mechanism to bring about national reconciliation to "victor's justice" or a way to legitimize the EPRDF.[14] As one Ethiopian put it, "Today's sentence makes a mockery of justice."[15] The moral ecology of imperial Ethiopia that bolstered restorative justice, with all its socio-political strength to reconcile, and juristic weaknesses that enabled verdicts to be flexible and adaptive to circumstances, was absent in post-Derg Ethiopia.

When and why did the EPRDF decide to pursue retributive justice instead of restorative justice in their effort to assert transitional justice? The "when" confirms the leadership's selection of a trial format well before entering the capital city victoriously. According to Meles Zenawi, the decision "that a legal accounting of what happened was the best way to go" was taken during the last stages of the war against the Derg when it was apparent that the EPRDF had seized the upper hand. The "why" Meles states has to do with the fact that truth commissions were unknown to them out in the bush circa 1989 through 1991,[16] even though they were already employed in Latin America.[17] The ignorance can be partially excused because South Africa's Truth and Reconciliation Commission was not to come about for another four years. Absent from his comments were references to or even knowledge of Ethiopia's own long history of restorative justice. Speculation surrounding why the EPRDF leadership did not consider "traditional" forms of restorative justice remains clouded;[18] however, three points should be taken into consideration. First, the EPRDF leadership, and for that matter all the student revolutionary groups of the 1970s to which they belonged, were rebelling against old traditions and customs, and the stifling authority of the Ethiopian Orthodox Church and the mon-

---

14 Demelash Shiferaw Reta, "National Prosecution and Transitional Justice: The Case of Ethiopia," Ph.D. dissertation, School of Law, University of Warwick (2014) for an assessment of the legal framework of the trials as well as their establishment of "truth." Also see Jima Dilbo Denbel, "Transitional Justice in the Context of Ethiopia," *International Letters of Social and Humanistic Sciences*, 10 (2013): 73–83.

15 "Life sentence for Ethiopia dictator," *Reuters* (January 11, 2007).

16 Kjetil Tronvoll interview with Prime Minister Meles Zenawi, in *Ethiopian Red Terror Trials*, 6.

17 Mark Ensalaco, "Truth Commissions for Chile and El Salvador: A Report and Assessment," *Human Rights Quarterly*, 16:4 (1994): 656–75.

18 Charles Schaefer "The Derg Trial versus Traditions of Restorative Justice in Ethiopia" in *The Ethiopian Red Terror Trials*, 68–72.

archy. To revert to traditional methods to restore peace and bring about reconciliation with all its Christian overtones would be tantamount to betraying their criticism of the ancien régime and Christian primacy. Second, EPRDF cadres were versed in Marxist/Leninist ideology which advocated the use of force and sought modern, scientific practices to advance the rights of the proletariat. Third, 1989 witnessed the collapse of the Soviet Union and in its place the ascendancy of Western insistence on democracy, transparency, and accountability. Translated into the political and judicial realms this meant holding free and fair elections and abiding by international law and the Geneva Conventions. To a great extent the global trend during this period emphasized retributive justice carried out in either national or international courts to resolve all human rights abuses and bring about reconciliation.[19] Certainly the United States exerted pressure on Ethiopia in this transitional period to opt for criminal prosecution, yet it appeared that the United States' insistence coincided with the EPRDF leadership's predilection to try Derg officials in a court of law.

Cry for Meaningful Justice

Whether "victor's justice" or not, even the defendants, who had been isolated in prison for nearly two decades, yearned for an opportunity to apologize to the Ethiopian people and repent.[20] The Red Terror trials' shortcomings were multistoried. Additionally, their legacy provided no foundation. A part of the transitional justice bricks and mortar attempts to commemorate travesties of the past to prevent repetition. Large memorials were erected in Adama, Bahir Dar, and Mekele, the regional capitals of Oromia, Amhara, and Tigray respectively, but while they memorialize lives lost, they are more about the valiant struggle the rebel parties of the 1980s waged against the totalitarian military regime.[21] The only real attempt to honor the victims of the Red Terror is through exhibits at the Red Terror Martyrs Memorial Museum in Meskel Square in Addis Ababa. Embodying memory is vital to dissipate the pain of genocide and allow society to move on.[22] Surprisingly, the museum was the inspiration of Nunu Tsige, a private citizen, and

---

19 Although Ruti Teitel's monograph is published well after this period, the study was first commissioned by the United States Institute for Peace in the early 1990s and convincingly argues the benefits of prosecutorial trials, see *Transitional Justice* (Oxford: Oxford University Press, 2000).

20 Girmachew Alemu Aneme, "Apology and Trials: The Case of the Red Terror Trials in Ethiopia," *African Human Rights Law Journal*, 6 (2006): 64–84.

21 Bridget Conley, *Memory from the Margins: Ethiopia's Red Terror Martyrs Memorial Museum* (Cham: Palgrave Macmillan, 2019), 98–109.

22 Rita Kesselring, *Bodies of Truth*, 77–94.

a dedicated band of volunteers who acquired land rights from the city government, raised sufficient funds, found architects and builders, and designed the exhibit narratives in keeping with the latest theories in memory museology.[23] Especially gripping are stacks of femurs, ribs, and sculls encased on glass shelves that trigger visceral responses. Unfortunately, between 2010 and the present, the Red Terror Martyrs Memorial Museum is overlooked by passersby, and more people appear to be drinking coffee at the coffeehouse just outside than going into the museum.

In 2011, the Patriarch of the Ethiopian Orthodox Tewahido Church, the Sheikh of the Ethiopian Muslim Affairs Supreme Council, the Archbishop of the Ethiopian Catholic Church, and the President of the Ethiopian Evangelical Church Mekane Yesus issued a communique calling for the pardon of sixteen top Derg officials thus shortening their life sentences. Evincing ecumenism and interreligious understanding, the religious leaders determined that twenty years imprisonment coupled with their demonstrated remorse was sufficient and it was time for the nation to show mercy by releasing them. As reported: "The intervention of religious leaders for mercy is widely accepted and promoted in church teachings."[24] It appears aspects of restorative justice still resided in Ethiopia's religious establishment.

This is not to say that the lament for peace and reconciliation is confined to religious leaders – anything but. Throughout the twenty-seven years of EPRDF rule there were occasional articles in the popular press proposing a national referendum, not dissimilar to the peace talks at the National Transitional Conference in late summer 1991 that led to the creation of the Provisional Government of Ethiopia, for everything was on the table then: who should be represented, how representatives would be elected and what form government would take. To an extent, there is a desire to go back to square one through a referendum that would recast Ethiopia to ensure a level playing field to bring about reconciliation.

These referendum articles have increased since Abiy Ahmed was elected Prime Minister by the Central Committee of the EPRDF in 2018, perhaps in part because Abiy promised reforms and had the credentials to back them up.[25] He defended his Ph.D. dissertation in 2016 which was on "Social Capital and Its Role in Traditional Conflict Resolution" using

---

23 Conley, *Memory from the Margins*, 112–67. Another exhibit exists outside Ethiopia commemorating the victims of the Red Terror at the Canadian Museum for Human Rights in Winnipeg, curated by Jeremy Maron and Charles Schaefer.

24 Solomon Bekele, "Sixteen former high Derg officials released," *Capital* (October 10, 2011).

25 Daniel Mekonnen, "Ethiopia's Transitional Justice Process Needs Restoration Work," *Ethiopia Insight* (February 1, 2019).

inter-religious conflicts in the Jimma Zone of Oromia as his case studies. Its bibliography is illuminating for it contains the top authorities in the subfields of conflict resolution, peace and reconciliation, and restorative justice.[26] It is unlikely any other head of state has studied reconciliation as thoroughly as Abiy Ahmed. The first year of this administration radiated possibilities. He renamed the Ministry of Federal Affairs the Ministry of Peace, which is either a bold scam or a brave reconceptualization of government. In December 2018 Abiy Ahmed's government established a Reconciliation Commission committed to seek "truth and justice," identify gross human rights violations, provide a forum for victims "to be heard and perpetrators to disclose," in order "to prevent future occurrence of such conflict."[27] He even won the Nobel Peace Prize in 2019 for forging a peace treaty with Eritrea after twenty-one years of hostilities often evolving into firefights. The years 2020 through 2024, however, were a disappointment. War consumed the country. Ethnic divisions deepened. Religious intolerance increased. National identity or, for that matter national unity, disappeared. The Reconciliation Commission was quietly dissolved in March of 2022.[28] At the time of this writing Ethiopia works to build its military, develop naval ports on the Red Sea, and deploy Turkish-made drones to suppress internal insurrection.

The cry for something – anything – to improve the situation in Ethiopia is resounding.[29] Either a referendum to resolve political issues or an improved transitional justice framework to ease social rupture are considered as possible solutions. In the call for improved transitional justice, it is widely believed that Ethiopia's previous experience – the Red Terror trials – did not live up to expectations.[30] The underlined question is "Can Justice Bring Peace to Ethiopia?"[31] To an extent Ethiopia

26 Abiy Ahmed, "Social Capital and its Role in Traditional Conflict Resolution: The Case of Inter-religious Conflict in Jimma Zone of the Oromia Regional State in Ethiopia," Ph.D. dissertation, Institute for Peace and Security Studies, Addis Ababa University (2016).

27 "A Proclamation to Establish Reconciliation Commission," *Federal Negarit Gazette*, Proclamation No. 1102/2018 (February 5, 2019).

28 "Ethiopian Reconciliation Commission Dissolves," *Addis Standard* (March 1, 2022).

29 Moussa Soumahoro and Fikir G. Mekonnen, "Beyond Cessation of Hostilities, Ethiopia Needs Comprehensive Peace," *Premium Times* (October 26, 2023); Tadesse Simie Metekia, "Ethiopia Urgently Needs a Transitional Justice Policy," *Institute for Security Studies* (August 1, 2022); and Michelle Gavin, "In Ethiopia, Peace Requires Domestic Reconciliation," *Council on Foreign Relations* (May 7, 2021).

30 Jeremy Sarkin, "Transitional Justice and the Prosecution Model: The Experience of Ethiopia," *Law, Democracy & Development*, 3:2 (1999): 253–66.

31 Patrick Vinck, Tadesse Simie Metekia, Geoff Dancy, Kathryn Sikkink, and Phuong N. Pham, "Can Justice Bring Peace to Ethiopia? How to Heal Division

is heeding the call and is patterning its transitional justice modalities after the African Union's 2019-adopted *Transitional Justice Policy* handbook.[32] Some progress has been made according to the news media,[33] but even before the framework was unveiled detractors criticized the direction it was taking.[34]

Tadesse Simie Metekia argues that by carefully analyzing and adopting aspects of *ubuntu* and *gacaca*, restorative justice could offer pathways to peace and reconciliation in Ethiopia.[35] Surprisingly, few are mining Ethiopia's own rich experience with restorative justice that has proven to be ingenious, flexible, and adaptable. Why borrow from South Africa or Rwanda or from the vast academic reservoir of restorative (transitional) justice literature when Ethiopia possesses abundant case studies that were understood by and meaningful to the Ethiopian population? The African Union's *Transitional Justice Policy* handbook offers an impressive toolkit yet one demonstrably hybridized.[36] Circumstances have changed dramatically, and the imperial examples described above may only offer suggestions. While the moral ecology of Ethiopia today appears ethnically fragmented, Ethiopian history should be studied to determine autochthonous solutions over imports from abroad. Five examples make this point, while the sixth shows the danger associated with retroactively applying historical solutions.

First, Ethiopia's historical understanding of justice was culturally defined – eyes wide open but faceless – demonstrating impartiality but also enabling judges to perceive ambiguity and contradictions in the administration of justice. Further, justice embodied the concept of *irq* that delivered verdicts that responded to socio-political realities and often contradicted strict legal interpretation. Could transitional justice take on Ethiopian features? Issues emerge, not least of which is which feature or which ethnic tradition? On the other hand, relying on foreign jurisprudence is tantamount to a copout. It absolves Ethiopian politicians and legal experts from scrutinizing their own legal systems and

---

After Decades of War," *Foreign Affairs* (November 15, 2023).

32 African Union, *Transitional Justice Policy*.

33 "Ethiopia to Make Available Draft Transitional Justice Policy for Public Review in a Month," *Addis Standard* (October 17, 2023). The Ethiopian government issued a Green Paper, "Transitional Justice Policy Options" in early 2023, based on the African Union's policy.

34 Seifudein Adem and Abadir Ibrahim, "Ethiopia Is Not Ready for Transitional Justice," *Foreign Policy* (March 14, 2023).

35 Tadesse Simie Metekia, "From Ubuntu to Gacaca: Traditional Justice could Benefit Ethiopia's Transition," *Institute for Security Studies* (October 16, 2023).

36 John G. Ikubaje, "African Union, Ethiopia, and New Developments on Transitional Justice in Africa," *The Cable* (May 13, 2024) https://www.thecable.ng/african-union-ethiopia-and-new-developments-on-transitional-justice-in-africa.

various Customary Dispute Resolution mechanisms to find workable systems that could be employed at the state level.

Second, the *Zemene Mesafint* suggests that, when a battle was prematurely stopped or its results ambiguous or forgiveness too freely given, peace was elusive. This was particularly the case when general amnesty or "forgive and forget" was decreed and rivals were allowed to return, unhindered, to their patrimonial lands and prepare once again for war. Under those circumstances, the aggrieved – which could have been both contenders but more likely the defeated party – were in a position to spend time rebuilding their armies in order to fight another day and regain their honor. "Forgive and forget" failed in Ethiopia and it took about a century for the political and judicial establishment to apply conditions to forgiveness.[37] Could studying history provide clues on how to end conflict and respect the vanquished by applying reasonable terms?

Third, conditional forgiveness was flexible; it allowed the state to modify sentences according to the perpetrators' willingness to abide by its decrees, thus reducing repetition. Conditional forgiveness also held out the possibility of complete reintegration into society and the political order for a multiplicity of reasons, including political changes, but foremost by the offender respecting and living by the terms associated with conditional forgiveness. Conversely today, the Cessation of Hostilities Agreement negotiated in Pretoria, South Africa, and signed by the government of Ethiopia and the Tigray People's Liberation Front (TPLF) has numerous clauses, many of which have not been implemented or have been abused by both signatories. The possibility that the agreement might collapse appears valid. The flexibility to rehash agreements and conditions associated with restorative justice may serve Ethiopia well as it moves forward.

Fourth, Ethiopia's traditions of restorative justice encouraged the state to consider leniency knowing that forgiveness was a two-way street where societal reconciliation often inhabited the median and where forgiveness at times could serve the long-term interests of the state and even promote national identity. Bedeviled with ethnic conflicts in the Amhara and Oromo regions that pit Ethiopian forces against the Amhara paramilitary group known as *Fano* and the Oromo military constellation referred to as the Oromo Liberation Army (OLF-Shane), the government could consider being sympathetic and even indulgent. The breakup of peace talks between Abiy Ahmed's Prosperity Party

37 For a longer examination of the policy implications of Ethiopia's traditions of restorative justice for inclusion in transitional justice policy today see, Charles Schaefer, "Restorative Justice Modalities: What Can Be Learned about Peace and Reconciliation from Imperial Ethiopia?" in *Ethiopia in the Wake of Political Reforms* (Los Angeles: Tsehai, 2020), 221–46.

and the Oromo Liberation Army in Arusha, Tanzania, had much to do with the government arriving with preset conditions and allegedly an unwillingness to listen and negotiate.[38] Ethiopian history reveals that harsh remedies were rarely perceived as just. Leniency can promote inclusion and national identity.[39]

Fifth, submission, formalized in the honor and shaming ceremony, was carried out in a public forum where the megaphone of gossip publicized the event: who submitted to whom and the conditions under which forgiveness and/or restitution were agreed upon. The courtroom did little to impart justice during the Derg trials. The Cessation of Hostilities Agreement, negotiated behind closed doors in Pretoria, is almost meaningless to the people of Tigray or the rest of Ethiopia. Transparency is a key element for transitional justice to succeed. In order to see the administration of justice there needs to be the possibility of public admission to wrongdoing in order to show contrition and shame. These are central to Ethiopian traditions of restorative justice as ceremonialized in *wurdet* – honor and shaming.

Sixth, the one that shows the dangers associated with retroactively applying historical solutions also involves shaming. Shaming is an element of restorative justice since truth-finding reveals a spectrum of human rights abuses from denial of free speech to extrajudicial killings. The modalities of shaming are culturally specific as historically attested to in highland Ethiopia's *wurdet* ceremony (see Chapter 1) where perpetrators often ritualistically cloaked themselves in a *shemma* and carried a millstone on their exposed shoulders as a sign of penitence. But cultural homogeneity – if it ever existed – died alongside imperial hegemony in 1974 with the Ethiopian Revolution. After the Derg, the Ethiopian People's Revolutionary Democratic Front (EPRDF) introduced "ethnic federalism," a bold experiment that gave agency to fourteen ethnically defined regions to promote their own languages, cultures, and governance. To some extent "ethnic federalism" encouraged cultural heterogeneity and, paraphrasing John Braithwaite, the development of subcultures – read ethnic ties – that conceived of crimes and justice in unique and sometimes incongruous ways.[40] Shaming, perhaps not surprisingly, can be reintegrative in favorable circumstances as well as disintegrative when the stigmatization is pushed too far. Under disintegrative circumstances the stigmatized individuals become convinced of their innocence and are spurred to

38 "Ethiopia Talks with Oromo Rebel Group End Without Deal for a Third Time," *Aljazeera* (November 22, 2023) https://www.aljazeera.com/news/2023/11/22/ethiopia-talks-with-rebel-group-ola-end-without-deal.

39 Mark Drumbl, "Punishment, Postgenocide: From Guilt to Shame to *Civis* in Rwanda," *New York University Law Review*, 75:5 (2000): 1221–1326.

40 Braithwaite, *Crime, Shame and Reintegration*, 65–8.

retaliate for their perception of wrongdoing against them.[41] Integrative shaming was the aim of Rwanda's *Gacaca* Courts although not always successfully.[42] Likewise, integrative shaming reflects the intent associated with restorative justice in Ethiopia. Disintegrative shaming may display the risks that attend implementing practices resurrected from the annals of history.

Peace Not War is about statecraft: how social advancement was attached to political loyalty or sometimes rebellion, how a feudal hierarchy honored its peasant base while exploiting them, how the state used biblical teachings as the progenitor of justice, how Ethiopians cultivated the ability to perceive ambiguity and find compromise (*irq*), how being magnanimous or vengeful as circumstances dictated served both the state and the people, and how the *zufan chilot* (Imperial Court) embraced ethnic and religious diversity although within formalized kinship and marriage structures. The lesson is Ethiopian resourcefulness. Circumstances have changed radically over the centuries from a feudal society based on a vertical hierarchical order with an emperor at the top and descending by rank to peasants at the bottom, to a centralized bureaucracy in the twenty-first century legitimized by elections that govern an ethnically divided nation where horizontal ties determine identity and allegiance. Yet despite these radical differences, it is hoped that this study of Ethiopian history encourages academics and policymakers to assess and possibly adopt ingenious and infinitely adaptable legal remedies devised and tested in imperial Ethiopia to augment the healthy discourse on transitional justice by asserting the documented, precolonial origins of restorative justice on the African continent.

41 Braithwaite, *Crime, Shame and Reintegration,* 67–8.
42 Drumbl, "Punishment, Postgenocide," 1263.

Glossary

Most Amharic words and names of people or places have been transliterated consistently without the use of diacritics. A decision was made to omit diacritical marks to ease reading and pronunciation for all readers. However, the spelling of certain common names that are near universally recognized or historically acknowledged, I have retained. I have also given weight to the spelling a historical figure uses in their own English publication for themselves. Spellings within quotes or in footnotes have not been changed.

abuna	Archbishop or head of the Ethiopian Orthodox Tewahido Church.
afa negus	'Mouth of the king' the supreme judge of the state under the king, equivalent to a chief justice.
askari	Eritrean or colonial soldiers in Italian pay.
atse serat	'The law of the sovereign.'
balabbat	Hereditary owner of *rest* land and local chief; after the nineteenth-century conquest of southern Ethiopia a hereditary chief.
chiqa shum	Village chief and/or tax collector for the *gult* holder.
dagna	Local judge or magistrate.
debtera	A highly educated but non-ordained cleric.
dejazmach	'Commander of the gate'; a political/military title below *ras.*
echage	Chief Prior of Debre Libanos monastery, who was the ecclesiastical head of all monasteries.
enderase	Regent.
fitawrari	'Commander of the vanguard' a military distinction conferring admittance into aristocratic ranks.

Fitha Negest	'Justice of the Kings.'
gebbi	Palace.
gizot	Connoted denunciation, demotion and relocation to the periphery of the empire.
gult	Non-hereditary right to demand tribute from peasants working the land.
irq	Possibility of negotiation between good and evil, or reconciliation between contending parties.
kebele	Neighborhood administration.
Kibre Negest	'The Glory of the Kings' the title of the fourteenth-century book about the biblical origins of the Solomonic dynasty.
ligaba	Protocol officer in charge of arranging visitation to the emperor.
lij	Child, also an honorific title used by sons of royal family and upper nobility.
mahber	Religious or community mutual self-help association.
mekwanint	High ruling class consisting of nobles, provincial governors, and high-ranking military.
Meshaf Bet	House of Books and Interpretation (perhaps equivalent to schools of theology).
mihret	Forgiveness or amnesty.
neggadras	'Head of merchants' with authority to collect customs and levy market taxes.
negus	King.
neguse negest	'King of kings'; emperor.
niftenya	Northern soldiers who settled in southern Ethiopia and were given hegemony over local populations.
qes atse	The Imperial Chaplain.
qiné	Liturgical form of poetry carrying a superficial "wax" level while indicating a contradictory "gold" level of meaning, eg. used in praising God or criticizing a ruler.
Qiné Bet	School of Poetry.
ras	Head; a title of nobility just below king; prince.
ras bitwedded	'The favorite,' head of the governors or princes.

rist	Peasant rights to cultivate lands through a usufruct system based on family lineage.
sem inna werq	"Wax and gold" a uniquely Ethiopian hermeneutic with ambiguous meanings. Its use extends beyond theology into secular discourse.
shaleqa fird bet	Governor's provincial court.
shemma	A heavy hand-woven cotton shawl.
shiftnet	An acknowledged form of banditry or rebellion.
shum shir	To shuffle governors and other government officials.
techiwoch	Comprised trusted members of the *mekwanint* (judges); act like a jury giving opinions about the final verdict.
Tewahido	Christological belief in the inseparability of Christ's human and divine natures.
wember	High judicial figure; *ras wember* infers superior judge.
Wara Sheh Mesfenate	Yejju rulers who governed Ethiopia from 1786 to 1853.
wurdet	Shaming in an honor and shaming ceremony.
Zema Bet	School of Church Music.
Zemene Mesafint	Era of the Princes, Era of the Judges, or the 'time of the nobility.'
zufan chilot	Imperial Court or Crown Court.

Index

Eastern Africa Series

Women's Land Rights & Privatization in Eastern Africa
BIRGIT ENGLERT & ELIZABETH DALEY (EDS)

War & the Politics of Identity in Ethiopia
KJETIL TRONVOLL

Moving People in Ethiopia
ALULA PANKHURST & FRANÇOIS PIGUET (EDS)

Living Terraces in Ethiopia
ELIZABETH E. WATSON

Eritrea
GAIM KIBREAB

Borders & Borderlands as Resources in the Horn of Africa
DEREJE FEYISSA & MARKUS VIRGIL HOEHNE (EDS)

After the Comprehensive Peace Agreement in Sudan
ELKE GRAWERT (ED.)

Land, Governance, Conflict & the Nuba of Sudan
GUMA KUNDA KOMEY

Ethiopia
JOHN MARKAKIS

Resurrecting Cannibals
HEIKE BEHREND

Pastoralism & Politics in Northern Kenya & Southern Ethiopia
GÜNTHER SCHLEE & ABDULLAHI A. SHONGOLO

Islam & Ethnicity in Northern Kenya & Southern Ethiopia
GÜNTHER SCHLEE with ABDULLAHI A. SHONGOLO

Foundations of an African Civilisation
DAVID W. PHILLIPSON

Regional Integration, Identity & Citizenship in the Greater Horn of Africa
KIDANE MENGISTEAB & REDIE BEREKETEAB (EDS)

Dealing with Government in South Sudan
CHERRY LEONARDI

The Quest for Socialist Utopia
BAHRU ZEWDE

Disrupting Territories
JÖRG GERTEL, RICHARD ROTTENBURG & SANDRA CALKINS (EDS)

The African Garrison State
KJETIL TRONVOLL & DANIEL R. MEKONNEN

The State of Post-conflict Reconstruction
NASEEM BADIEY

Gender, Home & Identity
KATARZYNA GRABSKA

Women, Land & Justice in Tanzania
HELEN DANCER

Remaking Mutirikwi
JOOST FONTEIN

The Oromo & the Christian Kingdom of Ethiopia
MOHAMMED HASSEN

Lost Nationalism
ELENA VEZZADINI

Darfur
CHRIS VAUGHAN

The Eritrean National Service
GAIM KIBREAB

Ploughing New Ground
GETNET BEKELE

Hawks & Doves in Sudan's Armed Conflict
SUAD M. E. MUSA

Ethiopian Warriorhood
TSEHAI BERHANE-SELASSIE

Land, Migration & Belonging
JOSEPH MUJERE

Land Tenure Security
SVEIN EGE (ED.)

Tanzanian Development
DAVID POTTS (ED.)

Nairobi in the Making
CONSTANCE SMITH

The Mission of Apolo Kivebulaya
EMMA WILD-WOOD

The Crisis of Democratization in the Greater Horn of Africa
KIDANE MENGISTEAB (ED.)

The Struggle for Land & Justice in Kenya
AMBREENA MANJI

Imperialism & Development
NICHOLAS WESTCOTT

Kamba Proverbs from Eastern Kenya
JEREMIAH M. KITUNDA

Sports & Modernity in Late Imperial Ethiopia
KATRIN BROMBER

Contested Sustainability
STEFANO PONTE, CHRISTINE NOE, DAN BROCKINGTON (EDS)

Decolonising State & Society in Uganda
KATHERINE BRUCE-LOCKHART, JONATHAN L. EARLE, NAKANYIKE B. MUSISI & EDGAR C. TAYLOR (EDS)

Reimagining the Gendered Nation
CHRISTINA KENNY

Kenya's and Zambia's Relations with China 1949–2019
JODIE YUZHOU SUN

A Political Ecology of Kenya's Mau Forest
LISA ELENA FUCHS

EASTERN AFRICAN STUDIES

These titles published in the United States and Canada by Ohio University Press

Revealing Prophets
Edited by DAVID M. ANDERSON & DOUGLAS H. JOHNSON

East African Expressions of Christianity
Edited by THOMAS SPEAR & ISARIA N. KIMAMBO

The Poor Are Not Us
Edited by DAVID M. ANDERSON & VIGDIS BROCH-DUE

Potent Brews
JUSTIN WILLIS

Swahili Origins
JAMES DE VERE ALLEN

Being Maasai
Edited by THOMAS SPEAR & RICHARD WALLER

Jua Kali Kenya
KENNETH KING

Control & Crisis in Colonial Kenya
BRUCE BERMAN

Unhappy Valley
Book One: State & Class
Book Two: Violence & Ethnicity
BRUCE BERMAN & JOHN LONSDALE

Mau Mau from Below
GREET KERSHAW

The Mau Mau War in Perspective
FRANK FUREDI

Squatters & the Roots of Mau Mau 1905–63
TABITHA KANOGO

Economic & Social Origins of Mau Mau 1945–53
DAVID W. THROUP

Multi-Party Politics in Kenya
DAVID W. THROUP & CHARLES HORNSBY

Empire State-Building
JOANNA LEWIS

Decolonization & Independence in Kenya 1940–93
Edited by B.A. OGOT & WILLIAM R. OCHIENG'

Eroding the Commons
DAVID ANDERSON

Penetration & Protest in Tanzania
ISARIA N. KIMAMBO

Custodians of the Land
Edited by GREGORY MADDOX, JAMES L. GIBLIN & ISARIA N. KIMAMBO

Education in the Development of Tanzania 1919–1990
LENE BUCHERT

The Second Economy in Tanzania
T.L. MALIYAMKONO & M.S.D. BAGACHWA

Ecology Control & Economic Development in East African History
HELGE KJEKSHUS

Siaya
DAVID WILLIAM COHEN & E.S. ATIENO ODHIAMBO

Uganda Now • Changing Uganda Developing Uganda • From Chaos to Order • Religion & Politics in East Africa
Edited by HOLGER BERNT HANSEN & MICHAEL TWADDLE

Kakungulu & the Creation of Uganda, 1868–1928
MICHAEL TWADDLE

Controlling Anger
SUZETTE HEALD

Kampala Women Getting By
SANDRA WALLMAN

Political Power in Pre-Colonial Buganda
RICHARD J. REID

Alice Lakwena & the Holy Spirits
HEIKE BEHREND

Slaves, Spices & Ivory in Zanzibar
ABDUL SHERIFF

Zanzibar Under Colonial Rule
Edited by ABDUL SHERIFF & ED FERGUSON

The History & Conservation of Zanzibar Stone Town
Edited by ABDUL SHERIFF

Pastimes & Politics
LAURA FAIR

Ethnicity & Conflict in the Horn of Africa
Edited by KATSUYOSHI FUKUI & JOHN MARKAKIS

Conflict, Age & Power in North East Africa
Edited by EISEI KURIMOTO & SIMON SIMONSE

Property Rights & Political Development in Ethiopia & Eritrea
SANDRA FULLERTON JOIREMAN

Revolution & Religion in Ethiopia
ØYVIND M. EIDE

Brothers at War
TEKESTE NEGASH & KJETIL TRONVOLL

From Guerrillas to Government
DAVID POOL

Mau Mau & Nationhood
Edited by E.S. ATIENO ODHIAMBO & JOHN LONSDALE

A History of Modern Ethiopia, 1855–1991 (2nd edn)
BAHRU ZEWDE

Pioneers of Change in Ethiopia
BAHRU ZEWDE

Remapping Ethiopia
Edited by W. JAMES, D. DONHAM, E. KURIMOTO & A. TRIULZI

Southern Marches of Imperial Ethiopia
Edited by DONALD L. DONHAM & WENDY JAMES

A Modern History of the Somali (4th edn)
I.M. LEWIS

Islands of Intensive Agriculture in East Africa
Edited by MATS WIDGREN & JOHN E.G. SUTTON

Leaf of Allah
EZEKIEL GEBISSA

Dhows & the Colonial Economy of Zanzibar 1860–1970
ERIK GILBERT

African Womanhood in Colonial Kenya
TABITHA KANOGO

African Underclass
ANDREW BURTON

In Search of a Nation
Edited by GREGORY H. MADDOX & JAMES L. GIBLIN

A History of the Excluded
JAMES L. GIBLIN

Black Poachers, White Hunters
EDWARD I. STEINHART

Ethnic Federalism
DAVID TURTON

Crisis & Decline in Bunyoro
SHANE DOYLE

Emancipation without Abolition in German East Africa
JAN-GEORG DEUTSCH

Women, Work & Domestic Virtue in Uganda 1900–2003
GRACE BANTEBYA KYOMUHENDO & MARJORIE KENISTON McINTOSH

Cultivating Success in Uganda
GRACE CARSWELL

War in Pre-Colonial Eastern Africa
RICHARD REID

Slavery in the Great Lakes Region of East Africa
Edited by HENRI MÉDARD & SHANE DOYLE

The Benefits of Famine
DAVID KEEN

Printed and bound by CPI Group (UK) Ltd, Croydon, CR0 4YY

13/09/2026

14961003-0002